The life and works of
Sister Mary Wilhelmina

Foundress of the
Benedictines of
Mary, Queen of Apostles

by her community

MMXX
Abbey of Our Lady of Ephesus

Printed in Kansas City, Missouri

First printing, August 15, 2020.

House of Ephesus™ Publishing Division
8005 Northwest 316th Street
Gower, Missouri 64454
United States of America
www.benedictinesofmary.org

All poems featured in this book are by Sr. Mary Wilhelmina.

Table of Contents

The Trinity
Is Unity
One God in Persons Three.

We worship Him
With gifts divine
Faith, Hope, and Charity.

With Prudence, too,
And justice, we
Try hard not to be rude;

But struggle on
With Temperance
And holy fortitude.

To live for God in peace and joy
One needs humility;
Obedience is crucial, too,
Your own guide NOT to be.
Putting your trust in God alone
The Great and Boundless Sea.
Fall back and float,
Relax and float,
Upon the Trinity.

God's love never changes;
That's why there's a Hell.
He waits for our loving Him
In return and well.

If you love Me, keep my laws
He advises me,
People land in Hell because
They think sin is glee.

Lord, please help me love Thee well,
Now, before I die,
Save me from the fires of Hell,
Bring me home on high!

+

PAX

GOD'S will, GOD'S will,
GOD'S will be done!
Praised be the Father,
Praised be the SON!
Praised be Divine Love, Lord Holy Ghost!
Praised be in union with the heavenly host!

One year after the death of our beloved foundress, the above poem still rings in our ears as though our beloved Sister Wilhelmina were still thumping her cane in time to the unforgettable rhythm of her own creation. This little poem encapsulates her name, her life, her purpose: to show that there is another Reality, no less real than what can be perceived around us; that there is indeed a loving God Who seeks only our good, our ultimate happiness, and that for all eternity.

Sister Wilhelmina understood that true holiness consists not in niceness or pleasant feelings, but a battle of wills; she was determined at all costs to surrender her strong will to an even stonger one: the will of God.

It was in the same spirit of the secondary love of her life, the love of her mother, the Blessed Virgin Mary, that she constantly gave her will over to God. In the Blessed Mother, the Word - Our Lord Jesus Christ - became flesh and dwelt among us. In the life of Sr. Wilhelmina, a new community took flesh for the succour of a suffering Mystical Body of Christ, the Church, in prayerful support of her priests.

We firmly believe that Sister Wilhelmina is the most timely and timeless to witness to an increasingly self-centered and narrow minded world. Her beautiful life led to a beautiful death after 95 years, 75 of which were vowed to God's service and glory. The staggering length of time was a simple composition of daily embraces of God's will at each moment, in a deep spirit of faith and loving perseverance.

Reams have been written in the last half century on the liturgical changes and fallout of the Second Vatican Council, on civil rights, on the rise in concern for social justice, but few have the all-encompassing lived experience of our dear Sister Wilhelmina. Her insuperable hope for humanity rested not on her laurels of service nor in her political views, but a vision that has been all but forgotten: that her Beloved Spouse, Our Lord Jesus Christ, came not as a secular leader but as a Suffering Servant. His death and Resurrection were meant to change our hearts and not our living circumstances. With her unshakeable faith, she never lost sight of the Divine Mission of her Spouse and of the Church: not to save bodies, but to save immortal souls. She understood that suffering, especially in union with Our Lord, was the most effective means to

GOD is the Source of Order,
Sin is the cause of pain;
We must endure pain gratefully
If we would Heaven gain.

this end. She spoke when necessary, but preached the Gospel far more eloquently in her peaceful and joyful life as a spouse of the Crucified.

We believe she will be reckoned with the great traditional witnesses of the last century, remembered not so much for her persuasive writings nor her genius, but rather by her very experience as a religious, holding on to the Faith amidst the terrible trials to which the Church has been subject, in resemblance to Christ crucified. From the very trenches, the very heart of the conflict, Sister endured all in union with her Divine Master. Hers was one of the few voices that was willing to point out the mistakes made, allowing water to seep into the Bark of Peter. Hers was the fortitude to emerge from the trenches of silence and suffering at nearly seventy-five years of age, to reclaim the Faith lost by almost all around her. She shared the story of a generation of "martyrs" whose suffering is known only to God. She was a true witness to hope in the authentic renewal of religious life for the future, with a clear vision of the Church's supernatural mission, and self-understanding as brides of Christ.

Sister Wilhelmina offered her life for the sacred priesthood, sadly disfigured in her time, by going back to the very Sacrifice to which it had laid claim for centuries. In the ancient liturgy, she found true union with God that surpassed all human efforts. She truly became one of God's cherished and devoted friends in her love for the unadulterated deposit of faith.

Now on the other side of the veil, Sister Wilhelmina dwells in the very reality to which her life continually pointed, that of the spiritual world. She belongs to the host of witnesses who, like the Divine Bridegroom, are so close to us and always ready to assist us in our own battles. She shows that holiness is possible even in this life, that saints are real, and that miracles do happen. And in her constant battle cry of "GOD'S will!" she attests to the infinite value of each passing moment for storing up treasures in heaven. We were privileged to know her, to dwell with her, and to be called her Sisters and intimate friends. We continue to strive to follow her Christ-like example, and we earnestly hope that you will come to love her too, and be aided by her powerful assistance from heaven. In the short time that we have been given on this earth, may we all endeavor to imitate Sister Wilhelmina, and seek above all else "GOD'S will!"

Chapter 1
Journeys of Faith

James Madden m. Mary Roberson (from St. Louis) (from Ste. Genevieve)
Theodore Granmot LaRose m. Mary Elizabeth (Domincano) (Cree/African)
William Lancaster m. Unknow (English) (Africa

Charles Joseph Madden m. Mary Louise Larose
William Lancaster

Ella Theresa Madden
Oscar Lancaste

The Lord is a helper in distress;
Of this truth the needy can be sure.
For God's grace, the poor man need not guess;
The Lord is a refuge for the poor.
They hope in the Lord who know His Name,
Who know Him as Father of us all;
The Lord does not leave His sons to shame,
Who seeking persistent heed His call.
Oh, sing to the Lord Who reigns above!
With joy tell the wonders He has done!
Always make return for His great Love,
The gift of His Well-beloved Son.

We are all supposed to live
In the golden ring of love,
But we have a lot of trouble
In so doing,

'Though we know that God loves us
And we hope that we love God,
All our sinfulness and selfishness
Eschewing.

But to love one's fellowman
Is a different sort of plan:
Deeds, not words, are needed here–
No evil brewing –

We must die to self to see
That bright ring of charity
Only high in Heaven is it
Clearly showing.

AND FREEDOM

Family History

nin Greene m. Unknown Slave
ı GEORGIA) (ETHIOPIAN?)

ietta Greene

Oh, what a joy it is to love Thee, Lord!
There is no sacrifice that is too hard
To bear with joy, my Love, for love of Thee!
Thou hast borne so much more for love of me.

DESCENDED FROM ROYAL BLOOD, *William Lancaster, son of an English landlord, ran away from his Georgian plantation with a slave girl. Through their clandestine marriage, the pair became the paternal great-grandparents of Sister Wilhelmina.*

the French-speaking settlers of Sainte-Genevieve, Missouri introduced black slavery to the state in 1719. As Sr. Wilhelmina's mother recounted, a large-scale awakening of consciences there led to emancipations before the Civil War, including that of her maternal great-grandmother, the newly-baptized Mary Roberson Madden.

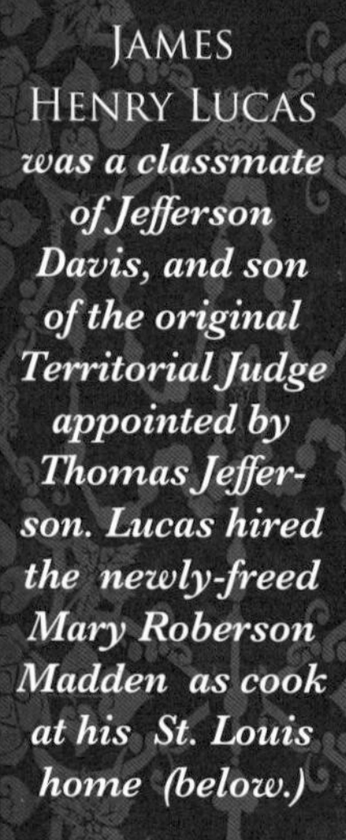

JAMES HENRY LUCAS *was a classmate of Jefferson Davis, and son of the original Territorial Judge appointed by Thomas Jefferson. Lucas hired the newly-freed Mary Roberson Madden as cook at his St. Louis home (below.)*

Although my family was materially poor and I had grown up in a segregated world, I did no feel myself to be disadvantaged in the least Our wealth was our Roman Catholic faith.

–*Sr. Wilhelmin*

When asked to recount her vocation story, Sister Wilhelmina, with her customary love of history, would begin with the seeds of the Catholic Faith that were sewn in her family three generations before her birth:

> The Faith had come down to me from my mother's side of the family. One of my maternal great-grandmothers, Mary Madden, had been the slave of a French property-holder in Ste. Genevieve, Missouri. When Mary became Catholic, her owner freed her. "I cannot keep you in slavery any longer," he told her. "Since you are now baptized, that would be like keeping Christ in slavery."

Mary then found work in nearby St. Louis as a cook fo the Lucases, a prominent French family. She met and mar ried a drayman, James Alexander Madden, and bore hir a son and a daughter, Charles Joseph and Ella Theres. Charles Joseph was to become the maternal grandfather o Sr. Wilhelmina. The Madden children were baptized at th church of St. Elizabeth of Hungary, the Jesuit parish dedi cated May 18, 1873, which served the Black Catholics of S Louis. Charles attended the parish school and served Mas there. It was the same church where his granddaughter, S Wilhelmina, would also be baptized and attend Mass as child. The Maddens were faithful parishioners of St. Eliza beth's, and very close to the parish priest, Fr. Ignatius Pank en, SJ. After Mary's death in 1883 and James' death in 188 Fr. Panken not only offered their Requiem Masses, but als buried them in his lot in Calvary Cemetery in St. Louis.

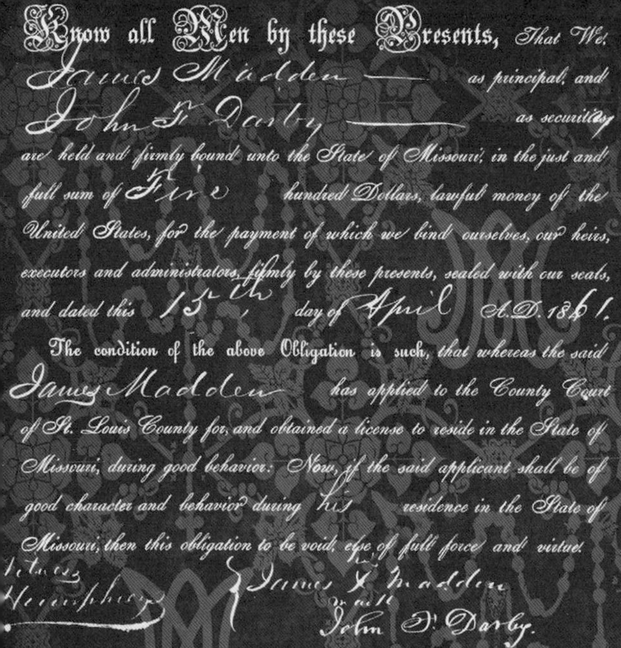

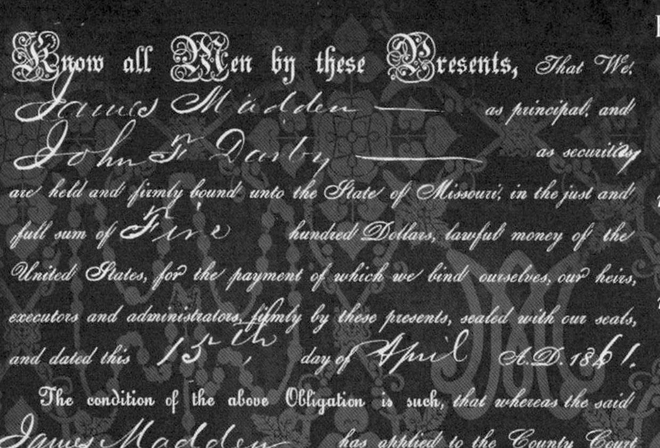

Know all Men by these Presents, That We James Madden —— as principal, and John F. Darby —— as securities are held and firmly bound unto the State of Missouri, in the just and full sum of Five hundred Dollars, lawful money of the United States, for the payment of which we bind ourselves, our heirs, executors and administrators, firmly by these presents, sealed with our seals, and dated this 15th day of April A.D. 1861.

The condition of the above Obligation is such, that whereas the said James Madden has applied to the County Court of St. Louis County for, and obtained a license to reside in the State of Missouri, during good behavior: Now, if the said applicant shall be of good character and behavior during his residence in the State of Missouri, then this obligation to be void; else of full force and virtue.

Witness [illegible] Humphrey

James X Madden (his mark)

John F. Darby

FREEDOM WAS NOT FREE *for James Madden, Sr. Wilhelmina's maternal great-grandfather. A bond of $500 released him in St. Louis, secured by the retired mayor, John Fletcher Darby. (above)*

THE ESTABLISHMENT OF ST. ELIZABETH PARISH *ubtlessly rejoiced the heart of the advocate of racial justice, r. Pierre de Smet, SJ (below.) When his failing health forced m to retire from his labors among the Native Americans to the Jesuit house in St. Louis, his associate, Fr. Ignatius Panken, SJ right) extended his ministry to the neglected Black Catholics nearby. To ensure their xclusive care, Fr. Panken obtained the right to deny Communion to white attendees. The parish became the spiritual center of Sr. Wilhelmina's family for four generations.*

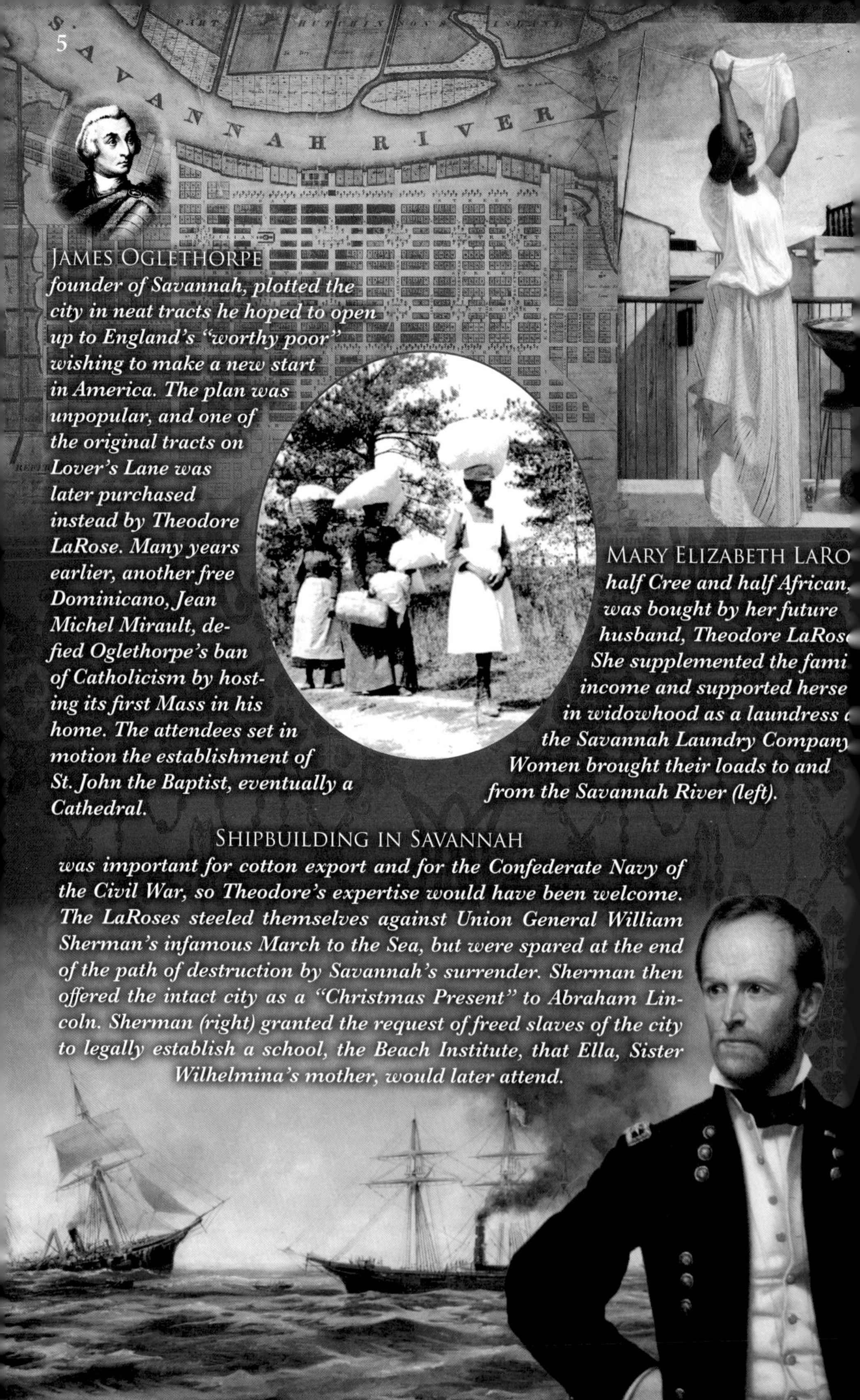

JAMES OGLETHORPE
founder of Savannah, plotted the city in neat tracts he hoped to open up to England's "worthy poor" wishing to make a new start in America. The plan was unpopular, and one of the original tracts on Lover's Lane was later purchased instead by Theodore LaRose. Many years earlier, another free Dominicano, Jean Michel Mirault, defied Oglethorpe's ban of Catholicism by hosting its first Mass in his home. The attendees set in motion the establishment of St. John the Baptist, eventually a Cathedral.

MARY ELIZABETH LARO
half Cree and half African, was bought by her future husband, Theodore LaRos She supplemented the fami income and supported herse in widowhood as a laundress the Savannah Laundry Company Women brought their loads to and from the Savannah River (left).

SHIPBUILDING IN SAVANNAH
was important for cotton export and for the Confederate Navy of the Civil War, so Theodore's expertise would have been welcome. The LaRoses steeled themselves against Union General William Sherman's infamous March to the Sea, but were spared at the end of the path of destruction by Savannah's surrender. Sherman then offered the intact city as a "Christmas Present" to Abraham Lincoln. Sherman (right) granted the request of freed slaves of the city to legally establish a school, the Beach Institute, that Ella, Sister Wilhelmina's mother, would later attend.

Some years before Charles' birth in 1866, Theodore Granmot LaRose, a free man of French and African descent who worked as a ship's carpenter, had come from his native island of Santo Domingo to the port of Savannah, Georgia. He decided to settle there, bought some land and then, as Sr. Wilhelmina put it, "set about looking for a bride." He bought a slave woman, Mary Elizabeth, the daughter of an African slave mother and a Cree Indian father; he introduced her to the Catholic Faith and made sure that she was baptized before he married her. It is not certain whether Mary Elizabeth was given this name at her birth or at her baptism, but Sr. Wilhelmina was her namesake, for Sr. Wilhelmina's mother, Ella Theresa, remembered her half-Indian grandmother fondly: "I knew her well and loved her, the only grandparent that I knew." Theodore LaRose and his wife, Mary Elizabeth, had two children, one of whom was named Mary Louise.

ABBOT BONIFACE WIMMER, *founder of Benedictine life in America, sent Fathers Oswald Moosmüller and Melchior Reichert from St. Vincent's Archabbey to begin a Savannah foundation and school, which he visited twice.*

How Mary Louise LaRose of Savannah met and married Charles Joseph Madden of St. Louis is a testimony to divine Providence. Their eldest daughter, Ella Theresa, told the story in a letter written for her grandchildren in the late 1960s. These maternal grandparents of Sr. Wilhelmina both desired to dedicate themselves to God's service: Mary Louise had seriously considered becoming an Oblate Sister of Providence, and Charles pursued a Benedictine vocation. Their granddaughter would fulfill both aspirations. Ella recounted her father's story:

> When Charles was seventeen years old, his mother died and he began to work at the church [of St. Elizabeth, St. Louis] assisting the sexton. He spent most of his time in the church basement after work, reading books loaned to him by Father Panken – most of them lives of the saints. He wanted to study for the priesthood and applied to the Benedictine Order. He was refused admission to the monastery, but was advised to go to a monastery on an island off the coast of Georgia. This was not a true monastery but a school for Negro boys. He spent two years there as a layman, teaching the youngest boys. Becoming dissatisfied with the conditions at the school, and told that he would not be sent to the regular novitiate house

THE FREEDMEN SCHOOL ON SKIDAWAY ISLAND *was a failure, much to the disappointment of Wimmer, who had hoped it would help blacks gain a foothold in society. Fr. Oswald held the boys to a strict monastic regimen, and natural misfortunes followed. Charles' entrance into monastic life was diverted to teaching until the closure. Fr. Oswald returned to St. Vincent's and wrote a biography of Wimmer, while Fr. Melchior remained in Savannah to minister to the black Catholics.*

TEACHING HIMSELF
after sixth grade under the eye of Father Panken, Charles Madden, maternal grandfather of Sr. Wilhelmina, remained a perpetual student in spite of his deep sufferings. He passed on his great love of reading to both his daughter and granddaughter.

DAILY

very day from
twelve to three,
I remember Calvary.
Pain of crucifixion fierce!
Sword that did my Mother pierce.
She stood motionless, in tears.
All around resounded jeers.

Every day from twelve to three,
I remember Calvary.
How my Lord hung there in pain,
So that I might Heaven gain;
Teaching me how to forgive;
Although dying, how to live.

Eerie darkness everywhere,
Yet a thief's brave public prayer;
So I try to pray and say:
"Make me, Lord, repent today."

So I honor Mother Mary
Who stands bravely, not contrary
To Our Heavenly Father's Will;
She keeps praying, praying still.

Let me, Lord, relieve Your thirst;
Of complaints this is Your first,
Only one on Calvary:
Thirst for souls, for souls like me.

DON'T STOP PRAYING!

Prayer is such a privilege!
Prayer is such a joy!
Those who hate us would by all mean
If they could, destroy.

Holy reading is the next thing
That our foes would stop;
We must listen to the Lord
And never good books drop.

St. Joseph's Infirmary *where Charles worked for the Sisters of Mercy.*

Mother Mathilda *fellow parishioner of the LaRoses may have inspired Mary Louise to consider a vocation.*

Father Melchior *Charles' Benedictine confrere performed the marriage of Charles and Mary Louise.*

St. Benedict the Moor *founded by Fr. Melchior hosted the marriage and aptisms of the Maddens. It was later the boyhood parish of Supreme Court Justice Clarence Thomas.*

because he stuttered, he left the island and went to Savannah, Georgia, the nearest city. He was now twenty-one years old. He had five dollars, and a recommendation for work.

He obtained work as an orderly in St. Joseph Catholic Hospital. His intention was to save enough money to return to St. Louis and his family and friends. During this time he met and fell in love with my mother, Mary Louise LaRose, and stayed in Georgia.

Although Charles' original dream of becoming a religious and a priest was not fulfilled, he did become a member of the Third Order of St. Francis. When he died in 1936 in St. Louis, he was buried in the brown Franciscan habit, and Franciscan brothers from St. Anthony Church attended his wake and recited the prayers for the dead.

Mary Louise's initial vocational discernment may have been sparked by Mother Mathilda Beasley, Georgia's first Black nun. Mary Louise learned to read and write at a time when educating Black children was illegal in Georgia. Mathilda was most likely Mary Louise's teacher at the secret school she began at their parish. Mathilda later entered the Franciscan Order at York, England, and returned to Savannah two years later to open an orphanage. She settled alongside St. Benedict the Moor parish, founded by Charles' sole remaining former confrere, Fr. Melchior. Mother Mathilda openly resumed teaching, and supported her own charitable works by sewing.

Perhaps initiated into sewing by Mother Mathilda, Mary Louise pursued this livelihood. As Charles boarded with Mary Louise's sewing instructor, the work occasioned their meeting. Ella related:

> My mother, a-seventeen-year-old, was an apprentice seamstress. On a particular night, the dressmaker had a lot of work that had to be gotten [done.] She kept my mother overtime. My father came home while Miss La Rose was still there at the dressmaker's shop. When my mother finished her work, the dressmaker asked Mr. Madden to take her home, and that budded into marriage.

After their marriage in 1890, Charles and Mary Louise Madden settled in Tennille, Georgia, where Charles bought land and built a frame-house, which the citizens called "the prettiest house in town." His daughter Ella recorded, "My father disliked being in debt. When the house was finished and he was given the keys, he paid the full cost in cash, $1000."

THE MADDEN HOME *in Tenille.*

The Maddens were the only Catholic family in Tennille, so the town had no Catholic church. Ella remembered:

> Once a month a priest visited another town, Sandersville, Georgia, three hours away by train, to celebrate Mass and hear confession. My parents made the trip each month to go to confession, hear Mass and receive Communion… Every other summer my mother took us to visit our grandmother [Mary Elizabeth] in Savannah for two weeks. We went to Mass at St. Benedict Catholic Church and the new baby was baptized.

Being the only Catholics in town led to interesting exchanges at Ella's one-room schoolhouse. During recess, the children would chant back and forth on the playground, "Baptist, Baptist is my name, I'm Baptist till I die! I've been baptized in the Baptist church, I'll stay on the Baptist side." "Methodist, Methodist is my name…" the other children would chant back in the same fashion. "Mama, are we Baptists or Methodists?" little Ella asked when she got home from school. "You're neither one. You're Catholic." Ella thoughtfully started washing the dishes. Then she remarked, "I know what I'll chant when I get to school: Catholic, Catholic is my name…" "Now, don't you go singin' that!" Her mother hastily checked her, fearing the backlash from anti-Catholic sentiment.

Charles and Mary Louise completed the secular education that their children received, instilling in them a deep love of their Catholic Faith and also a zeal for learning. As Ella later remembered:

CHARLES JOSEPH MADDEN *Sister Wilhelmina's maternal grandfather*

THE NEWLY BUILT SAINT ELIZABETH CONVENT *(left) was where St. Katharine Drexel (below) received Mary Josephine Doley, having just moved from the temporary convent of St. Michel.*

My father taught me my catechism. My mother taught me my prayers. My father was a student all his life and constantly added books to our home library. He read children's books to me long before I was old enough to attend school. These were happy Sunday afternoons.

When Ella was only ten years old, she lost her beloved grandmother, mother, and three siblings in a single year: Mary Elizabeth died of a stroke, Mary Louise in childbirth with twins, and her baby sister of pneumonia at the age of two. After a few years, Charles entered a second marriage with Mary Josephine Doley, "a fine woman," Ella called her. Like Charles and his late wife, Mary Josephine also was a devout Catholic who had pursued a religious vocation. Orphaned at the age of ten, she had been entrusted to St. Katharine Drexel and the Sisters of the Blessed Sacrament at their convent in Cornwells, Pennsylvania. She actually entered the community as a sister, but left at the age of twenty. She met and married Charles Madden a few years later in 1905. Mary Josephine's formation under the hand of Mother Drexel, along with her experience of religious life, doubtless contributed to the strong Catholic formation of Sr. Wilhelmina's mother.

This second marriage of Charles Madden also makes another connection between Sr. Wilhelmina's family history and her life as a religious, both as an Oblate Sister of Providence and as a Benedictine. St. Katharine Drexel had begun her new order, the Sisters of the Blessed Sacrament, at her blood sister's home in Torresdale, Pennsylvania. She called the temporary convent St. Michel. In the meantime, a new convent, St. Elizabeth's, was built two miles down the road from St. Michel, where Mother Drexel received Sr. Wilhelmina's step-grandmother. Bishop Ryan of

MARY JOSEPHINE DOLEY *second wife of Charles Madden, pictured later in life.*

SANCTUARY OF CHAPEL
SHRINE OF THE TRUE CROSS
TORRESDALE PA.

Philadelphia gave Mother Drexel a precious relic of the True Cross that had belonged to St. John Neumann, a friend and part-time chaplain of the Oblate Sisters of Providence. Mother Drexel then encouraged her sister to convert the old convent at St. Michel into a shrine for the relic of the True Cross, which she did. Many years later, the shrine closed, and the pews were sent to the newly founded community of the Benedictines of Mary in 2002. The next year, by God's Providence, Sr. Wilhelmina happened upon the grounds of St. Michel, so close to the place where her step-grandmother was raised. Without knowing where she was, Sister Wilhelmina found the grave of a priest who would have known Mother Drexel and perhaps also her young charges. Sister was mysteriously moved to recite Psalm 129, "Out of the Depths," the traditional prayer for the dead, with great devotion.

Charles Madden's work transferred him back to St. Louis in 1912, where Ella attended Sumner High School, the oldest and most renowned high school for Black students, with many notable alumni in the fields of music, sports and education. There Ella first met her future husband, Oscar Lee Lancaster.

THE RELIC OF THE TRUE CROSS *belonging to St. John Neumann was given to Mother Katharine Drexel by Bishop Ryan of Philadelphia. When vacating St. Michel to move to St. Elizabeth's convent and receive Sr. Wilhelmina's step-grandmother, Mother Katharine asked her Sister to convert the former convent into a shrine to house the relic. The pews from this shrine (upper left) now face the altar at the Abbey of Our Lady of Ephesus, which contains a relic of Saint John Neumann (above.)*

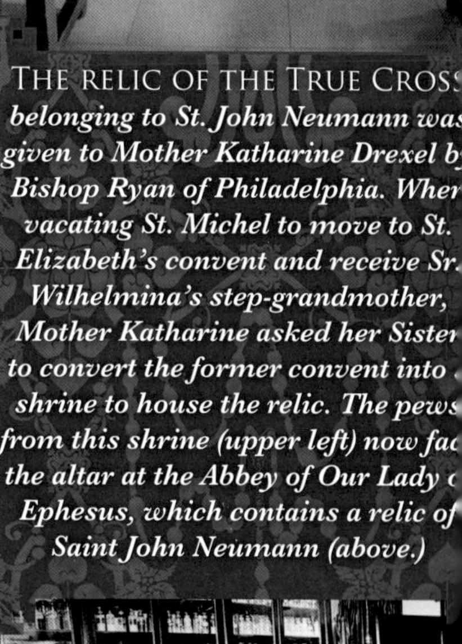

THE SISTERS OF MERCY *whom Charles Madden assisted in Savannah, assisted him in turn at his death at St. Mary's Infirmary in St. Louis, 1935.*

Mrs. Carpenter

So many days'd been spent in
building and repairing,
While Mary served and cooked,
and cooked and served;
With love and lightsome step
the family bore the load
Of daily toil. It'd been the mother's
constant joy
To feed and clothe the two:
her man, her Boy,
And driving nails they did almost
from morn 'til night,
While muscles strong developed
in that arm of might.

Then suddenly He said goodbye,
the shop was closed;
His father lay in peace under the hill;
And left alone
she was remembering until
She heard of His arrest.
Then straight she went
To stand close by His side;
She'd be His caring mother 'til He died.

She met Him on the road
carrying that log
To which He would be nailed –
How her heart quailed! The
sight gave her a start
Of tears that flowed in tor-
rents tart;
It was the hammering,
the hammering,
that broke her heart.

THE HOUSE OF LANCASTER *overtook the Crown of England in the War of the Roses, and placed three sovereigns on the throne: Henry IV, V and VI. Its seat, the Roman coastal city of Lancaster, centered around a 9th Century Benedictine Priory. (opposite) The Lancasters of western Georgia were closely descended from the royal line, and the rose was later incorporated into Sister Wilhelmina's personal coat of arms.*

THE BATTLE OF AGINCORT *decisively established the Lancastrian Rule over France on St. Crispin's Day 1415. France's freedom was regained through the call of St. Joan of Arc to expel the English forces.*

In the war that is raging
Between wrong and right
Please help us, Sweet Mother,
On your side to fight!

Confederate Soldier
eighteen-year-old John Lancaster, brother of William, lost an arm at Thoroughfare Gap while coming to aid of Stonewall Jackson (above).

Oscar came from a very different family background. His grandfather, William Lancaster, was an English overseer who had eloped with a slave. Their only son, William Jr., strongly resembled his white father, and consequently did not suffer any discrimination from the local white society in Tifton, Georgia. As Sr. Wilhelmina told the story, however, "William Jr. disappointed his white neighbors when he followed his father's example by marrying black-as-coal Henrietta Greene," the daughter of Baptist minister Rev. Benjamin Greene. They had two sons, the eldest being Oscar Lee Lancaster.

By the age of six, Oscar had lost both his mother and little brother. At the age of twelve, he ran into trouble with his father, who had recently remarried, but the details of the conflict remain unknown. At that point, Oscar had also gotten as far in his education as the little country school for Blacks could take him. Consequently, at the young age of twelve, he ran away from home.

William Lancaster Jr.
Sr. Wilhelmina's paternal grandfather.

Tifton, Georgia
birthplace of Sister Wilhelmina's father-was named for its founder, Nelson Tift (upper left) who began a sawmill at which William Lancaster Jr. worked.

Chapter 2
Meet Me In

A family is trinity of father, mother, child –
Begun in love and promise true
By husband and his wife –
An indissoluble event beyond
Opposing strife –
In sight of God, true holiness,
Both parties undefiled.

Baptized and filled with grace of God,
They start their marriage right;
And side by side they kneel to pray
Each morning and each night;
For God is first and uppermost
In everything they do,
And with God's help they hope to be
To one another true.

A marriage is a one-time thing,
That's how a family starts;
But children come in multiples:
Twins, triplets, even quarts.
And all of these must welcomed be,
And taught to work and pray,
To speak their language skillfully
And by all means obey.

June is that famous month worldwide,
When families begin;
God wants them to begin in grace
And not in mortal sin.

Let all who marry truthfully
Receive the Sacrament;
Then God will bless what they begin,
And they will be content.

Saint Louis

Oscar & Ella Lancaster

THE EYES OF THE WORLD WERE ON ST. LOUIS IN 1904 *when the city hosted the World's Fair and the extended Olympics of that year, eighty couples having their weddings in the great Ferris wheel. An estimated 20 million people flocked to the "Most American City" in 1904 alone. Many followed, as St. Louis became a primary destination in "the Great Migration" of Blacks from the South, seeking education and employment. Oscar Lancaster and Ella Madden were among them.*

When man and woman
make their vows
And he gives her a ring,
They do what God
to them allows:
A holy, lasting thing.

They do a great
momentous thing,
That cannot be undone:
Accepting all
that life will bring,
Their children, every one.

They who love God,
keep God's commands,
No matter what the pain;
They share together,
clasping hands,
In sunshine and in rain.

And children all,
who come to them
They bravely educate
To know the Lord
and well love Him
Throughout their
worldly state.

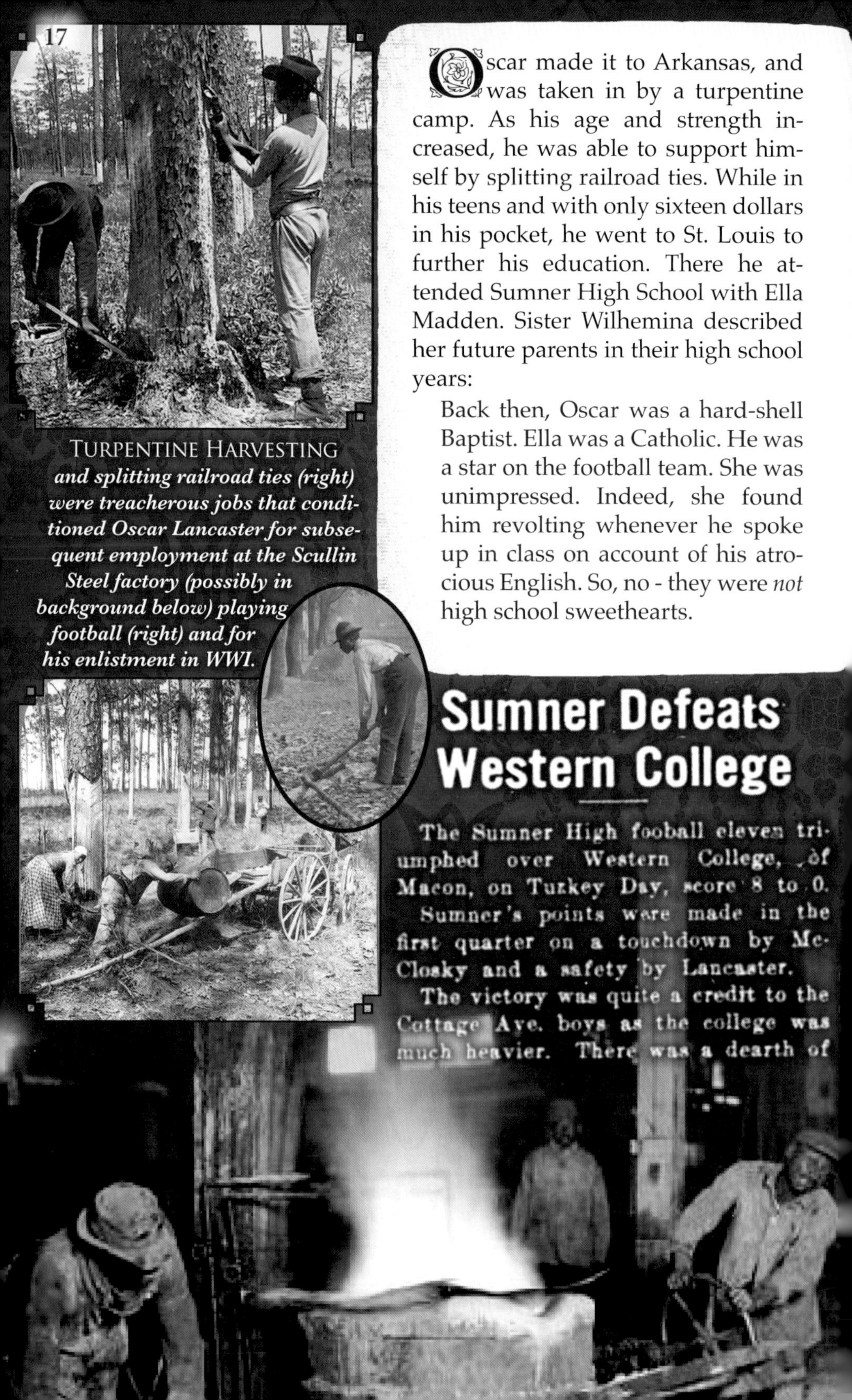

Oscar made it to Arkansas, and was taken in by a turpentine camp. As his age and strength increased, he was able to support himself by splitting railroad ties. While in his teens and with only sixteen dollars in his pocket, he went to St. Louis to further his education. There he attended Sumner High School with Ella Madden. Sister Wilhemina described her future parents in their high school years:

> Back then, Oscar was a hard-shell Baptist. Ella was a Catholic. He was a star on the football team. She was unimpressed. Indeed, she found him revolting whenever he spoke up in class on account of his atrocious English. So, no - they were *not* high school sweethearts.

TURPENTINE HARVESTING ***and splitting railroad ties (right) were treacherous jobs that conditioned Oscar Lancaster for subsequent employment at the Scullin Steel factory (possibly in background below) playing football (right) and for his enlistment in WWI.***

Sumner Defeats Western College

The Sumner High fooball eleven triumphed over Western College, of Macon, on Tukey Day, score 8 to 0.

Sumner's points were made in the first quarter on a touchdown by McClosky and a safety by Lancaster.

The victory was quite a credit to the Cottage Ave. boys as the college was much heavier. There was a dearth of

west of the Mississippi was the main reason many young people made their way to St. Louis: to graduate alongside outstanding contibutors to art, music, sports, military, business and culture.

Girls Head Home
after school at the corner of Sumner High School in Ella's freshman year.

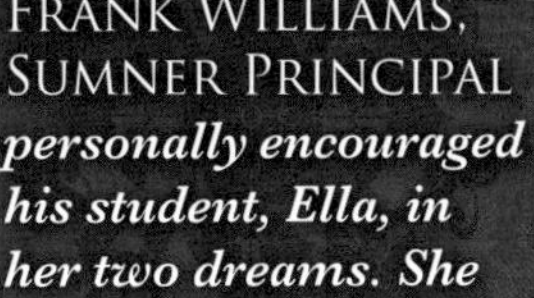

Frank Williams, Sumner Principal
personally encouraged his student, Ella, in her two dreams. She attended the teaching college (below) served as intern at the new practice classrooms added on to Sumner (lower left) and wrote short stories. One of her first known works, "A Girl's Will" had heavily autobiographical references. It was published in the February 1920 Brownies' Book. (below) The heroine was Helen LaRose, eldest child of a mail clerk who lost her mother and sacrificed herself for the sake of her family.

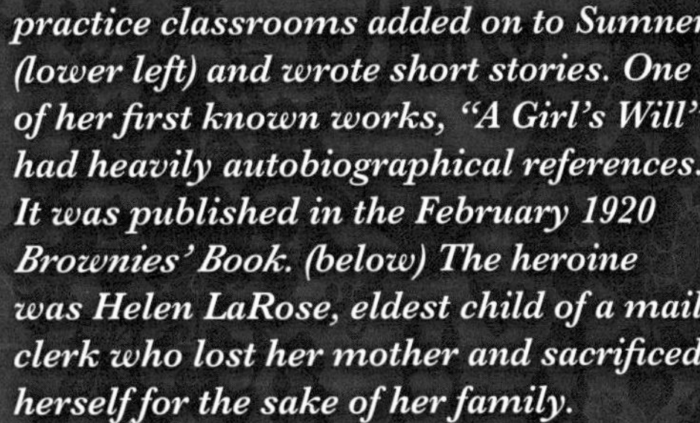

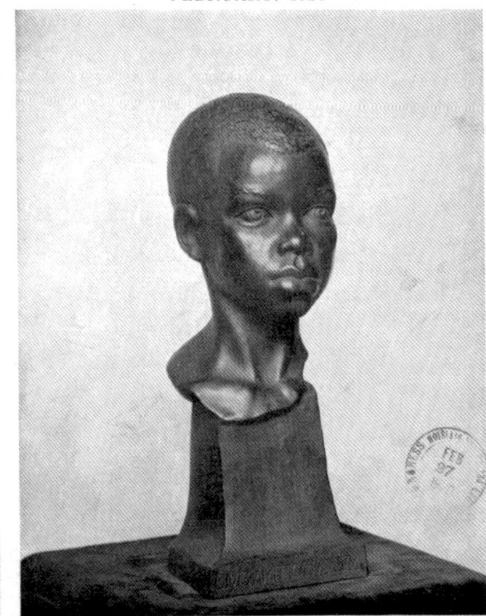

The Brownies' Book

FEBRUARY, 1920

One Dollar and a Half a Year

"I am an American Citizen"

Fifteen Cents a Copy

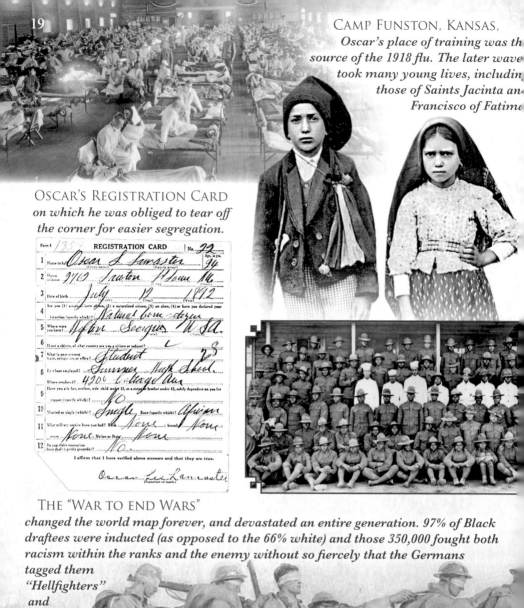

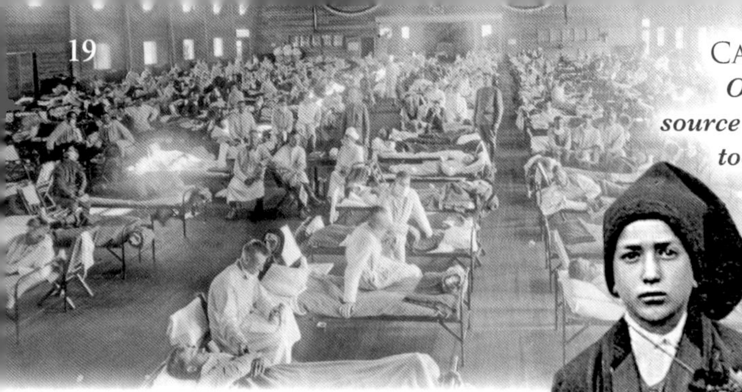

Camp Funston, Kansas,

Oscar's place of training was th source of the 1918 flu. The later wave took many young lives, includin those of Saints Jacinta an Francisco of Fatim

Oscar's Registration Card

on which he was obliged to tear off the corner for easier segregation.

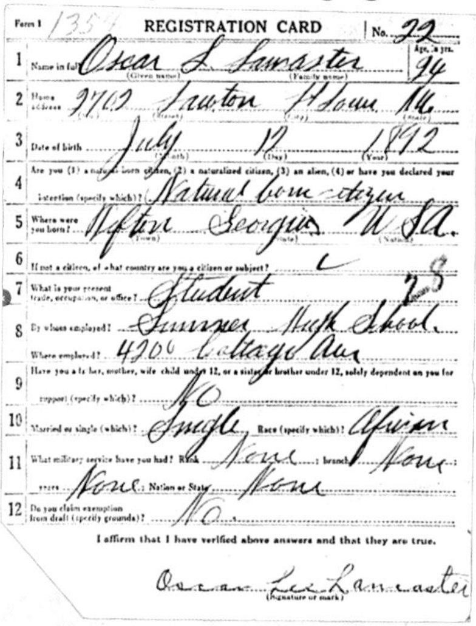

Form 1 1354 **REGISTRATION CARD** No. 22

1 Name in full Oscar L Lancaster (Given name) (Family name) Age, in yrs. 24

2 Home address 9709 Lawton St Louis Mo (No.) (Street) (City) (State)

3 Date of birth July 12 1892 (Month) (Day) (Year)

4 Are you (1) a natural-born citizen, (2) a naturalized citizen, (3) an alien, (4) or have you declared your intention (specify which)? Natural born citizen

5 Where were you born? Upton Georgia U.S.A. (Town) (State) (Nation)

6 If not a citizen, of what country are you a citizen or subject?

7 What is your present trade, occupation, or office? Student

8 By whom employed? Sumner High School
Where employed? 4206 Cottage Ave

9 Have you a father, mother, wife, child under 12, or a sister or brother under 12, solely dependent on you for support (specify which)? No

10 Married or single (which)? Single Race (specify which)? African

11 What military service have you had? Rank None ; branch None ;
years None ; Nation or State None

12 Do you claim exemption from draft (specify grounds)? No

I affirm that I have verified above answers and that they are true.

Oscar Lee Lancaster (Signature or mark)

The "War to end Wars"

changed the world map forever, and devastated an entire generation. 97% of Black draftees were inducted (as opposed to the 66% white) and those 350,000 fought both racism within the ranks and the enemy without so fiercely that the Germans tagged them "Hellfighters" and "black devils."

THE USS AGAMMEMNON *bearing Oscar from Upton to France.*

HE "BUFFALOES" ARRIVE IN FRANCE. *Oscar served briefly in the Engineer Corps, then at Headquarters (below.)*

After high school, Oscar enlisted in a Black regiment for World War I, serving for two years and eight months overseas in France. He trained first in Camp Funston, Kansas, and then Camp Upton, New York with the famous "Buffalo Soldiers," the 92nd Division. He served first in the Engineer Corps and then Quartermaster Corps of the 367th Infantry, and was promoted to the rank of sergeant. The company was involved in the horrific Meuse-Argonne offensive that effectively brought about the Armistice. Meanwhile, back in St. Louis, Ella pursued her dream to become a teacher. "All my life," she recalled, "I have had two ambitions: to teach and to write stories." After the war, she became reacquainted with Oscar and introduced him to the Catholic Faith. Sister Wilhelmina affirmed that Ella sought to bring Oscar into the Church without the intention of marrying him. On the contrary, Ella had no intention of marrying at all, for in those days the schools in St. Louis did not hire married women as teachers, and she wanted to remain a teacher.

Upon his return to St. Louis, Oscar was hired as business manager for a publishing company, the St. Louis Tribune. Oscar approached Ella as a company sales representative, and Ella confessed "I bought a share just to get rid of him." Nevertheless, Oscar persisted in his Catholic interest, and decided to enter the Church in 1921. Ironically, the Antioch Baptist Church to which he belonged was just about to name him minister.

THE TRIUMPHANT 367TH INFANTRY *arrives home in St. Louis.*

ANTIOCH BAPTIST CHURCH *nearly named Oscar pastor in 192*

OSCAR LEE LANCASTER *Sister Wilhelmina's father*

DR. HERMAN DREER *editor of the St. Louis Tribune hired Oscar as business manager, which occasioned Oscar's pursuit both of his faith and his future bride.*

A woman's power o'er a man
Is awesome! Let me tell:
She either leads him up to heav'n or
drags him down to hell.

Ella jubilantly brought him to Fr. Joseph P. Lynam, SJ, at the Black parish of St. Elizabeth of Hungary, saying, "This young man wishes to be received into the Church, and I would like to be his godmother." The wise priest looked at her, then looked at him, and stated, "No, you may not be his godmother." He knew that according to the Code of Canon Law at that time, such a relationship would be a spiritual impediment if they would eventually wish to marry.

Ella recounted: "I didn't fall in love with Oscar until after he became Catholic. I realized afterwards, that whenever we talked (when we went to school together) he would ask me questions about the Catholic Church and I answered them." Father Lynam's foresight was salutary; Ella and Oscar were indeed married on July 29, 1922 at St. Elizabeth's with Fr. Lynam presiding.

Oscar and Ella settled at 4315 Garfield Street in a Black neighborhood of St. Louis, where he worked long, hard hours as a life insurance salesman. Ella ended her teaching career in order to raise their five children: Oscar Lee, Jr., Mary Elizabeth, William Charles (Billy), Christine Marie, and Benjamin Greene.

ELLA THERESA MADDEN LANCASTER
Sister Wilhelmina's mother and model

SAINT ELIZABETH OF HUNGARY, PRINCESS *and Third Order Franciscan of the early 13th Century was patroness of the parish and Sr. Wilhelmina's baptismal patroness, after the Blessed Virgin Mary.*

Mother Mary, help!
Help me to behave!
Make me a true saint
Now before my grave.

CERTIFICATE OF BAPTISM
CHURCH OF St. Elizabeth

CHILD
NAME Mary Elizabeth Lancaster
RESIDENCE
DATE OF BIRTH April 13 / 1924
DATE OF BAPTISM May 30 / 1924

FATHER'S NAME Oscar L. Lancaster
BIRTHPLACE

MOTHER'S MAIDEN NAME Ella T. Madden
BIRTHPLACE

SPONSORS Ella T. Holloman

PRIEST WHO BAPTIZED THE CHILD: Rev. Jos. P. Lynam, S.J.

HE THAT BELIEVETH AND IS BAPTIZED, SHALL BE SAVED. MK. 16:16

Mary Elizabeth, who would grow up to become Sr. Wilhelmina, was born on Palm Sunday, April 13, 1924, and baptized at the church of St. Elizabeth's, where her parents had been married and where her grandfather Charles Madden had been raised.

THE BAPTISM OF MARY ELIZABETH ***by Father Joseph Lynam (above) took place May 30, 1924, six weeks after her birth on April 13, 1924 at Barnes Hospital (below.) Charles Joseph Madden's sister, Ella Theresa Holloman, stood as godmother.***

"I lived with both my parents – along with three brothers and one sister – at 4315 Garfield for seventeen straight years from my birth in Barnes Hospital on April 13, 1924, until my departure for the novitiate of the Oblate Sisters of Providence in September 1941," Sister Wilhelmina remembered. "We shared joys and sorrows, struggles and hardships; we skimped, saved and sacrificed, with my mother carrying the greater portion of the cross."

Make me daily
follow Thee!
Save me from
all evil strife:
All misfortune,
and misery.
Lord! The Way,
the Truth, the Life!

Almighty Father, in this place
I offer Thee the Holy Face
Of Thy Beloved Jesus Christ
With Whom I always wouldst keep tryst.

Please shower down Thy blessings great
Upon each neighborhood and state,
Converting us from war to peace
And making all our vices cease.

TODAY

Precious pain!
Let me not complain
Of thee;
Jesus died!
He was crucified
For me.

Heaven waits
While I pass thru straits
So gray;
God alone
Leads me to my throne
Today.

MRS. GEORGE BRANTLEY *(above) was entertained by Ella and her son George by the young Lancasters when visiting.*

BERTY LIFE
SURANCE CO

FRANK GILLESPIE *Sumner Graduate, sought out he most talented en he could find for his Company, Liberty ife Insurance. A erger left Oscar nemployed~but only for a day.*

Despite her life-long ambitions to teach and to write, Ella subordinated them to her new roles as wife and mother. Sister Wilhelmina gratefully recalled that despite the children being "somewhat boisterous," Ella "bravely made the sacrifice of staying at home with us throughout all our growing up years. We could converse with her at any time; she had the patience, humility and heroic charity to listen to all our childish notions."

Ella's school friends used to visit, Sr. Wilhelmina reminisced, "to give her advice on how to enjoy life and not be dominated by drab, domestic drudgery."

> I remember one visitor very vividly. She was the wife of a high school principal. Laden with perfume and furs she would come with her five-year-old son whom Oscar, Billy and I had to take outside in the backyard with us and entertain. Meanwhile she sat in our plain, sofaless, living room, chatting with her old friend "Ella T," then wearing a plain gingham house dress and old house shoes. After a while this lady stopped coming; my mother had not been able to return her visits.

The years during the Great Depression were especially difficult for the Lancasters. Sister Wilhelmina recalled one evening at the dinner table, when they had no bread. "My brothers and sister and I, we were laughing and playing; we didn't even notice something was missing." Later that night, however, little Mary overheard her mother sobbing, "I have not fed my children today! I have not fed my children today!"

Sister Wilhelmina also described the warm summer day in 1930 when her father came home "crushed with sorrow at the loss of his job as insurance salesman for Liberty Life."

> His world seemed to have come to an end. The insurance company for which he worked had folded. Ella was cooking in the kitchen; and from lines anchored to posts of the back porch there were clothes flapping in the summer breeze. Oscar was sitting in a chair at the kitchen table. He saw his shirt on the line."I guess that's my last shirt," he said aloud. Ella laughed. She was nearly jovial. "Nonsense!" She cried. "You're not that kind of man." Indeed he wasn't. He went out and got another job with another insurance company – Atlanta Life – the very next day. He went out with the backing of a woman who believed in him, a woman who had laughed aloud at his fears, and who had gone on with home duty as usual.

OSCAR LEE LANCASTER JR.
1923-1979

CHRISTINE MARIE LANCASTER JACKSON
1929-1998

Ella Lancaster never consented to take a job herself or to receive welfare money from the government, knowing what a humiliation that would have been to her husband. She preferred to endure their poverty bravely rather than call into question her husband's ability to provide for their family. As her daughter remembered,

> Friends would say that it was a shame she couldn't go to work and thus supplement her husband's income. Ella wouldn't hear of such a course of action. Nor would she think of applying for government relief as many of the neighbors were doing. She was determined to live on her husband's income. He wanted to be the provider and she would not crush his manhood.

Oscar used their material hardships as occasions to teach their children responsibility. When Oscar Jr. was six years old and Mary was five, Sr. Wilhelmina remembered, they would sometimes ask their father for a nickel, which he always gave them. But before they could run off with it, Oscar would be called back.

> "Now, Oscar," his father would say, "How are you going to spend that nickel? I'll give you a nickel every week, but you must learn to budget it. You can't just run off and buy candy with it. You should change it to pennies. You have to save, put some of those pennies aside. Look at your shoes; won't you need shoe strings? You have to save to buy yourself new shoe strings!"

Sr. Wilhelmina concluded the story, "It was no wonder that Oscar grew up to become an eminently successful public accountant."

In addition to their struggle with poverty, the Lancaster family had to endure the hardship of segregation. The Lancasters attended St. Elizabeth's, just as the Maddens had a generation before. The Black parish at this time was blessed with a zealous pastor, Fr. William Markoe, in whose honor Sr. Wilhelmina would eventually receive her religious name.

CHARLES WILLIAM LANCASTER
1925-1983

BENJAMIN GREENE LANCASTER
1930-2015

THE LANCASTER HOME *was split for a time with the top floor rented out in the early years of their marriage. In time, the family took up the whole house. Ella lived here until being moved to assisted living shortly before her death in 1986.*

"THE VILLE REVOLVED AROUND ANNIE MALONE" *a chemist, foundress of Poro Beauty College and philanthropist. She encouraged married women to take up work in the beauty industry, but Ella remained at home, devoted to her children.*

MARY LOUISE MADDEN *(left) remained close to her half-sister Ella in Saint Louis.*

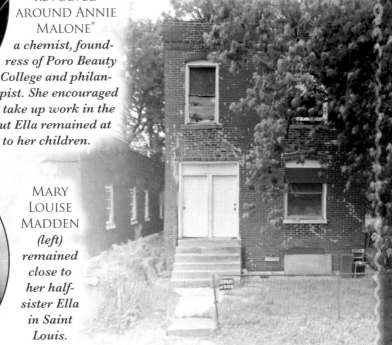

EXCERPT FROM A LETTER FROM OSCAR TO POLICY HOLDERS *reveals the strength of his faith.*

My Dear Policyholders and Friends:

May 3, 1934, we opened St. Louis District No. 2 to give service to the large colored population of Metropolitan St. Louis and suburban towns surrounding thereto. It was right in the heat of the depression. The outlook was very dark. Small institutions with insufficient capital and reserve to tide them over were failing on either side. I was told by many of my cautious friends that an ordinary agency could not be built during such crisis. I did not believe this story, so I worked day and night with my friends and people who thought different about the whole situation.

Again, I want to thank you for your attention and fine cooperation. Without your help the occasion which we are now enjoying, would have been impossible. Please remember me in your prayers and I will remember you each time I approach the Holy Communion rail and receive the body and blood of our Savior.

O. L. LANCASTER

Chapter 3

The Fighting

A Black

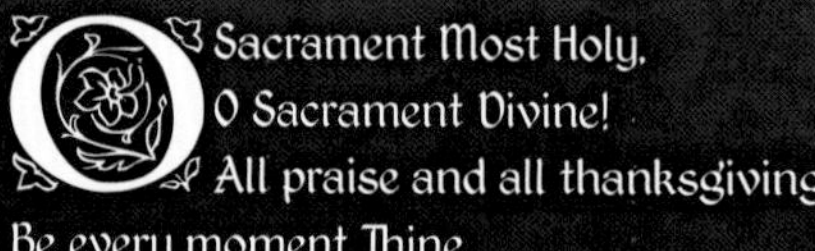

O Sacrament Most Holy,
O Sacrament Divine!
All praise and all thanksgiving
Be every moment Thine.

Thank You for coming to us
O Loving Savior dear,
Have mercy on all people
Especially those here.

Like snow that falls from heaven,
Thy coming is to men:
That we may be forgiven
And never sin again.

Have mercy on poor sinners,
Who lie and steal and cheat;
Change them
to heaven winners,
Adoring at Thy feet.

Let pagans come
to know Thee,
To kneel before Thy face:
O Sacrament Most Holy,
Please fill us with Thy grace.

Now what must Heaven be like,
Since this is only earth,
Where God has made the present
Of His Son's human birth.

Surrounded now with beauty
'Though hidden be Thy face,
We strive to do our duty
Sweet Sacrament of grace.

Oh, let us run to meet Him!
He's coming in the Mass!
Be sure then to receive Him,
And do not let Him pass!

O Sacrament Most Holy,
O Sacrament Divine!
Bless all the little children
For all of them are Thine!

O Love! O Love Eternal!
O Fire! O Ocean deep!
You give us gifts supernal,
And even while we sleep!

Sweet Heart of Jesus, thank Y
For life and liberty!
But I must be Your captive
For so I want to be.

Have mercy on the dying
The sinners and the sain
Bring them to Heaven fl
With no selfish complain

Lord, bless Thy
faithful chaplain,
Who serves us in Thy Name;
Make him Thy true apostle,
Exempt from filth and shame.

Grant us true love, O Jesus,
For one another here,
And exercising kindness
Help all to persevere.

Let's learn to love, O Jesus,
And truly humble be
With chief consideration
For ev'ry enemy.

Our ev'ry fault confessing
To the community,
We humbly ask God's blessing
In burning charity

MARKOES & White World

FATHER WILLIAM MARKOE *(below) was Sr. Wilhelmina's eponym and inspiration toward a life of prayer for priests. With his brother, Father John (left) he served St. Elizabeth's parish for many years.*

.ord, make us firm and stable!
Oon't let us gypsies be!
3ut work as we are able
ſo build this house for Thee.

ʼour Will be done, Lord Jesus,
lo matter what You say;
ʼou are our Lord and Savior
ʼoday and every day.

.ord, help us
oray the Office
\s You would have us do
n love and adoration,
ı joy and penance true.

ternal thanks to Jesus
\re due from you and me;
e suffered awful torture,
e suffered lovingly.

Vhen company is coming
et each one do her part
o give them royal welcome
Vith a true and loving heart.

et us do fervent penance
or all our filthy sins
nd be one of those children
Vho highest heaven wins.

ear not! Run! Be a martyr!
ccept each passing pain!
ou have a throne in Heaven;
orever you will reign.

ring priests to reach salvation,
epentant of all sin,
ejecting all temptation,
hen help them start again.

I want to quench Thy thirst, Lord;
So let me limpid be,
Refreshing, pure so Thou canst
Drink all Thou wilt of me.

We want to quench Thy thirst, Lord,
So let us limpid be
Refreshing, pure so Thou canst
Drink for eternity.

Divine and Loving Mercy,
Fill us with trust in Thee!
That we may love like
children
And reach eternity!

Divine and Loving Mercy!
Help souls departed who
Lived all their lives
in blindness,
Not really knowing You!

If enemies are hungry,
Or if they suffer thirst,
Lord! Hasten to their rescue!
And save them from the worst.

Thank You, Lord Jesus, thank You!
For all that You have done!
You are the Son of Mary!
Make each priest Mary's son.

Make strong each priest, each deacon!
Make strong each bishop, too!
Don't let him ever weaken
Who acts in place of You.

The days are getting longer,
I see at Holy Hour;
My gratitude grows stronger
As Jesus shows His power.

Without Him,
You can nothing do.
While with Him,
You can do all things;
Fear not!
Your Father cares for you!
From Heart of Christ
His mercy springs.

At labor hard
and sacrificed
With heart and mind
and body spent,
We leave all
blossoming to Christ,
Secure against
discouragement.

O Heart of Love!
That grew below
The Heart of Mary pure!
Glory to Thee
Forevermore
That makest
salvation sure!

Jesus, Love!
Jesus, Sweet!
Let me daily of You eat!
Love!
Sweetheart!
Lord and King!
Let me daily of You sing!

Make me daily follow Thee!
Save me from all evil strife:
All misfortune, and misery.
Lord! The Way, the Truth, the Life!

Glory to
Thy Precious
Blood, Lord!
Glory to
Thy Sacred Heart!
Help us to follow
Thee to Heaven,
There to have
a lasting part!

THE SACRED HEART
enthroned by Cardinal Burke at the Abbey of Our Lady of Ephesus 2017.

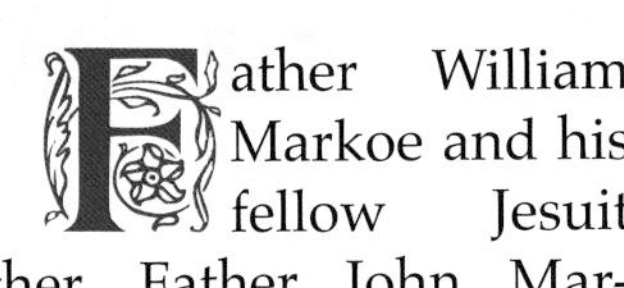

Father William Markoe and his fellow Jesuit priest-brother, Father John Markoe, were devoted apostles to the Black population of St. Louis. On the feast of the Assumption of the Blessed Virgin Mary, August 15, 1917, several weeks after the East St. Louis massacre which left about one hundred Black people dead and hundreds more homeless, Fathers William and John Markoe made the following vow:

> O Jesus, we, the undersigned, resolve and determine, in honor of Thy Sacred Heart, Thy Holy Mother, our Guardian Angels and all our Patron Saints, especially Saint Ignatius and Saint Peter Claver, to give and dedicate our whole lives and all our energies, as far as we are able, and it is not contrary to a pure spirit of pure indifference and obedience, for the work of the salvation of the Negroes in the United States; and though altogether unworthy, we trust in the Sacred Hearts, O Jesus and Mary, to obtain for us the priceless favor of doing so. And do thou, O St. Peter Claver, pray for us. Amen. Also, daily to repeat this resolution, for the fulfillment of our expectations and desires.

Frenzied Mobs Wreak Vengeance on Negroes of East St. Louis; Martial Law Declared by Illinois

TORCH APPLIED TO SECTION OF CITY INHABITED BY COLORED PEOPLE AND SCORES WERE SHOT DOWN AS THEY TRIED TO ESCAPE FROM THE FIRE AND MANY OTHERS LYNCHED—MARTIAL LAW DECLARED UNDER ILLINOIS AUTHORITY.

"A NATIONAL DISGRACE," *the bloodshed and brutality of the July 1917 riots sent many homeless into the western side of St. Louis. Their plight led to the vow of the Markoe brothers.*

Once a priest,
Always a priest,
Mother Mary, help him!
He is sick,
And can no longer
Hold the Sacred Chalice,
Can no longer lead the Feast
In service at the altar:
He who is Our Lady's slave
Does by no means falter.

Glory to the Face of
Jesus,
Glory to His Holy Name!
Honor to His every breath –
And may He save
This priest
From shame!

May God bless priests
who have the power
To consecrate the Host!
They give us comfort
in death's hour
When we all need God most!

Born in the 1890s in Minnesota, the Markoe brothers had virtually no contact with Blacks in their youth, but they each became devoted to the Black people early on. John, the elder of the two, entered West Point, where he became a football star, playing alongside the future President Eisenhower and against Knute Rockne. As a young cadet, John defended the only Black cadet at the school. He went on to be assigned to a Black regiment, until he was discharged for a scene of public drunkenness. He consequently entered the Minnesota National Guard and served honorably in the southwest.

"THE CLASS THE STARS FELL ON" ***was the nickname of John Markoe's West Point class of 1915. Dwight Eisenhower, Omar Bradley (bottom row, far left) and 57 others became generals. John Markoe is pictured at right as a young cadet in 1914.***

Holy Confessors of the Lord,
Help us make good confessions!
And never to tepidity
Make any sad concessions.

Hail, Priests in Heaven, pray for us!
Hail, Priests in Purgatory!
We pray for you and those on earth
Till all are joined in glory!

Thy priests, dear Lord!
Thy precious priests!
May peace to each be given!
Don't let them languish in the fire,
But bring them all to heaven!

Let us do all we can to get
Souls out of Purgatory;
They are the friends of God who yet
Will enter into glory;
That priests are there, I think it true,
For God is the All-Holy,
And priests are men like me and you,
Inclined to earth and lowly.

NO NATION CAN ENDURE HALF-SLAVE AND HALF-FREE
VOTE NO ON SEGREGATION FEB.29

SEGREGATION IN ST. LOUIS *was approved by the vote of the city in 1916. The legislature and ensuing 1917 riots drew national criticism.*

"MR. PRESIDENT, WHY NOT MAKE AMERICA SAFE FOR DEMOCRACY?"

THE WORLD MUST BE MADE SAFE FOR DEMOCRACY

SAINT STANISLAUS SEMINARY, FLORISSANT
cradle of half of the Jesuit missions in America.

Meanwhile, his younger brother William studied for a year at St. Louis University before entering the Jesuit novitiate in Florissant, Missouri, in 1913. As a novice he frequented the crowded and impoverished Black communities of downtown St. Louis, bringing them religious instruction as well as material assistance. He wrote to his brother John, then fighting on the Mexican border, about his work with the Black Catholics of St. Louis, which made an impression on his older brother. Soon John left the military to join his brother as a Jesuit in 1917.

This was a particularly turbulent time for the Blacks of St. Louis. The 1916 vote on segregation confined a large section of the Black population to the Ville, just north of the Cathedral Basilica of St. Louis. The tension ensuing this vote culminated in the 1917 massacre. This turbulence in the early part of the twentieth century gave St. Louis a reputation for being a hotbed of interracial

Eternal Wisdom,
With no restraint,
Almighty God: make
This priest a saint.

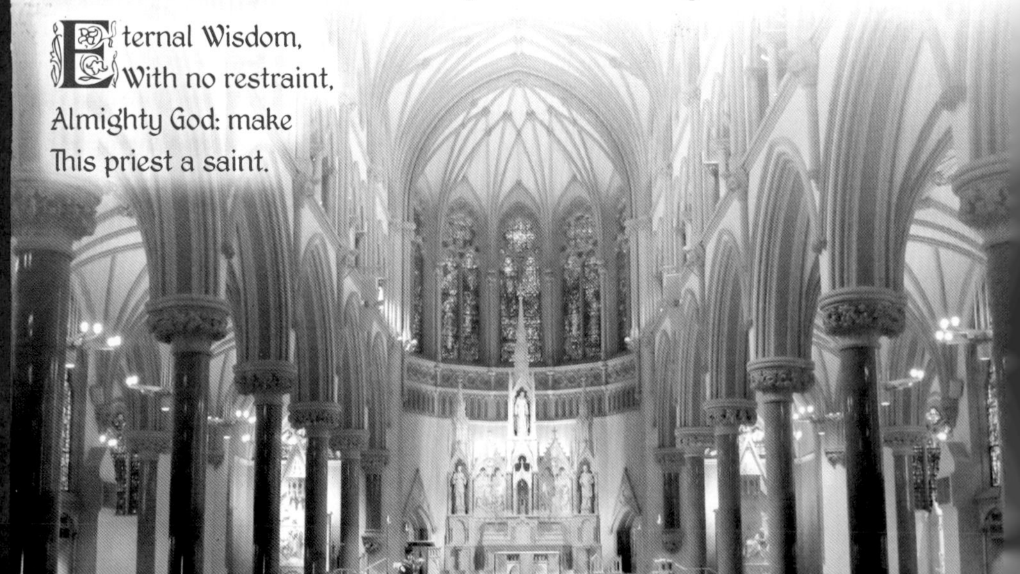

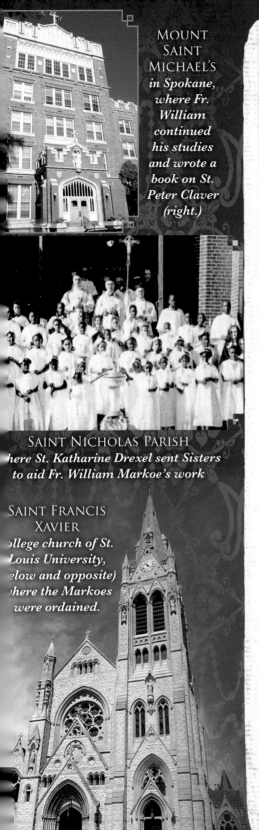

Mount Saint Michael's *in Spokane, where Fr. William continued his studies and wrote a book on St. Peter Claver (right.)*

Saint Nicholas Parish *here St. Katharine Drexel sent Sisters to aid Fr. William Markoe's work*

Saint Francis Xavier *ollege church of St. Louis University, elow and opposite) here the Markoes were ordained.*

strife. In response to this violence, the Markoe brothers made their vow and dedicated the rest of their lives to the service of the Black people.

William furthered his studies in Spokane, where he continued his Black ministry and authored a book on St. Peter Claver, *The Slave of the Negroes*. Returning to St. Louis in 1923, before he was even ordained a priest, he made 200 Black converts in nine months, largely by walking through Black neighborhoods, calling on families and bringing food and supplies. That same year, he wrote to Mother Katharine Drexel, begging her to send sisters to St. Louis. She consented, sending Blessed Sacrament Sisters the next year to aid him at St. Nicholas parish where he catechized many souls.

Fr. William was ordained at St. Francis Xavier Church at St. Louis University in 1926. Many Black people attended, despite the initial refusal of Fr. William's superiors. The following

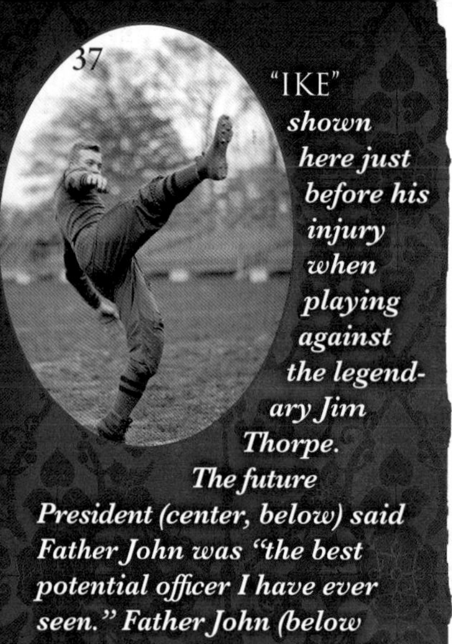

"IKE" *shown here just before his injury when playing against the legendary Jim Thorpe. The future President (center, below) said Father John was "the best potential officer I have ever seen." Father John (below left) in turn later praised his former classmate in the oval office, writing to congratulate him on "the tremendous good you have accomplished" in the area of civil rights, "more good in a few years than the combined efforts of many over the years."*

FATHER JOHN *at far left, Eisenhower at center.*

Adown
the centuries
the persecutions roll,
Intent to kill each pure,
believing soul;
Intent to kill each
cardinal, bishop, priest,
Those most well-known
and other known
the least.

year, he was made pastor of St. Elizabeth's, where Father John would also eventually be assigned. Fr. William served as pastor there until 1941, with only a brief interval away, in service to Black organizations. He devoted a tireless amount of energy into the parish. After the 1927 tornado severely damaged the old church building, Fr. William acquired a former mansion on Pine Street to use as a new setting for the parish. The new location, about an hour's walk from the Lancasters' home, was outside the Black sector of St. Louis. The projected movement of a Black parish to a white sector led to a protest meeting. Fr. William recalled in his autobiography:

> We held a council of war. My brother being a West Pointer and an old army man was a good strategist. He had also played football on the same squad with Ike Eisenhower. We decided we should cover the un-Catholic anti-Negro meeting.

THE NEW LOCATION OF SAINT ELIZABETH'S *(right) allowed Fr. William to lead retreats such as th attended by Mary Elizabeth and Ella (at far right.*

Fr. John and another friend attended the protest meeting in civilian dress in order to remain incognito, taking down and then publishing the speeches which criticized not only Fr. William Markoe, but also the Archbishop of St. Louis, who had given his approval to the parish's relocation. As a result, the leaders of the opposition were shamed into silence, and the parish move continued unimpeded.

ST. ELIZABETH'S CHURCH, 2721 PINE ST., ST. LOUIS, MO.

MSGR. FLAVIN, PASTOR OF VISITATION *(left) hosted Sr. Wilhelmina's high school reunion, attended by her parents and family. Visitation parish absorbed Saint Elizabeth's parish in the days of integration.*

FR. JOHN LA FAR *later editor of Amer son of an artist an stained glass pion*

The new parish also lay within the boundaries of Visitation Parish, which would host the reunion for the alumni of the St. Joseph Catholic High School for Negroes, which Ella and Oscar Lancaster would help to found. The pastor of Visitation Parish was Msgr. Cornelius Flavin, the brother of Bishop Glennon Flavin of Lincoln and the pastor of the future Cardinal Dolan. In addition to sponsoring the St. Joseph Reunion, Msgr. Flavin was a vigorous champion of racial integration.

Fr. William began *The St. Elizabeth's Chronicle*, which eventually became the *Interracial Review*, taken over by Fr. John LaFarge. Father LaFarge was son of the artist who pioneered the stained-glass style eventually attributed to Louis Comfort Tiffany. Father LaFarge, future editor of *America* magazine, was originally a great ally of the Markoes, but they eventually distanced themselves since they felt he was too condescending in his approach to ministry among the Black population.

Fr. Daniel Lord
wholeheartedly supported the Markoes and St. Elizabeth's parish.

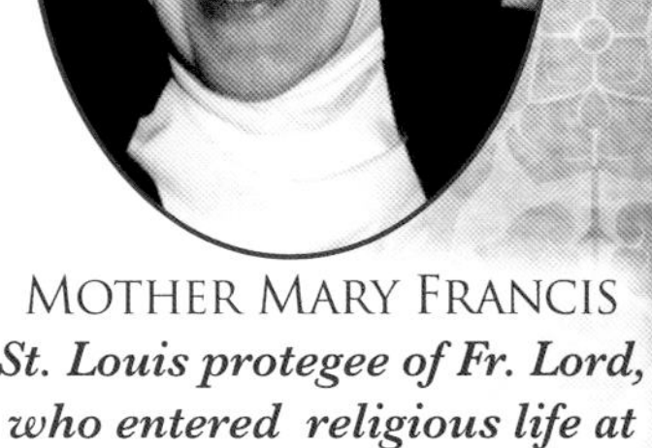

Mother Mary Francis
St. Louis protegee of Fr. Lord, who entered religious life at same time as Sr. Wilhelmina

Fr. Claude Heithaus
confrere and co-worker of the Markoes

Another ally was the great writer and playwright, Fr. Daniel Lord, SJ, who frequented St. Elizabeth's Parish and made a point of including its parishioners in his productions. In her later years, Sr. Wilhelmina still lit up whenever anyone sang Fr. Lord's hymn to Christ the King, and she would join in with gusto. An unknown but tantalizing question, is whether Sr. Wilhelmina ever crossed paths with the future Mother Mary Francis, PCC. Mother Mary Francis, Abbess of the Poor Clare Monastery in Roswell, New Mexico, and brave defender of traditional religious life during the 1970s and 1980s, was herself a native of St. Louis, three years older than Sr. Wilhelmina, and also closely associated with Fr. Daniel Lord at that time.

A later and powerful friend was Fr. Claude Heithaus, SJ, whose explosive sermon at St. Francis Xavier College Church in 1944, attacked the continuing practice of rejecting Black applicants to college, even as one of Sr. Wilhemina's classmates had been rejected on account of her race. Sister Wilhelmina's own sister Christine benefited from Fr. Heithaus' efforts. She was one of the first Black

FATHER WILLIAM'S FAREWELL DINNER *honored the pastor (seated third from the left) but Father John (at left and on the left his brother) continued his work alone in St. Louis for a few years until he was sent to Creighton University in Nebraska. Both employed peaceful means taken up by the Ci Rights movement decades later after it becan more popular.*

Priests, Lord! Priests, Lord!
Each poor priest!
Don't let him fail You
In the least!

MOTHER MARY!
HELP YOUR SON!
BRING HIM HOME WHEN
WORK IS DONE!

FATHER WILLIAM *pictured just before his departure.*

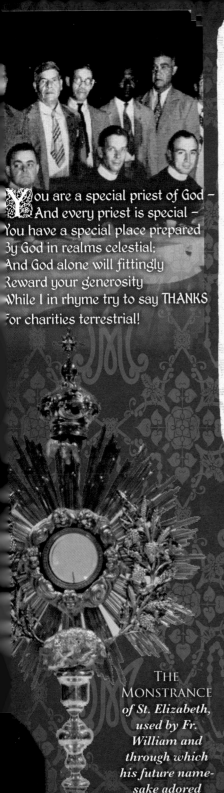

women admitted to the University of Saint Louis in the years that followed, even being offered a scholarship.

Apart from these rare exceptions, the Markoes were not supported by the hierarchy nor by their fellow priests. In 1941, Fr. William was reassigned to Mankato, Minnesota, where he lamented that "not a single Negro lived." Sr. Wilhelmina was therefore the last young woman whom Fr. William Markoe directed to the religious life before his northern exile, following St. Elizabeth Parishioners Sr. Claude, Sr. Philomena, Sr. Incarnata, and Sr. Eulalia. Father William briefly took up his work later in his assignment in Denver, but was then assigned to teach theology at Marquette, again limiting his apostolate. He supported his brother's work in Omaha from a distance until his death in Milwaukee in 1969.

You are a special priest of God –
And every priest is special –
You have a special place prepared
By God in realms celestial;
And God alone will fittingly
Reward your generosity
While I in rhyme try to say THANKS
For charities terrestrial!

I feel drawn to succor the souls of priests in Purgatory.

Console Thy priests who sigh, Lord!
Give them eternal rest
With Thee, in Heaven high, Lord!
The Kingdom of the Blest.

THE MONSTRANCE *of St. Elizabeth, used by Fr. William and through which his future namesake adored her Eucharistic Lord.*

Chapter 4
My Heart

Although we'd rather play than pray,
You kindly call us still,
Holding a big reward in store for
Those who do God's Will.

Thy Will be done,
Lord Jesus dear!
Life is such fun
For You are here!

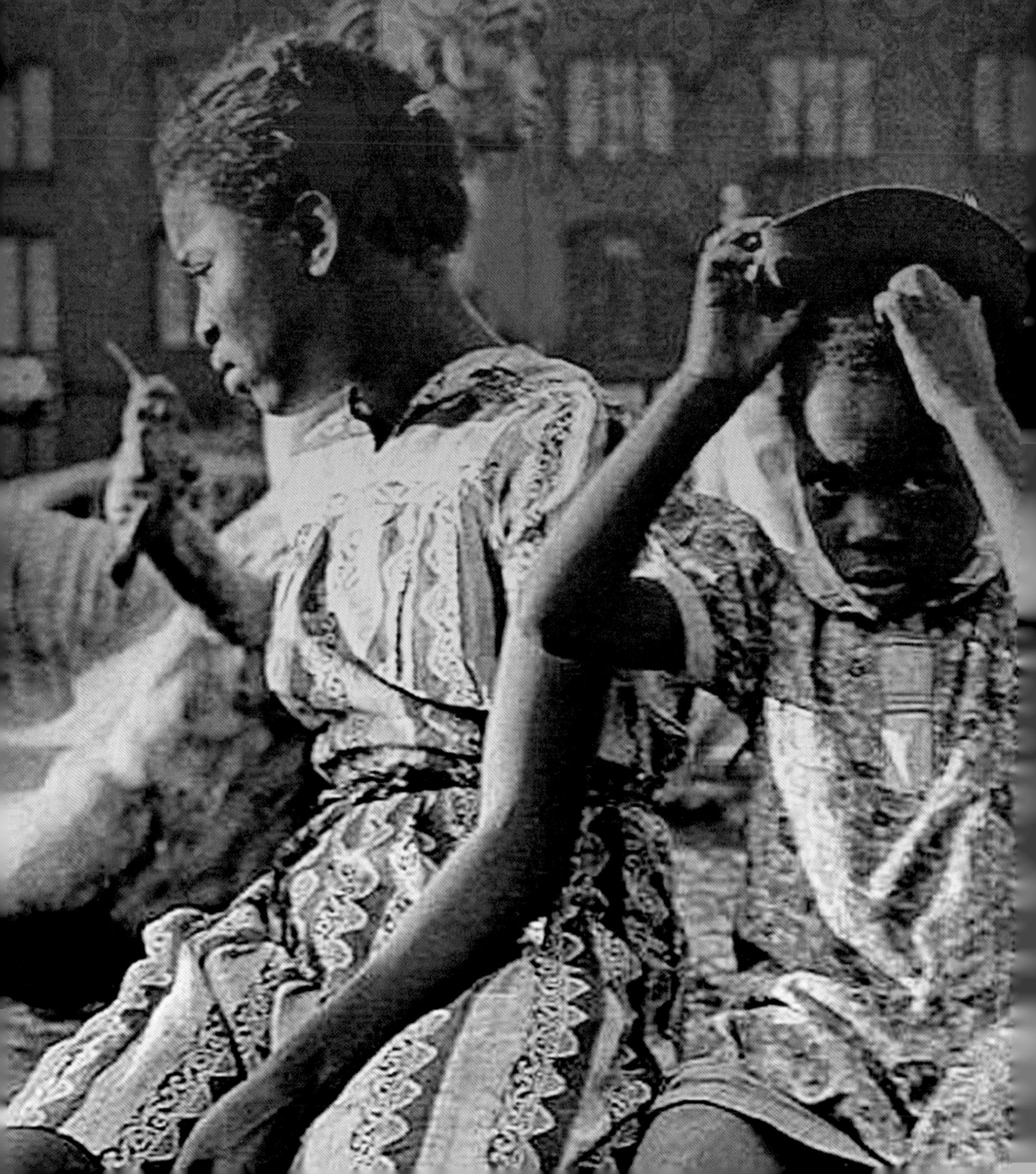

The School of Love Is Set

How sweet You are,
my Lord, my Love!
How beautiful! How good!
Please let me serve You lovingly
And suffer as I should!
Until we are in Heaven joined
In bliss beyond compare,
Until that moment comes I live
As if already there.

Jesus, Love,
Thy Will be done!
Keep on having
Heav'nly fun!

Growing up in a poor Black neighborhood amidst all the turbulence of interracial strife, Mary did not become a bitter victim of discrimination. Much later, as an elderly nun, she composed a couplet that no doubt echoed her own childhood: "A child's business is to play; without it he has lost the day." As a little girl, she and her brother had to pass through a white neighborhood to get to the library. "And we were runnin'!" she vividly recalled, lest they, as Black children, should get into trouble in a white neighborhood. A little white boy sitting on his front porch called to the pair, "Hiya, chocolate drops!" Without skipping a beat, she called back, "Hello, marshmallow!" When asked how the remarked was received, Sister said,"I don't know, we just kept on runnin'!" Another asked if the white boy spoke unkindly. Sister punned, "oh no, he was a *sweet* boy!"

No doubt Sister inherited her buoyant spirit and strength of soul from her parents. In her later years, Sr. Wilhelmina copied the oft-quoted poem by Edward Tuck, to which she added the title, "Ella Theresa Madden Lancaster's PHILOSOPHY":

Age is a quality of mind.
If you have left your dreams behind,
If hope is cold,
If you no longer look ahead,
If your ambitions' fires are dead,
Then you are old.

But if from life you take the best,
And if in life you keep the jest,
If love you hold,
No matter how the years go by,
No matter how the birthdays fly,
You are not old.

THE CABANNE BRANCH LIBRARY

one of seven St. Louis libraries built by Andrew Carnegie (left) was the favorite haunt of young Mary after her parishes. It is still functioning.

ELLA VOLUNTEERED *[fo]r events at St. Elizabeth's, and in the later 1940s for [th]e Sisters of the Helpers of [th]e Holy Souls (below) when [t]hey opened Sacred Heart Center on Garfield Ave.*

Despite segregation and material hardships, the Lancasters found their wealth and their dignity in their Faith. While her children attended catechism classes at St. Elizabeth's on Sunday, Ella Lancaster attended an informal course on theology for the laity taught by Fr. William Markoe. She later wrote:

> It was joy for me. When the opportunity came to help neighbors who came to me for counsel I was able to help. Many came to learn about the Catholic religion, or rather to discuss what they thought about white Catholics – prejudice, bigotry, Negro pride, etc. In time many decided they wanted instruction in Catholic Christian doctrine but did not want to go to a priest. Father Markoe gave me permission and I became an authorized catechist.

In an essay entitled "The Negro Looks at Catholicism," published in *The Interracial Review*, Ella wrote that many Black people considered the Catholic Church in America as the white man's church. She observed that the real obstacle to conversion was not doctrine, but prejudice:

> Those who have studied with me have had no difficulty in accepting the Catholic Church as the one true Church established by Christ for the salvation of men. Acts of prejudice perpetrated against them by white Catholics have been the obstacle that made it difficult for them to enter the Church. If all Catholics in America, white and Negro, kept the two great commandments of love of God and love of neighbor, I believe we would see in America in our day mass conversion of the Negro to Catholicism.

Ella Lancaster practiced what she preached. "My father was the first convert that my mother helped to make." Sr. Wilhelmina recounted. "Before her death in 1986, she had helped to make at least a hundred more."

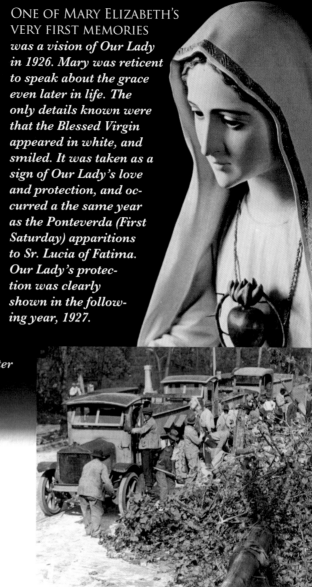

ONE OF MARY ELIZABETH'S VERY FIRST MEMORIES *was a vision of Our Lady in 1926. Mary was reticent to speak about the grace even later in life. The only details known were that the Blessed Virgin appeared in white, and smiled. It was taken as a sign of Our Lady's love and protection, and occurred a the same year as the Ponteverda (First Saturday) apparitions to Sr. Lucia of Fatima. Our Lady's protection was clearly shown in the following year, 1927.*

"LIKE A MATCH LIGHTING A BONFIRE" *was how the surprised St. Louis air mail clerk and inventor Charles Lindbergh described the world's reaction to his transatlantic flight of May 20-21, 1927, which shot him to stardom overnight. Greater spiritual forces were at work in his home town.*

Little Mary was particularly affected by her mother's zeal and also by a tender love for the Blessed Virgin Mary. One of her earliest memories was a vision of Our Lady: when Mary was only two years old and sitting in her high chair, she saw the Blessed Virgin Mary appear to her and smile at her. The rest of her family remembered this event and handed down the story, as one of Sr. Wilhelmina's nieces recalled more than ninety years later.

SEPTEMBER 29, 1927: THE PATH OF ST. LOUIS' SECOND DEADLIEST TORNADO

covered a seven mile stretch, including the Ville (left.) In five minutes, 78 were left dead, and 550 injured. The Lancasters home was spared (marked by a star, above) as was the new Cathedral (below, at center back of the photo) dedicated only the year before. But Saint Elizabeth's parish suffered damage, giving rise to a relocation.

Sr. Wilhelmina's most beloved way of honoring the Blessed Mother was the recitation of the Most Holy Rosary. Even as a seven-year-old child, Mary asked her siblings and playmates to pray the Rosary with her. When they refused, she tearfully had recourse to her mother, who replied that she should pray it by herself, which she did. This was the occasion of her second encounter with the Blessed Mother, who appeared to her and thanked her.

On another occasion, her brothers, Oscar and Billy had gone off to the river to fish while their sister was at home playing in the yard. Suddenly, Mary bolted into the house, exclaiming, "Mama, we've got

DOLLS OF MANY LANDS
a play produced at John Marshall Elementary School when Mary was in first grade there.

to pray the Rosary right now!" Her mother hesitated, surprised at her daughter's outburst, but Mary insisted that they must pray immediately for her brothers. So Ella consented and prayed the Rosary with her little daughter. When the boys returned, their mother asked them about their fishing excursion. At first, they replied that it had been fine, but when she persisted in her questioning, they confessed that the boat had capsized, and they had been afraid that they would drown. They were not sure why or how, but they managed to get back to the shore safely.

"Did it happen at such-and-such a time?" Ella queried, citing the time at which time Mary had rushed into the house."Yes, it was at that time," the boys answered. "Well, your sister was praying for you, that's why." Ella replied.

Sr. Wilhelmina remained a faithful and zealous proponent of the Holy Rosary all her life, even adding it to her religious name when she took vows as a Benedictine of Mary, becoming Sr. Mary Wilhelmina of the Most Holy Rosary.

Ella continued bringing up her children with a deep spirit of piety. One prayer Sr. Wilhelmina particularly remembered her teaching the youngsters was:

> Jesus, Mary and Joseph I give you my heart and my soul;
> Jesus, Mary, and Joseph, assist me in my last agony.
> Jesus, Mary and Joseph may I breathe forth my spirit in peace with you. Amen.

After repeating the prayer with them, Oscar suddenly looked up and said "Mama, is Benjamin gonna die?" Ella then explained that the prayer was to help them when they *would* die.

Priests, Lord!
Priests, Lord!
Save your priest!
Bring him to the
Heavenly feast!

Children! Children!
Like to play!
May they do so
In God's way.

Father! Mister!
Head of House!
Please be faithful
To your spouse!

Mother! Woman!
Save your soul!
Pray and practice
Self-control.

All religious
Please repent!
Lest to fiery Hell
You're sent!

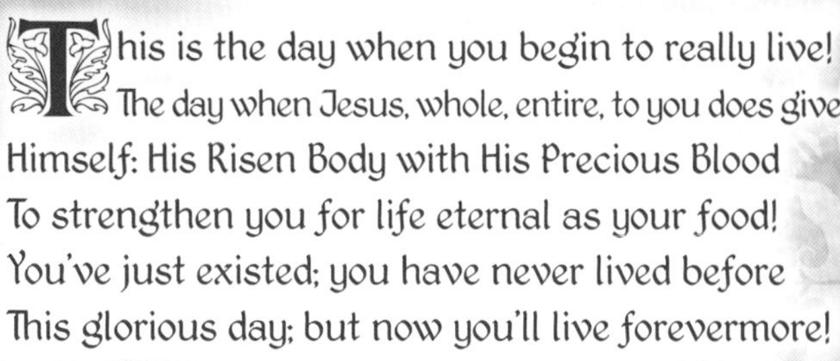

This is the day when you begin to really live!
The day when Jesus, whole, entire, to you does give
Himself: His Risen Body with His Precious Blood
To strengthen you for life eternal as your food!
You've just existed; you have never lived before
This glorious day; but now you'll live forevermore!

Being raised strong in the Faith, little Mary was well prepared for the grace of a religious vocation. This call came very early, with her first reception of Holy Communion, and her response was immediate and irrevocable. In her own words:

> I had scarlet fever when I was eight, so I couldn't make my first Communion 'til I was nine. I received my vocation on my First Communion day. On April 2, 1934, I made my first Holy Communion, an unforgettable experience, when Our Lord asked me, "Will you be mine?" He seemed to be such a handsome and wonderful man, I agreed immediately. Then He told me to meet Him every Sunday at Holy Communion: "You come to Communion every time you come to Mass," He said. I said nothing about this conversation to anyone, believing that everyone that went to Holy Communion heard Our Lord talk to them."

Sr. Wilhelmina continued the story of her first Holy Communion:

> Well, the next week, I got up and got a drink of water like I usually did. Back then, water broke the fast required for Holy Communion. I went crying to my mother, "Mama, I broke my fast, I can't receive Communion." "Now you stop that foolishness," Mama replied, "You can receive Communion next week."

This commonsense reply did not console Mary, and as she remained in her pew while everyone else went up to receive Communion, she could not check her tears. This was more than her father

MARY ELIZABETH LANCASTER
at age nine.

GOD of Beauty!
GOD of Love!
Reigning High
in Heaven above,
FATHER, SON
and SPIRIT DOVE!
ONLY ONE
I'm thinking of!

At Communion Time

Oh, the beauty of our God!
He reigns in that ransomed soul
Who the path of penance trod
And doth practice self-control;
Who has humbly bowed to grace
And accepted heav'nly light
God for now has won the race,
Makes His loved one judge aright.
"'Tis no longer I that live,"
Cries the soul, "Christ lives in me!"
Steadfast, com-mu-ni-ca-tive,
Joined forever, let them be.

could bear, so he ran after the priest to ask for a dispensation for his little daughter. Whether he obtained this dispensation is not recorded, but Sr. Wilhelmina never forgot the tender solicitude of her father in this attempt. "That same, unfortunate, drink-water Sunday, April 9," Sister Wilhelmina concluded her memories of that day, "I was confirmed."

JOHN MARSHALL ELEMENTARY SCHOOL *where Ella taught before her marriage. It was later attended by Mary from Kindergarten through eighth grade.*

Mary remained faithful to her weekly meetings with Our Lord at Holy Communion, but as she later confessed, "In those days I hardly knew what belonging to Our Lord meant." The seed of a religious vocation lay hidden for several years.

Mary's faith helped her face the opposition both of segregation on the one hand and anti-Catholic sentiment on the other. She wrote:

> The public school that I attended– John Marshall Elementary- was only two blocks away from my house. Also two blocks away, in another direction, was Holy Ghost Catholic Church. Although long ago demolished, that church and its atmosphere are still vivid in my memory. What a difference a few steps from the sidewalk made! Once across the threshold, I was awestruck by that quiet place where sunlight streamed through multi-colored glass windows and played upon dark oaken pew and marble columns. The church had been built by Germans years before. The neighborhood had once been their neighborhood. In my childhood the congregation was still for the most part German: they returned in their cars every Sunday to worship there. My family and a few

HOLY GHOST CHURCH *photographed by Arteaga Studios. This parish was closer than St. Elizabeth's after the latter parish's relocation.*

THE INTERIOR OF HOLY GHOST
photographed by Arteaga Studios.

FR. LAWRENCE ROST
the first to suggest a religious vocation to Mary.

others like us sat in the rear of the church on the left side. The people in this section were the last ones to approach the Communion rail, but when I knelt to receive the Lord I felt no loss or deprivation whatever. My mother had taught me from my infancy that the church was God's house, and that the Lord Jesus Christ was truly present in the most holy Sacrament of the Altar. "What does it matter," she would say when talk of discrimination against us arose, "whether you are first or last in line, you receive the Lord!"

I was taunted at times by my schoolmates for my adherence to Catholicism. Words of ridicule and disapproval still resound: "You fool! You are going to the white man's church!" I would stand up to them with the emphatic reply "I belong to the Church that Christ established for all people! Of course the children would laugh at me…

At last, several years later, my confessor, Father Lawrence Rost, whom I saw every Saturday at Holy Ghost Church two blocks up the street, asked if I ever thought about being a Sister. I had not of course, but he thought I could be a good Sister. I went to work on the idea right away and wrote to the superior of the Oblate Sisters of Providence in Baltimore, Maryland for direction.

MARY ELIZABETH WITH FRIENDS
including future high schoolmates Mary Aloyse Foster (second from left) and Modean Jones (center.)

From day to day
We are not the same,
As we play with God
His eternal game;
We either get better
Or somewhat worse;

But God is the Judge
And He carries the purse.
He will repay us
For what we do here;
He loves us truly
And counts ev'ry tear.

MOTHER CONSUELLA CLIFFORD
recipient of the letter

This letter, preserved by the Oblate Sisters of Providence, displays Mary's single-heartedness and forthrightness, which remained two of her most signal characteristics. It is also written in her flawless penmanship, which she maintained to the end of her life:

4315 Garfield
St. Louis, Missouri
May, 6, 1937

Dear Mother Superior;

I am a girl, thirteen years old, and I would like to become a nun. I plan to come to your convent as soon as possible. I will graduate from Grade School next month. What I want to know is, whether you have to bring anything to the convent and what it is you have to bring. I hope I am not troubling you any, but I have my heart set on becoming a nun. (Of course I am a Catholic.)

God bless you and those under your command.

Respectfully,
Mary Elizabeth Lancaster

Sr. Wilhelmina recalled the Superior's response:

> Mother Mary Consuella Clifford wrote me back, told me that I was too young to enter the convent and advised that I finish high school first. She advised that I go to the Blessed Sacrament Sisters' school in Rock Castle, Virginia. The odd part about this advice is that the Oblate Sisters of Providence had a school for girls right there in St. Louis: St. Rita's Academy.

So Mary's pursuit of her vocation was delayed until her secondary education was completed, but the few Catholic options necessitated a new school.

ROCK CASTLE
the common name for St. Francis de Sales girls Academy in Virginia founded by Mother Drexel.

Chapter 5

Ite Ad

St. Joseph's High School in the Ville *founded by the Sisters of St. Joseph (with the help of the Lancasters) was the first High School for Black Catholics in Missouri. Fr. Patrick Malloy (center) started the St. Joseph's athletics program, introducing integrated sports into the Archdiocese and state.*

Go to Joseph!
He's the man!
Does each job
As best he can,
Best as any
Can be done:
All for Mary
And her Son.

Joseph

Saints Prepare the Way

O St. Joseph, great protector,
Strong and prompt before God's throne,
See all my desires and interests,
Take them for thy very own.

O St. Joseph, please assist me,
And from Jesus Christ obtain
Heaven's blessings and thanksgiving
For relief from earthly pain.

O St. Joseph, Jesus sleeping
In thy arms, I contemplate;
Kiss His dear head I beseech thee
While for His reward I wait;

I look forward to my passing
Through that penance
we call death;
Ask Him to give me His kisses
When I draw my parting breath.

ST. JOSEPH'S STUDENTS *in 1940, Mary Elizabeth and Oscar at center*

Around the time of Mary's graduation from Marshall and her letter to Mother Consuella, Ella and Oscar were enlisted in an enterprise. The Sisters of St. Joseph of Carondelet staffed St. Matthew's School in the Ville. One of them, Sister Anna Joseph Bercherer, saw the urgent need for continuity in a Black Catholic high school. This urgency increased after the Christian Brothers' McBride High School denied the entrance of a group of Black boys in 1937. Obtaining the support and permission of her superior, Mother Tarcisia, Sr. Anna Joseph approached the Lancasters to help establish a Black Catholic high school in that same year, 1937. Though Marshall was a public school, Sr. Wilhelmina recalled, "My parents, who did not want me to go to the public high school, got to work and founded St. Joseph's Catholic High School for Negroes which lasted until Archbishop Ritter put an end to segregation of Negroes in the Diocese." All five of the Lancaster children graduated from this school that their parents founded.

SR. ANNA JOSEP *foundress of St. Joseph's*

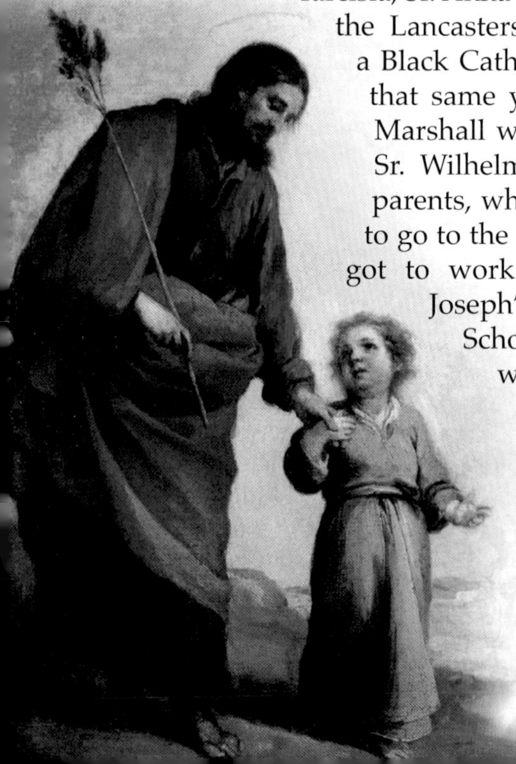

R. MARY RICARDA
low) Sister's History
nd French teacher

Others generously contributed their help and expertise, such as Redemptorist Fr. Donald Corrigan, who took on responsibilities at the new school along with his duties teaching Latin and math at St. Joseph College and Seminary. Seminarian Patrick Malloy led a formidable athletics department, playing its way into integration by challenging local white schools. It went on to become the first Black team to enter the State High School Athletic Association. Fr. Malloy continued his work at St. Joseph's after his ordination. Mary began her studies at St. Joseph's High School in its inaugural year.

During my four years in high school I sort of put the idea of becoming a Sister on the back burner, and applied myself to learning as much as I could about everything there was to learn. Unfortunately, my parents spoiled me and let me sit down much too much to books and papers when I should have been up cooking, sewing and doing household work. My mother was a bookworm, too, and she is mentioned in the little book, Negro Catholic Writers, which mentions her as being deceased many years before her death actually happened. Underground or along with the religious desire was my desire to become a writer. I wrote my first poem, or rhyme, when I was in the 4th grade and was made it over for someone special. I soon had a notebook full of rhymes, but this was not what I really wanted. I wanted to write stories, good fiction, like Little Women, and so on.

LITTLE WOMEN
as listed as one of Sr.
ilhelmina's five books
it most influenced her
as late as 2004.

LITTLE WOMEN
A STORY FOR GIRLS
By L. M. ALCOTT

HAROLD COPPING

POPULAR EDITION

LONDON
THE RELIGIOUS TRACT SOCIETY

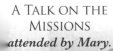

A TALK ON THE
MISSIONS
attended by Mary.

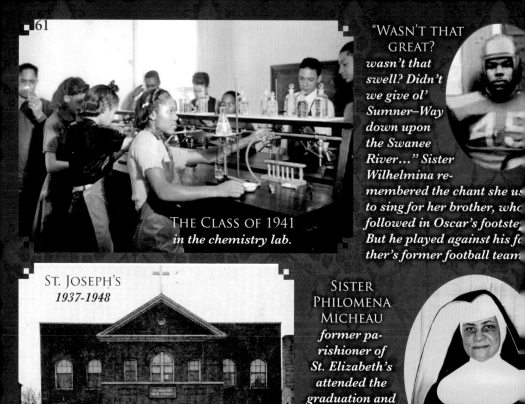

THE CLASS OF 1941
in the chemistry lab.

"WASN'T THAT GREAT? ***wasn't that swell? Didn't we give ol' Sumner–Way down upon the Swanee River…" Sister Wilhelmina remembered the chant she us to sing for her brother, who followed in Oscar's footste But he played against his fa ther's former football team***

ST. JOSEPH'S
1937-1948

SISTER PHILOMENA MICHEAU
former parishioner of St. Elizabeth's attended the graduation and received Mary Elizabeth's announcement.

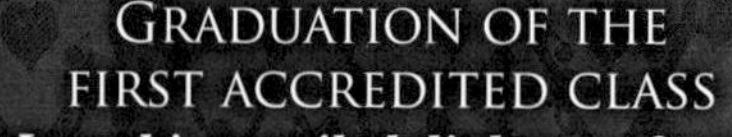

GRADUATION OF THE FIRST ACCREDITED CLASS
of St. Joseph's entailed diplomas from Fr. Charles Helmsing and congratulations from Senator Sullivan. Mary Elizabeth is at far right, Modean Jones to the left of her, Mary Aloyse Foster back center and Thomas Micheau front center.

THE CATHOLIC HIGH SCHOOL ASSOCIAT
OF THE
ARCHDIOCESE OF SAINT LOUIS
UPON RECOMMENDATION OF THE FACULTY OF
SAINT JOSEPH HIGH SCHOOL FOR NEGR
CERTIFIES THAT
MARY ELIZABETH LANCASTER
HAS SATISFACTORILY COMPLETED THE COURSE OF STUDY PRESCRIBE
AWARDED THIS
DIPLOMA
GIVEN THIS ST DAY OF JUNE, ONE THOUSAND NINE HUNDRED FO
SUPERINTENDENT
Charles H.
SECRETARY OF T

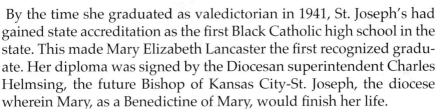

Mary never lost her love of words; she continued to write verses throughout her religious life, filling many notebooks with poetry to succeed this first one written during her childhood years.

By the time she graduated as valedictorian in 1941, St. Joseph's had gained state accreditation as the first Black Catholic high school in the state. This made Mary Elizabeth Lancaster the first recognized graduate. Her diploma was signed by the Diocesan superintendent Charles Helmsing, the future Bishop of Kansas City-St. Joseph, the diocese wherein Mary, as a Benedictine of Mary, would finish her life.

BISHOP CHARLES HELMSING
head of St. Louis schools and later Bishop of Kansas City and Springfield-Cape Girardeau.

The struggle for integration continued on the college level. Following their graduation, one of Mary's classmates, Mary Aloyse Foster, was denied admission to Webster College near St. Louis. Father John Markoe used this refusal as ammunition to break down the racial educational barrier in St. Louis, where even Catholic colleges such as Webster refused admission of Blacks. Ironically, Sr. Wilhelmina studied music at Webster College from 1953 until 1955, twelve years after Mary Aloyse was refused. Ethel Mattie Williams, another schoolmate of Mary, finally succeeded in being among the first five Blacks admitted to St. Louis University in 1944. This motivated Archbishop Ritter to begin integration of schools in his Diocese, threatening excommunication for resistance. He ordered all Catholics to attend the parish closest to them, which effectively closed St. Elizabeth's Parish for Blacks in 1949.

Two Oblate Sisters of Providence attended Mary's graduation on June 1, 1941. One of them was twenty-two-year-old Sr. Philomena Micheau, then stationed at the Oblates' school in St. Louis. Her brother was a member of Mary's graduating class. Sister Wilhelmina recalled their meeting, which manifests again her customary forthrightness:

> The day of my graduation from high school, two Oblate Sisters of Providence were present. When I walked out of the church, I went straight to them standing in the vestibule and told them that I wanted to be one of them. They were shocked, and I was satisfied that I had done what had to be done.

Saint Joseph
was not only patron of the Lancaster's new High School, but also of the Novitiate of the Oblate Sisters of Providence.

Honor St. Joseph's
Fidelity
to grace!
That you may
come at last
To see God's face.

Honor St. Joseph's
Fidelity
to interior life!
That you may
overcome
In all your
earthly strife.

Honor St. Joseph's
Love for Mary!
That to God's Will
You never
be contrary.

Honor St. Joseph's
Love for
the Holy Child!
That you pass
through life
Pure and undefiled.

Servant of God Mother Mary Lange
(top right) Foundress of the Oblate Sisters of Providence with Fr. Joubert (above right.) He received the vows of Mother Mary and Mother Theresa Duchemin (center right, later foundress of the Immaculate Heart of Mary Sisters) in the lower chapel of St. Mary's Seminary in Baltimore (far right). The vows of St. Elizabeth Ann Seton (right) were also received here. Mother Seton went on to found the Sisters of Charity of Saint Joseph in Emmitsbug, Maryland. Statues of Mother Seton and Mother Lange flank the altar in St. Mary's crypt.

We must do
all we can to feed
The hungry men
about us,
And succouring
their every need,
No parsimony
clout us.

At the time, there were only two religious orders for Black or Hispanic women in the United States. Fr. William Markoe, guided her to one, the Oblate Sisters of Providence. Mother Mary Elizabeth Lange founded this active community of Black sisters in the early 19th century, primarily for the Christian education of Black children.

Mother Lange was born Elizabeth Clarisse Lange in a Haitian community in Cuba around 1784, and received an excellent education. The slave uprising in Haiti in the late 1700s led to her departure from Cuba to the United States. Travelling up the southern states, she settled in Baltimore in 1813.

Baltimore's free Black population already outnumbered the slave population, and there was also a sizeable French-speaking African Caribbean population that had fled the Haitian revolt. Baltimore had few educational opportunities for Black children, especially for the poor. There were no free public schools for Black children in Baltimore until 1866. The few Protestant schools for Black students could not meet the demands of Baltimore's growing free Black population, especially the Catholics. Elizabeth Lange recognized the urgent need, and opened a free school in her home in the Fells Point area of the city with the help of another Carribean woman.

Elizabeth Lange met a Sulpician priest at Baltimore in 1828: Fr. James Marie Hector Nicholas Joubert de la Muraille, a native Frenchman and former soldier. He had also fled the Haitian slave revolt, and headed off teaching catechism to the young refugees who attended Mass at the Lower Chapel at Saint Mary's Seminary. Their illiteracy made for slow progress, so Fr. Joubert asked Elizabeth to consider founding an order of Sisters to teach and care for Black children. With the addition of two more women, a community began to form, and gained Diocesan approval in 1829.

Your Heart must truly triumph,
Immaculate, Serene,
And recognized by everyone
As Mother and as Queen.

In a document composed for the 160th anniversary of the Oblates' foundation in 1989 entitled "A Sesquicentennial Salute," Sr. Wilhelmina takes up the story of these humble origins of her community:

> Just as Americans in this late Twentieth Century are divided over the question of whether or not a child in his mother's womb is a human being with a right to life, so in the early Nineteenth Century people were divided over the question of whether or not the slaves had souls. It was in this milieu that the Oblate Sisters of Providence were founded, as a religious institute, July 2, 1829.
>
> Their original oblation was a promise of obedience to the Archbishop of Baltimore, at that time the Most Reverend James Whitfield, and to their superior chosen from among themselves, she then being Sister Mary, the former Elizabeth Lange.
>
> Three years later, on July 2, 1832, the Sisters made vows of poverty, chastity and obedience.
>
> A significant step in between these two events – these two wonderful July seconds – was the community's entry into the association of Holy Slavery of Mary the Mother of God, or, their formal inauguration of the practice of the True Devotion taught by St. Louis Marie Grignon de Montfort. (He was Venerable then.) It happened on July 2, 1830: the entrants were altogether nine persons, including the founder, Reverend James Marie Hector Nicholas Joubert de la Muraille. July second, throughout the years, has been regarded by the Oblate Sisters of Providence as their day of triple consecration, the fountainhead of all their spirituality which has ensued.

O Mother mine!
I am all thine!
Immaculate!
I'm thine Oblate.
Tell thy Divine
His Will is mine.

As the founding superior, Mother Mary Lange entrusted the new community to the patronage of St. Frances of Rome, a widow and Benedictine oblate. Sister Wilhelmina adds a note about St. Frances of Rome in the same essay:

Waste not a minute
Not praying!
Or you war in it
Betraying.

SAINTS LOUIS DE MONTFORT AND FRANCES OF ROME *patrons of the Oblates of Providence (left and below.)*

Francesca, daughter of Paul and Jacobella Bussa, was born in Rome in the year 1384. Her mother was a very devout person, in the habit of visiting every day some of the churches. Francesca, from her infancy, was a pious child. She wanted to give herself completely to God as a religious, but her father refused to go along with this desire and ordered her, when she was twelve years old, to marry the wealthy nobleman, Lorenzo Ponziano. Guided by her confessor, Don Antonio Savello, Francesca made the sacrifice of her own will to God's will and married Lorenzo, to whom she bore six children.

While Francesca was a married woman seeing to the education of her children and working in behalf of her sick, poor neighbors, God assigned an archangel to her as a visible guardian. She saw him always for the remainder of her life, which was long and full of trials. Francesca never gave up assiduous prayer.

Four of her six children having died as infants and her husband's health having begun to decline, Francesca began laying the foundation of the Oblates of Mary of Mount Olivet of the Benedictine Order. Other women, under Francesca's encouragement and guidance, gave themselves to fasting, to prayer and to charitable services. Consecrating themselves to the Blessed Virgin Mary on the feast of the Assumption in the year 1425, they eventually became the original members of this group. Not until after the death of her husband several years later was Francesca able to join the community which she herself had founded. Today she is hailed as a model for young girls, the example of a devout matron, and finally a true widow, according to the very pattern drawn up by St. Paul.

5 St. Mary's Court
the Oblates' first school in Baltimore

Perhaps Mother Mary Lange's choice of this patroness was St. Frances' devotion to the education of her children and to corporal and spiritual works of mercy for the poor. The very Rule of the Oblate Sisters of Providence had many Benedictine practices and overtones, and also a special consecration to the Blessed Virgin, as did St. Frances' community of Oblates. This Benedictine and Marian influence formed Mother Mary's spiritual daughter, Sr. Wilhelmina, who in God's providence would one day become a foundress herself of a new community of Oblates, the future Benedictines of Mary.

With just the four founding sisters and twenty students, Mother Mary Lange opened a Catholic school for girls in a rented house at 5 St. Mary's Court in Baltimore. Thus began St. Frances Academy, the oldest continuously operating school for Black Catholic children in the United States. The academy continues to educate children in Baltimore to this day.

Enduring untold hardships, the Oblate Sisters sought to evangelize the Black community through Catholic education. In addition to schools, the sisters later conducted night classes for women, vocational and career training, and established homes for widows and orphans.

They also gave themselves generously to other acts of charity. A cholera epidemic broke out in Baltimore in 1832, when the community numbered just eleven members. The city officials had asked the Sisters of Charity

The Cholera Epidemic of 1832
threatened the newly formed Oblates of Providence

for eight sisters to serve the victims of the epidemic, but had only received four. They then sought help from Fr. Joubert, who approached the little community of the Oblates of Providence. The Sisters of Charity were, by the spirit of their institute, obliged to look after the sick, he told the sisters. The Oblates of Providence were dedicated to the education of Black children, but he hoped that the Oblates "would not have less charity than the daughters of St. Paul." When he then asked for volunteers to risk their lives in nursing the cholera victims, the entire community rose. He only chose four, however: Mother Mary Lange herself and three companions. So great was the danger of death, that the only sister who had not yet made religious profession was allowed to do so at the morning Mass the next day before setting out to minister to the sick and dying. Fr. Joubert later recalled his sermon to the sisters at that Mass:

> I addressed a few words to them on the good work they were about to undertake, on the merits attached to the sacrifice they were making to God of the life He had given them. I pointed out to them the dangers to which they were obliged to expose themselves in thus devoting themselves to the service of the sick poor... I told them that if God permitted that they should be victims of their zeal, they would die martyrs of charity.

One of these heroic Oblates of Providence did indeed obtain such a martyrdom of charity.

Father Saint Benedict
Help us to humbly pray
The Work of God
throughout each day;
Keeping silence as we should
Doing our manual labor
Loving God and loving too
Each needy neighbor.

Father Saint Benedict
Help us to bravely seek
God's Will and learning
of Jesus meek,
Following obedient
Each given true command
Holding with heart,
mind and soul
Our Blessed Mother's hand.

St. Benedict! St. Benedict!
Please help all those who are sick!

THE RULE OF SAINT BENEDICT
inspired the Rule and way of life of the Oblates of Providence.

Lord, strengthen,
assist and save
Thy bishops,
priests and deacons
He who puts
his trust in Thee
Ne'er falters, halts
nor weakens.

God's priest!
God's priest!
What can we do?
That be he holy!
That he be true!
Give him to his mother
Mary Our Queen!
She will see that he behaves
And reaches Life Serene.

The death of Fr. Joubert in 1843 was a crisis for the Oblates, who no longer had a chaplain to offer daily Mass for them and to support them in their struggle to maintain their fledging community. Not many were supportive of the small convent of Black sisters. Yet Divine Providence intervened: the sisters' convent adjoined a Redemptorist parish, in the care of St. John Neumann, who not only served the sisters' spiritual needs, but also introduced them to another Redemptorist priest named Fr. Thaddeus Anwander. So great was Fr. Anwander's concern for the Oblates that on his knees he begged St. John Neumann, his superior, to serve as the Oblates' chaplain. He proved to be a second father and founder of the Oblates.

FATHER ANWANDER *a classmate of Blessed Francis Xavier Seelos (below) begged St. John Neumann (left) to serve as the Oblates' chaplain.*

From the community's inception in 1829 until her death on February 3, 1882, Mother Mary Lange never ceased to spend herself for the community. For some years she even worked as a domestic servant at St. Mary's Seminary in Baltimore to help support her sisters. The community's diary records the delicate balance that the Black sisters strove to maintain as religious while undertaking such menial work:

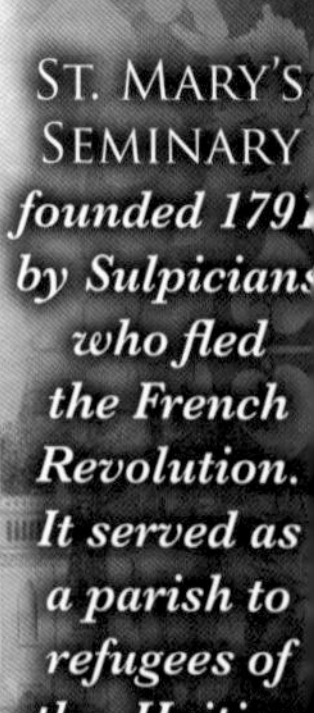

ST. MARY'S SEMINARY *founded 1791 by Sulpicians who fled the French Revolution. It served as a parish to refugees of the Haitian Revolution.*

In 1879 *the Oblates gathered for a group photo beneath a portrait of Fr. Joubert one year before Sisters were sent to St. Elizabeth's parish. The Sisters adopted a veil in 1906.*

We do not conceal the difficulty of our situation as persons of color and religious at the same time, and we wish to conciliate these two qualities in such a manner as not to appear too arrogant on the one hand and on the other, not to miss the respect which is due to the state we have embraced and the holy habit which we have the honor to wear.

Sr. Wilhelmina inherited from her spiritual mother this humble self-effacement united to a deep understanding of the dignity of her religious state, particularly as manifested in the holy habit.

The difficult beginning of the Oblate Sisters, with challenges from poverty, racial discrimination and periods without a chaplain, was not without consolations and even times of lightheartedness. Sister Wilhelmina gladly shared one of these stories, preserved through the Oblates' oral tradition: at a profession ceremony in the very early days of the community, when the Oblates' chapel was located on a busy inner-city street of Baltimore, the chaplain, possibly Fr. Joubert himself, solemnly asked the sisters about to make profession, "Beloved daughters, what do you wish?" But before they could respond with the formal request to profess vows, the raucous call of a street vendor blared through the open chapel window for all to hear: "HOT DEVILLED CRABS!" The community and congregation burst into laughter, and Sr. Wilhelmina herself could never re-tell this story without a chuckle.

Jesus, my Love
I love Thee Love!
lease may I love Thee more
oday my Love
han I have ever
oved Thee, Love, before!

Chapter 6

See That

What God wants is what I want,
And nothing else besides!
God Almighty knows the end
Of all our earthly rides.

Expect the unexpected
While you stay well-connected
To all the goings-on within
Your holy family;
Protect the unprotected –
Although quite unsuspected –
The urgent need, day in, day out,
For flexibility.

A Train Pulls Out *of the station at Relay, Maryland, in the early 1940s just as it would have done after leaving Mary Elizabeth Lancaster to her Novitiate there.*

Mary, my Mother, you are so meek and strong,
So zealous, prudent, never in the wrong;
Humble, courageous, fruitful and so pure;
Renouncing self, I give myself to you entire.

You are the mold of God; every perfection –
The Holy Ghost has formed His own confection;
In my small measure I must gaze and imitate,
Admiring God's mold, so exclusive and so great!

O Garden Paradise of the New Adam,
Where He was formed of your immaculate earth,
There, planted by the hand of God and watered
By His unction, you gave us His day of birth.

O Eastern Gate by which our High Priest entered!
O fountain sealed, by which He shall return!
You are my means mysterious for finding JESUS
For you alone, I fight, I work, I live, I learn.

Door? Going Forth to Meet the Bridegroom

He speaks
Of His eternal love,
His love that never changes;
And everything that happens,
Happens just as He arranges;
So we should never worried be
About our circumstances,
For Love of God eternally
Is greatest of romances.

You are in it!
See, you're in it
If you've giv'n yourself to God!
Just be faithful,
Ever faithful
While you live upon earth's sod.

The Parable of the Ten Virgins

one of the final parables of Christ, was one that Sister particularly loved.

O all ye holy Virgins, help us to be prudent, wise
While waiting for the Groom's return, with watchful open eyes.
But if we nod and fall asleep because of heavy toil
Make sure we carry lighted lamps and vast supplies of oil!

Queen of Apostles,
Mystical Rose,
Help us to bravely
Never oppose
God's Will for us, but –
Lamps lighted bright –
Follow Christ bravely
All through this night.

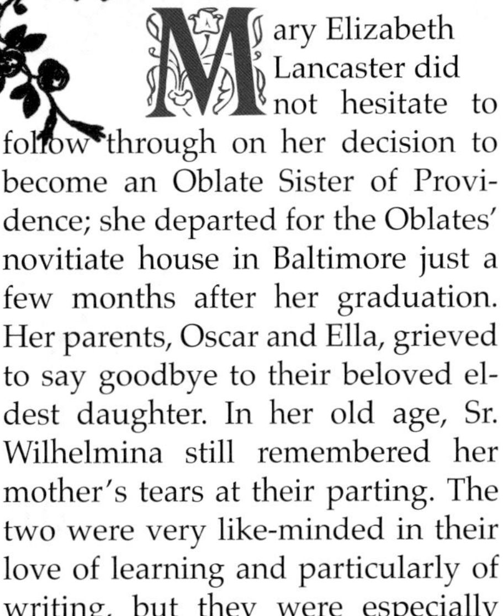

Mary Elizabeth Lancaster did not hesitate to follow through on her decision to become an Oblate Sister of Providence; she departed for the Oblates' novitiate house in Baltimore just a few months after her graduation. Her parents, Oscar and Ella, grieved to say goodbye to their beloved eldest daughter. In her old age, Sr. Wilhelmina still remembered her mother's tears at their parting. The two were very like-minded in their love of learning and particularly of writing, but they were especially close through their mutual devotion to their Catholic Faith. This Faith, however, strengthened them to make the sacrifice of parting, and Mary boarded the train to follow the Lord wherever He would lead her.

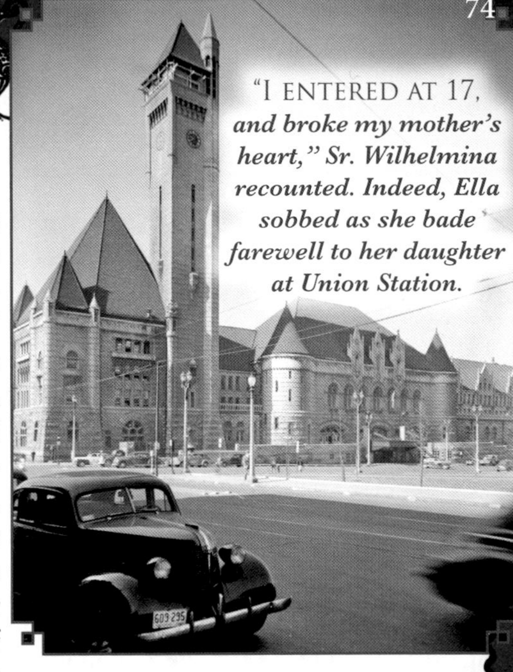

"I ENTERED AT 17, *and broke my mother's heart," Sr. Wilhelmina recounted. Indeed, Ella sobbed as she bade farewell to her daughter at Union Station.*

> So that September, at age 17, I left my parents' house for Baltimore, Maryland. Sister Philomena Micheau, one of the sisters who attended my graduation and who was superior of St. Frances Home for Girls in Normandy, gave me a trunk. Two of her sisters who happened to be going to Baltimore accompanied me on my journey there in September.

Mary had no illusions about the challenges of the novitiate. She recalled in later years, "I knew that the novitiate was a time of trial during which the community would look me over and decide whether I had a vocation to it or not." When she and her band of classmates arrived at the Oblates' novitiate house at Relay, Maryland, they were greeted by the novice mistress, Sr. Mary Inez Calthirst. "See that door?" Sr. Inez turned to the newly arrived group of postulants and pointed with a foreboding air to the door through which they had just entered to commence their novitiate. "It swings both ways!"

THE MANNING ESTATE *at Relay served as the Oblates' Novitiate until a fire destroyed it in 1945.*

My Jesus Christ

There is no man so
handsome and so grand,
As Jesus Christ, the Godman,
Whom I love;
His head is as the finest gold,
His hand
Shall yet embrace
His precious little dove.
His eyes as doves
upon the flowing streams,
His cheeks all spiced,
His lips filled with choice myrrh;
His ivory belly
sapphire-studded gleams;
His form of Libanus,
excellent as the fir;
His throat most sweet,
and He Himself delight;
My Love I love
and He my Love loves me
From thousands chosen,
ruddy red and white,
He is the King for all eternity.
Ah, then He shall embrace
His little dove,
My Jesus Christ! My Nazarene!
The Man I love

Sister Philomena, who had seen Mary to the station in St. Louis, became novice mistress of the community just after Sr. Wilhelmina's profession. Sister Wilhelmina probably would have preferred to have been formed by her, having already known her as a fellow St. Louisan, but accepted God's Providence in her formation under Sr. Inez. She nevertheless carried Sr. Philomena's promise of prayer with her for the remainder of her life. A visible reminder of this was the cross Sr. Philomena gave Sr. Wilhelmina, which was affixed to her rosary. Sister Wilhelmina cherished the gift and used the rosary until misplacing it in 2001.

Sr. Inez, on the other hand, had deep psychological problems made especially manifest the year after Sr. Wilhelmina's profession and after the novitiate building burned down. Some of Sr. Wilhelmina's stories about her novitiate days hinted at Sr. Inez' strict discipline, but Sr. Wilhelmina never made a complaint about her. Rather, she seemed grateful for the sense of sacrifice that Sr. Inez instilled in her novices.

Sister Wilhelmina's faith in the Lord's personal love for her sustained her from the very first day of her novitiate. Years later, she recalled:

> That September day, when I entered the novitiate chapel for the first time, that same Lord Who spoke to me in my First Communion, welcomed me lovingly, put His arms around me and promised that from then on I would be His.

OBLATE POSTULANTS
eager to begin.

St. William the Abbot, Sister's patron.

In March 1942, after the initial period of postulancy, Mary exchanged a white bridal gown for her religious habit, which she treasured until the day of her death; the sign of her consecration as a Bride of Christ. All the postulants were allowed to submit three suggestions for their religious name. Mary's great devotion to St. John the Baptist prompted her to write "Sr. Mary Baptista." But her formators advised her, "No, you should ask for 'Wilhelmina,' since you are the last sister sent by Fr. William Markoe." So the young postulant tearfully added, "Sr. Mary Wilhelmina," as a second choice. This was the name she received, much to her disappointment, as she later admitted. Here again, however, Divine Providence entrusted her to the patronage of a great Benedictine, St. William the Abbot.

As a novice, Sr. Mary Wilhelmina eagerly studied the Rule and history of her community. She developed a deep and trusting abandonment to Divine Providence. As an old nun, she would walk the halls of the convent, beating time with her cane and chanting her "Marching Song":

GOD's will, GOD's will,
GOD's will be done!
Praised be the Father!
Praised be the Son!

Praised be Divine Love,
Lord HO-ly Ghost!
Praised be in union
with the heavenly host!

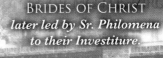

BRIDES OF CHRIST
later led by Sr. Philomena to their Investiture.

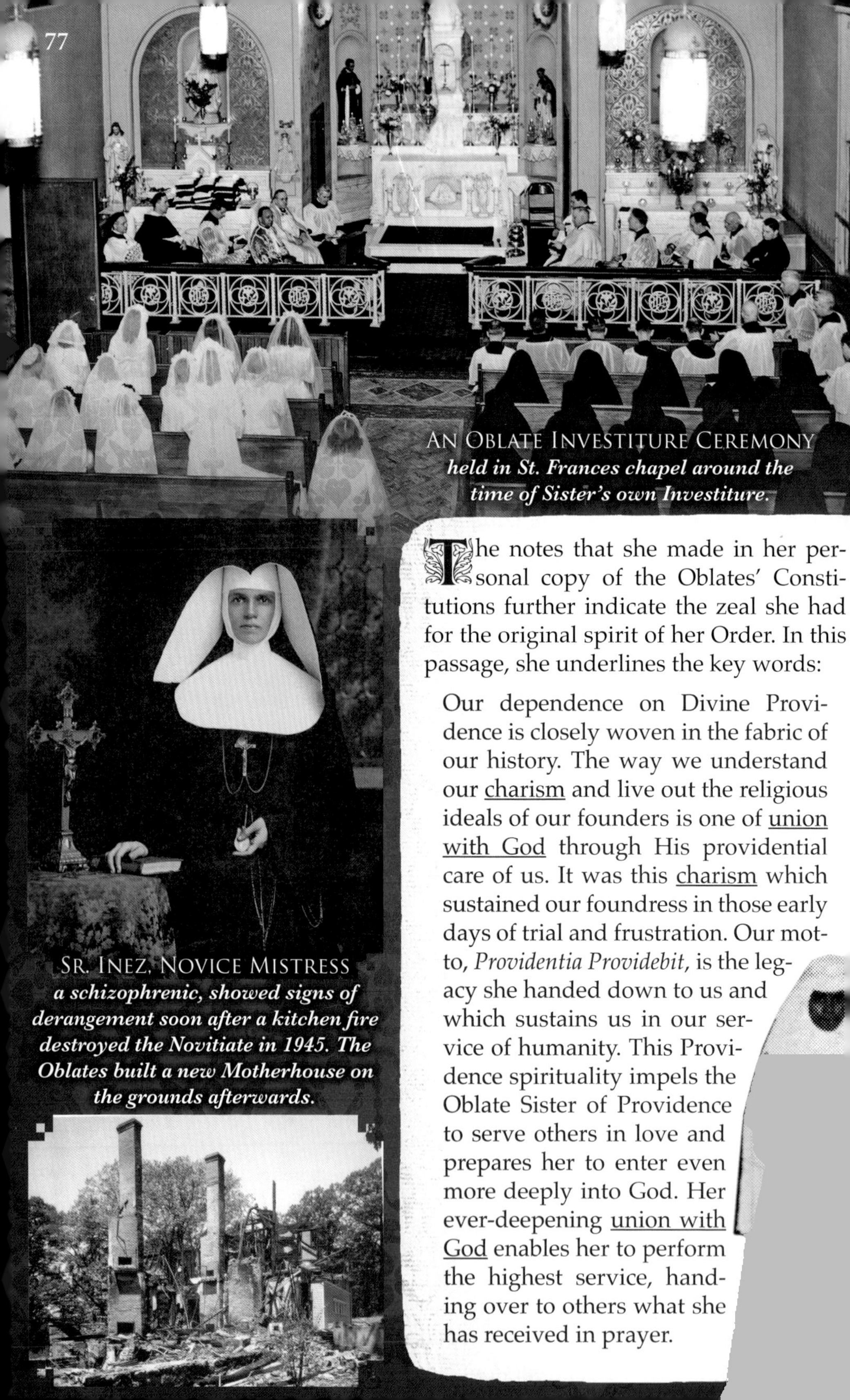

AN OBLATE INVESTITURE CEREMONY *held in St. Frances chapel around the time of Sister's own Investiture.*

SR. INEZ, NOVICE MISTRESS *a schizophrenic, showed signs of derangement soon after a kitchen fire destroyed the Novitiate in 1945. The Oblates built a new Motherhouse on the grounds afterwards.*

The notes that she made in her personal copy of the Oblates' Constitutions further indicate the zeal she had for the original spirit of her Order. In this passage, she underlines the key words:

> Our dependence on Divine Providence is closely woven in the fabric of our history. The way we understand our charism and live out the religious ideals of our founders is one of union with God through His providential care of us. It was this charism which sustained our foundress in those early days of trial and frustration. Our motto, *Providentia Providebit*, is the legacy she handed down to us and which sustains us in our service of humanity. This Providence spirituality impels the Oblate Sister of Providence to serve others in love and prepares her to enter even more deeply into God. Her ever-deepening union with God enables her to perform the highest service, handing over to others what she has received in prayer.

"GET WOOD,"
was often the sole order Sr. Wilhelmina id her companions received in the morn-g when reporting to Sr. Inez for the day's vork assignment. They would proceed to ie woods surrounding Relay (above) and chop firewood the whole day long.

God wills that each day I work:
First of all there's manual labor,
Which should help my needy neighbor.
This expands to Opus Dei
And INTERIOR ASCETICISM
Must be sure and not a maybe.
None of these three kinds I shirk.

These words, "charism" and "union with God," profoundly resonated with her who had embraced religious life as a life of fidelity to the Lord with whom she was so deeply in love.

In the margins of this copy of the constitutions, she adds in her own hand, "Our <u>first</u> constitution, drawn up by Fathers Joubert and Tessier, stated: "The sisters shall form but one class, and all shall wish with joy to do the meanest work." Throughout her religious life, Sr. Wilhelmina never shirked any task given her, no matter how tedious or unpleasant. As a novice, she had no teaching engagements, but much training in domestic chores. "We did a lot of SWIC," she remembered, "Sweeping, Washing, Ironing and Cooking." "Get wood," was the command she most frequently received. So off she would go, no matter the weather, to chop and split wood all day.

THE BAND ON THEIR INVESTITURE DAY,
Sister Wilhelmina (center left) loved her companions dearly. All persevered in their vocations.

SR. DOROTHY, ONE OF FOUR *Burks sisters who entered the Oblates, and one of Sister's band.*

Sister kept her high spirits at all times, even after her newly earned driver's license was taken away. "It felt so *good* to be out driving," she recalled. "The problem was that I turned right when I *saw* the intersection… right into a man's parked car." The gentleman came out of the store furiously yelling in Spanish. "He did not know I understood, and I wouldn't repeat it," she said. Years later, when a novice took Sr. Wilhelmina, then in her eighties, for a car ride, the novice asked her if she would like to take the wheel. Sr. Wilhelmina replied, "Not unless you want to go up one side of the tree and down the other!"

SR. KATHARINE *outlived her other band members, celebrating her 100th birthday (above) just before this writing.*

She often recalled another novitiate misadventure: "I got new high-top boots. I was so proud of them until I fell down the stairs with a whole stack of plates." If a sister broke anything, her penance would be to kneel in the refectory holding the broken item before being permitted to eat, so the other novices cried out, "Oh, Sr. Wilhelmina, how're you gonna hold all those?" As her novice mistress inspected Sr. Wilhelmina's wrist, lacerated by the broken dishes, Sr. Wilhelmina quoted their monthly meditation on the Passion: "And the red blood ran down!" To which Sr. Inez retorted, "When you get better, I'm gonna punish you!" Returning to her companions, Sr. Wilhelmina continued quoting the meditation, "I have trodden the wine press alone." Telling the story years later, she would add confidentially, in light of Sr. Inez' reproach, "And I never *did* get better!"

SR. MICHAEL *much loved by Sister, was the prominent musician of her band, pictured above in a music class*

On another occasion, some newspapers were accidentally delivered to the novitiate. The young sisters in formation had limited contact with the outside world, especially through secular media, and so decided to take advantage of this rare occurrence. The group of them immediately found and divided the comic strips, which they were enjoying when Sr. Inez unexpectedly appeared. Sister Wilhelmina imitated her terse assessment of the situation: "I don't think you're gonna find those funnies as funny as you think you are!"

IN OLD AGE *Sister could not resist "the funnies" even amidst donated "packing paper."*

Although Sr. Wilhelmina did not return to St. Louis until years later as a professed sister, she maintained her precious family ties. One of her joys as a novice, she recalled, was a letter about her father, who, sharing his wife's missionary zeal, brought his own father into the Catholic Church:

> I learned that my father had gone back to Georgia to help his own father, William Lancaster, Jr., on his deathbed. My grandfather had lived his life without any religious faith to speak of, interested only in raising hogs and corn and making regular visits to the saloon in town. My father found the nearest Catholic priest and brought him to the bedridden old man. With my father's encouragement, Grandfather Lancaster received instruction in the Catholic faith and was baptized by the priest. He died peacefully the next day.

Sr. Wilhelmina's time of formation included growth in her devotion to the Blessed Mother:

> My two and a half years in the novitiate were a happy time, during which I learned from a fellow novice, thirteen years older than I was, about True Devotion to Mary taught by St. Louis de Montfort. We had no book about it; Sr. Alma simply reiterated emphatically that I had no true devotion to Mary because I did not belong to her as her slave. I was so moved by this that I went to the novice-mistress, Sr. Inez, and asked if I could become a slave of Mary, like Sr. Alma was. Sister Inez, amused, grabbed the chain I was wearing and said that this was the sign that all Oblates were slaves of Mary. The miraculous medal and chain were placed around the neck of each novice when she received the habit.

SR. ALMA *another band member, encouraged Sr. Wilhemina in the Montfortian Consecration*

TRUE DEVOTION

We stand with Mother
Church who once
Was founded on a Rock;
The Church is one, and
We are one
No matter what the shock.
We stand together by the Church
On bloody Calvary;
In her we live, for her we die
Oblations, who will be
Her saints forever through her help
For all eternity.

SEAT OF WISDOM *by Henri Bouriche was associated with the Sulpicians. Sr. Wilhelmina received this replica in her formative years and kept it always in her cell until her death. Bouriche also created the altarpiece of Notre Dame in Montreal, later visited by Sister.*

Sr. Wilhelmina wore her beloved miraculous medal through her entire religious life, including her last years as a Benedictine of Mary. Her new order continued the tradition of placing the blessed medal and chain around the neck of each young woman being received into the community. As an elderly sister, she would devoutly kiss the medal whenever she put it on in the morning or took it off at night and would pray the inscription aloud, "O Mary, conceived without sin, pray for us who have recourse to thee!" She never failed to add her own intentions: "And for those who do NOT have recourse to thee, especially Freemasons, atheists, abortionists..." In her late eighties and early nineties, she always concluded with, "Obama and his wife and daughters!" And in the very last years of her life, "and for Donald Trump and his family!"

Sr. Wilhelmina also brought her love of writing with her into religious life and dedicated it to the service of her Beloved Lord and His Blessed Mother. Her earliest extant poem dates from around 1944:

MIRACULOUS MEDAL *revealed to St. Catherine Laboure*

Saturday Prayer

Sweet Lady, thanks for all your care for us!
You've been so good- we have no right to fuss.
Yet we entreat thee not to think us grown
And reach out all on our own.
We are thy babes, in diapers, not in silk;
We're but newborn and howling for thy milk;
Nay! We are in thy womb, frail seed, unborn:
Oh, bear us Christlike some bright winter morn!

MARYLAND SNOWS *provided much fun for the young Sisters.*

THE SILVER JUBILEE REUNION
***Seated left to right:** Sr. M. Dorothy Burks, Sr. M. Katharine Brent, Sr. M. Michael Grant, Sr. M. Robert Rodgers, Sr. M. Wilhelmina Lancaster.*
***Standing left to right:** Sr. M. Immaculate (later Sr. Naomi) Smith, Sr. M. Augustine Green, Sr. M. Denise Blocker, Sr. M. Alma Richardson.*

This bright winter morn was realized for her in a special way on the day of her profession, on the feast of the Benedictine Oblate, St. Frances of Rome:

> I was allowed to make vows of poverty, chastity and obedience on March 9, 1944. "Beloved daughters, what do you wish?" my novitiate companions and I were asked that day in 1944 when we took our first vows in St. Frances Chapel in Baltimore. "Right Reverend Monsignor," we responded in unison, "the goodness of God has shown me the nothingness of this world and all that the world holds dear. I desire to consecrate myself to Jesus Christ, to serve Him with all my heart in this pious association of which I promise to observe the rules with an entire fidelity."

More than 50 years after the day of her first profession of religious vows, as she set out to found a new order of sisters, Sr. Wilhelmina recalled these words of petition, declaring, "I desire that no less today."

Sister made her final profession as an Oblate Sister of Providence on the feast of the Assumption, August 15, 1950. It was the same day on which St. Frances of Rome had made her consecration to Our Lady in 1425. It was also the 33rd anniversary of the vow that her spiritual director, Fr. William Markoe, had made to devote his life to the service of the Black people. On that day in 1950, Sr. Wilhelmina received a silver nuptial ring espousing her forever to Jesus Christ. Inscribed in her ring were the date and the simple initials: "JMJF," signifying her devotion to Jesus, Mary, Joseph and the order's special patroness, the Benedictine Oblate St. Frances of Rome.

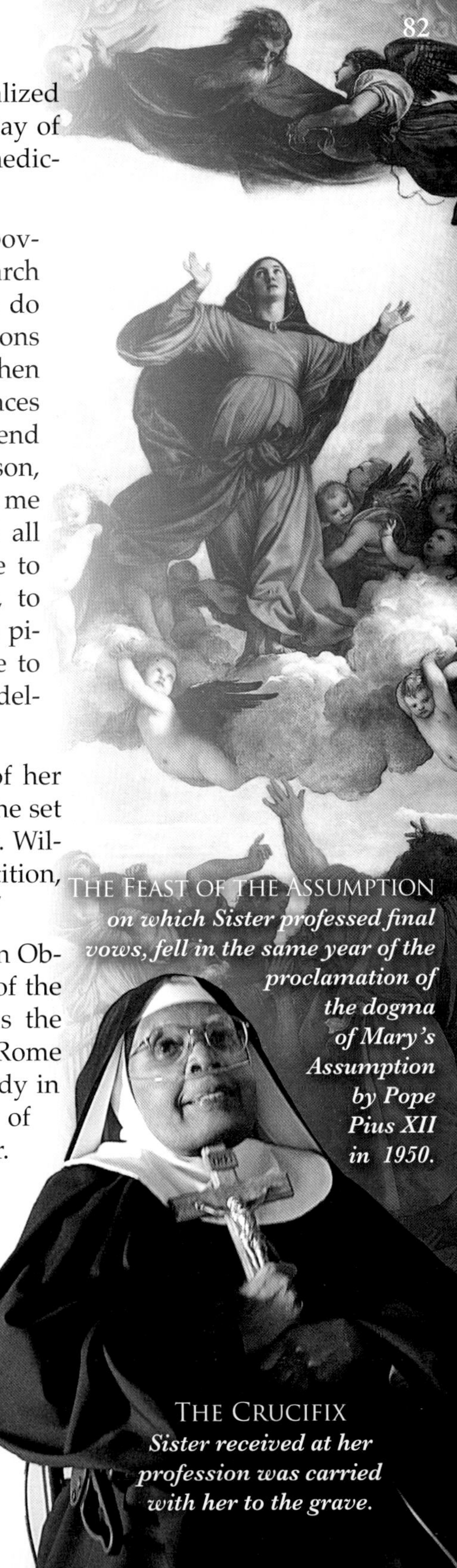

THE FEAST OF THE ASSUMPTION *on which Sister professed final vows, fell in the same year of the proclamation of the dogma of Mary's Assumption by Pope Pius XII in 1950.*

THE CRUCIFIX *Sister received at her profession was carried with her to the grave.*

Chapter 7
Kaleidoscop

We are to love, and not to judge,
We are to hope and pray!
From charity we're not to budge,
United more, each day!

Our home eternal Heaven is
If we accept Christ's rule,
Patiently bearing earth's business
While scholars in His school.

St. Pius V School in Baltimore
was Sister's longest assignment in her extensive teaching career.

Experience

Teaching and Taught

Not what I do, but WHY I do it –
Soul, learn to LOVE – or you will rue it.

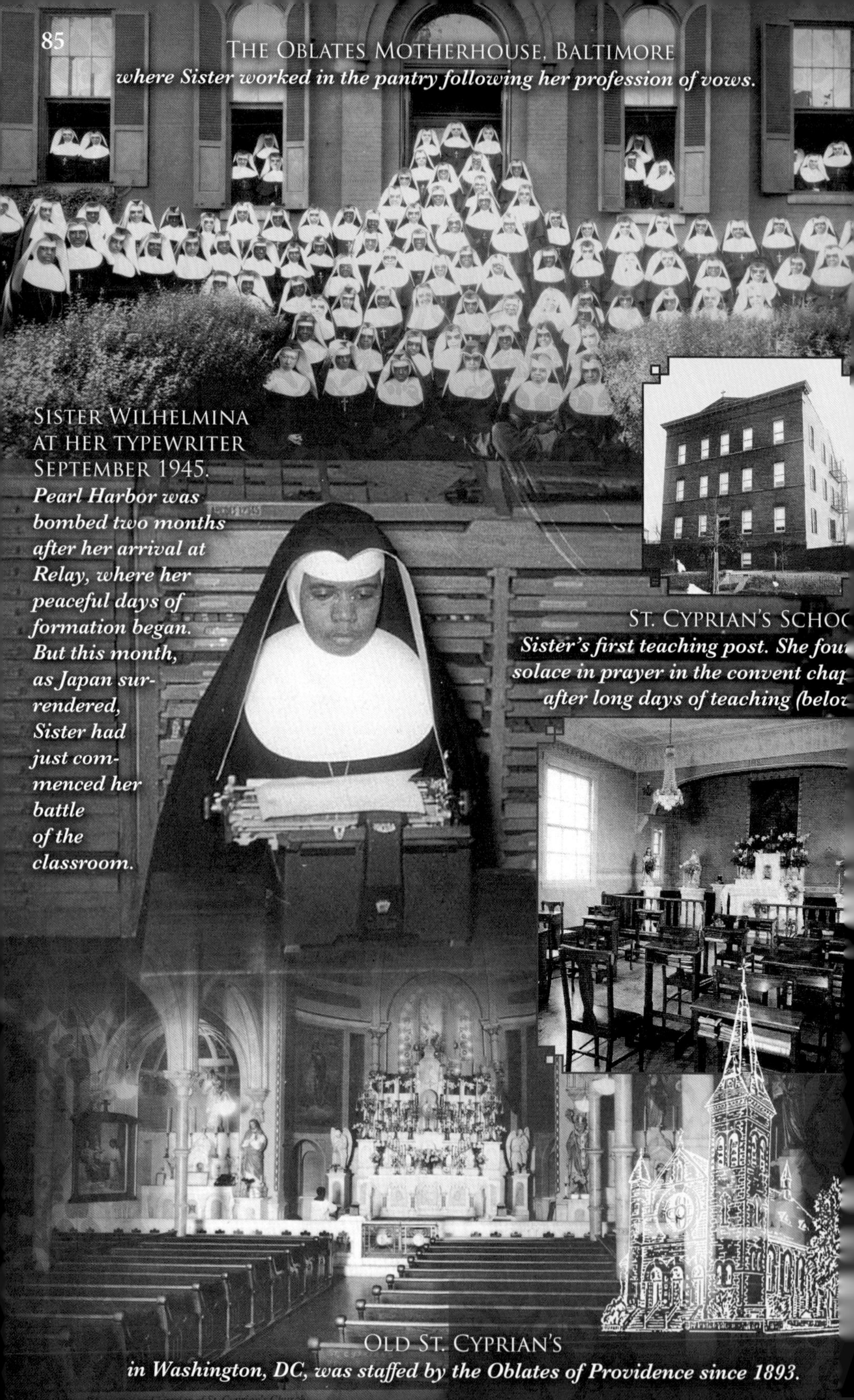

The Oblates Motherhouse, Baltimore
where Sister worked in the pantry following her profession of vows.

Sister Wilhelmina at her typewriter September 1945.
Pearl Harbor was bombed two months after her arrival at Relay, where her peaceful days of formation began. But this month, as Japan surrendered, Sister had just commenced her battle of the classroom.

St. Cyprian's Schoo
Sister's first teaching post. She fou solace in prayer in the convent chap after long days of teaching (belo

Old St. Cyprian's
in Washington, DC, was staffed by the Oblates of Providence since 1893.

SECOND GRADE *at St. Cyprian's, 1946. Sister remained until 1948.*

Although Sr. Wilhelmina relished her studies, she soon found that the community apostolate of educating children was a very different experience. Life in the classroom was a challenge, teaching children from impoverished and often troubled backgrounds from the inner-cities of Baltimore, Washington D.C., St. Louis, Pennsylvania, Maryland, South Carolina and Florida. Sister wrote:

> In September 1944, I was brought to the Motherhouse and assigned to work in the pantry. Soon after New Year's, I was given a fourth-grade class whose teacher was being transferred elsewhere. So my teaching career began, a kaleidoscope of good days and bad days that I was constantly praying to be delivered from. I loved study and school, but not teaching. During the 22 years between 1944 and 1966 I had a short, happy stint at housework - mainly cleaning - at St. Rita's Residence in St. Louis and then at

FIRST COMMUNION *at St. Rita's while Sister was first assigned there.*

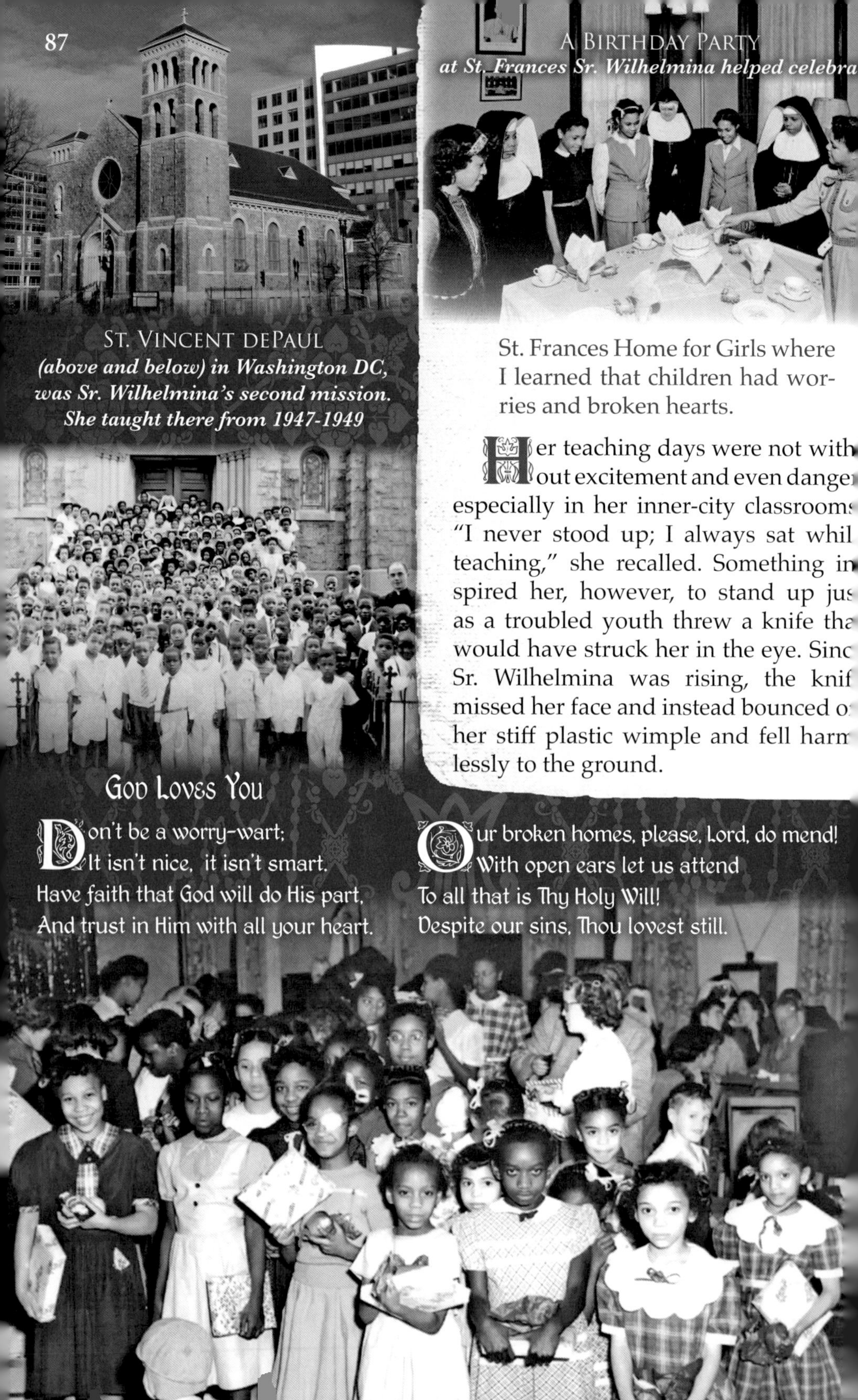

St. Vincent dePaul
(above and below) in Washington DC, was Sr. Wilhelmina's second mission. She taught there from 1947-1949

A Birthday Party
at St. Frances Sr. Wilhelmina helped celebra

St. Frances Home for Girls where I learned that children had worries and broken hearts.

Her teaching days were not without excitement and even dange especially in her inner-city classroom "I never stood up; I always sat whil teaching," she recalled. Something in spired her, however, to stand up jus as a troubled youth threw a knife tha would have struck her in the eye. Sinc Sr. Wilhelmina was rising, the knif missed her face and instead bounced o her stiff plastic wimple and fell harm lessly to the ground.

God Loves You

Don't be a worry-wart;
It isn't nice, it isn't smart.
Have faith that God will do His part,
And trust in Him with all your heart.

Our broken homes, please, Lord, do mend!
With open ears let us attend
To all that is Thy Holy Will!
Despite our sins, Thou lovest still.

T. FRANCES' HOME *hile Sister was there. : was located in Nor- nandy, MO, named hus by James Lucas' Norman father, Jean- Baptiste.*

The mid-twentieth century brought many cultural changes and technological innovations, including television. Sister Wilhelmina was shrewd in her appraisal of this new means of communication and entertainment:

> Television came into my life during the fifties when I was at St. Rita's, and I wondered how I had lived so many years without it. Recreation in the evening consisted in sitting down before it and listening to everything it had to say. After some years I was thoroughly disenchanted with it because one couldn't talk back to it but had to be completely on the receiving end, taking in both error and foolishness.

R. WILHELMINA LOOKED ON *left, from the background) at St. Rita's in St. Louis as Christmas fts were presented, including the elevision. Sister spent time first t St. Rita's, then at St. Frances' etween teaching jobs and while working on her degree.*

Somehow we must get
back to loving truly;
Unselfishly,
with all things shared,
That we may live and grow
and prosper duly;
Our broken family
must be repaired.

We really don't
need TV in the parlor,
Nor any place where we
should sit and talk;
And silence isn't bad
when we side by side,
Or travel the same way
along the walk.

No more the fights,
the arguments, the lying;
But we to one another
will be true
And sacrificing 'till
the day we're dying
We want to see God
up above the blue

We left Grandmother
in that nursing center
Her heart was broken
in that bright new place
Without the love of kin
her room was winter
While strangers coldly
wore the daily face.

In church let's kneel and
promise God together
We'll kill no more and trust
Him to forgive;
Let's you and I forgive; no
stormy weather
Shall hinder children
whom God would have
live.

The Mystery of Love
alone unites us;
God is almighty, all things
He can do;
He doesn't force, He lov-
ingly invites us.
If we're transformed it's up
to me and you.

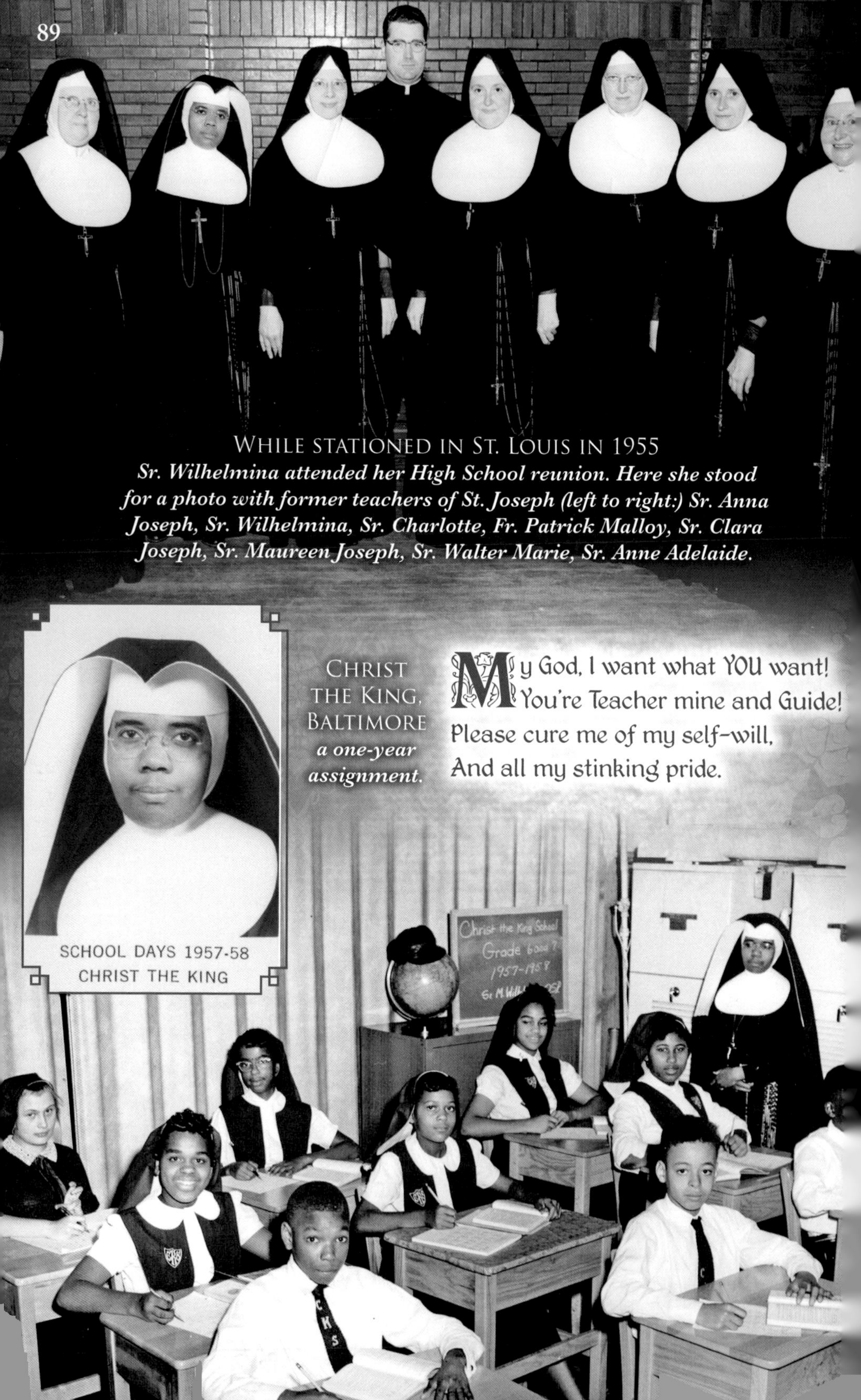

WHILE STATIONED IN ST. LOUIS IN 1955

Sr. Wilhelmina attended her High School reunion. Here she stood for a photo with former teachers of St. Joseph (left to right:) Sr. Anna Joseph, Sr. Wilhelmina, Sr. Charlotte, Fr. Patrick Malloy, Sr. Clara Joseph, Sr. Maureen Joseph, Sr. Walter Marie, Sr. Anne Adelaide.

CHRIST THE KING, BALTIMORE *a one-year assignment.*

My God, I want what YOU want!
You're Teacher mine and Guide!
Please cure me of my self-will,
And all my stinking pride.

MASS is the greatest thing –the greatest thing – on earth!
[S]howing us Jesus from the moment of [Hi]s birth!
[C]hrist comes to dies for us, to heal us and To save!
[Gi]ving us resurrection with Him, from The grave!

[T]HE HOLY SACRIFICE OF THE MASS
[i]s the center of Sr. Wil[h]elmina's existence, to [wh]ich her writings, songs [and] years of teaching attest.

SAINT PIUS V *where Sister served from 1958-1970, with a brief interval back at St. Frances. The patron of the parish was an apt one for her, being an Apostle of the Tridentine Missal and the rosary in light of the Victory at Lepanto shown to him.*

Sr. Wilhelmina wrote years later that, in spite of her dislike for teaching, her love for the True Presence of Our Lord in the Eucharist was her primary motivator in entering the Oblate Sisters of Providence. Teaching about the Mass and Sacraments proved to be a joy:

> Attendance at Mass took on a different aspect as I sat behind rows of squirming fourth-graders, some of whom were not Catholic. Like a mother hen hovering over her brood, I was anxious—perhaps too anxious—that they have the same regard for this awesome sacrifice as I had. I wanted the children to appreciate the Mass and to get all possible benefit from it; but alas, some of them

DODGE BALL *with Sr. Wilhelmina and the girls of Pius V.*

Joy is God's gifts to souls of men
Who are living in His grace;
Be sorry for your sins, dear soul,
And seek His Holy Face.

III

5. Credo in unum De- um, Patrem omni-pot-éntem,

were not even baptized. Was I expecting too much? I sometimes wondered. In those days the Ward method of teaching music was being introduced, and one could step from it very easily into Gregorian Chant. The grand accomplishment of a fourth-grader before he passed into fifth was to sing Credo III. I am amazed as I remember how much Latin the children learned and sang with seeming pride and satisfaction. It was also my duty to teach the rudiments of Latin pronunciation—mainly the necessary Mass responses—to those fourth-grade boys who hoped to become altar boys the next year. *Ad Deum qui laetificat juventutem meam.* How proudly they would say the words so that they could join the club! Faithful altar boys were taken on special trips by the grateful pastor. While eighth-grade boys were cocks-of-the-walk as altar boys, the eighth-grade girls were in demand as a choir for funerals. They had a perfect mastery of the Requiem Mass, including the *Dies Irae,* which they sang as if they understood every phrase.

A NON-CATHOLIC STUDENT ***of Sister's at Pius V from 1969 (above) sent his picture and deep thanks to her in 1981.***

THE WARD METHOD ***developed by Justine Ward and Dom André Mocquereau (above right) to teach children sight reading and Gregorian Chant was incorporated by the Oblates in their music curriculum.***

When is a woman greatest?
Someone asked me the other day.
You speak now of three occasions,
I responded right away:
At the bedside of the dying,
at the crib of her young child,
And while helping at a marriage feast,
although the guests be wild.
These are the times when Mary was
the greatest woman e'er,
Giving birth in an old stable,
without worry, without care;
Then supplying help at marriage feast
when there was need of wine,
Mary caused her Son to demonstrate
that He was God Divine.
Last of all when He hung dying
on the cross in cruel pain,
She stood bravely by His side
and now in Heav'n
with Him does reign.

Thank you, Lord,
for the gift of faith;
Thank you, Lord,
for Mother dear.
Thank you, Lord,
for staying with us
As we struggle for
You here.

SAINT REMIGIUS

(opposite) whose feast was removed from the new calendar, baptized and crowned King Clovis. He was cited by Sr. Wilhelmina in her thesis. In light of the Civil Rights movement around her, she insisted that the evangelization of her people was the sole solution to the racial tensions she herself suffered.

In August 1966, Sr. Wilhelmina finished her degree at the College of Notre Dame of Maryland, majoring in history. Her thesis had the arresting title, "The Tragedy of Christianity," which she held to be that "so much evil has been done in the name of Christ," such as the oppression and enslavement of entire peoples. Consequently, she observed, oppressed races have not, for the most part, received the redemptive Blood of Christ, poured out for the salvation of every race. In this paper, she showed herself to be both a true daughter of Ella Madden Lancaster and a true spiritual daughter of Mother Mary Lange, in her zeal for the evangelization of her people.

> Christ has been identified by many brown-skinned people of this planet as "the white man's God," having no concern for the black and coloured peoples of the earth. Yet Christ was born in Asia, and learned to walk in Egypt; it was upon African soil that Christ first set foot. It is strange that these two continents are still, majoritatively [*sic*] speaking, alienated from Him. It is the tragedy of Christianity that these millions of human beings, for whom He lived, suffered, taught and died, should live and die untaught, not knowing Him, enthralled in ignorance and moral degradation, blinded by the example of those who claim to have taught and to know, as well as by their own innate perversity, the heritage of the fall of Adam.

Sister understood that true freedom was that of the children of God, to be found only in the bosom of Holy Mother Church. The path to true freedom is through enlightening the mind, for "those who refuse to think are usually ruled by others who do their thinking for them," she wrote. Once the mind is freed from ignorance, then the will is freed to choose the good and to respond to grace of faith.

> Faith is a free gift from God and can no more be forced upon anyone than a rosebud can be forced to open by violent pressure from without... It was, and it still is, a great blessing to be a Christian, to be engrafted into a living, eternal organism, that is moving – like some planet in space – out of the trappings of time into the Parousia of eternity! True progress and betterment are assured for the individual who, gifted with the light of faith, freely elects to abide by the teachings and example of the Divine Master, and who thereby embraces the Christian commitment: to belong to Christ and to love all whom He loves, to be divinized, incorporated into Him as flesh of His flesh and blood of His blood, to be outcast no longer, to be elevated to a unique and eternal nobility, to be imbued with His Spirit, His Ideals, His very Life, and to be, thereby, saved. This is the viewpoint of faith.

Those who already possess the precious gift of faith have the rave responsibility to share this gift with others; thus she quotes t. Remigius, speaking to King Clovis when he ascended the hrone, "With the riches left you by your father, ransom the aptives and deliver them from the yoke of slavery." Siser could have addressed these words to herself, having eceived the riches of her Faith and evangelical zeal from oth her natural and her spiritual mothers.

This Diploma makes known that

The College of Notre Dame of Maryland

has admitted

Sister Mary Wilhelmina Lancaster, O.S.P.

to the degree of

Bachelor of Arts

and that she is entitled to all the Honors, Rights and Privileges to that degree appertaining.

Given in the City of Baltimore, in the State of Maryland, this fifth day of Aug., in the year of Our Lord one thousand nine hundred and sixty-six.

In Witness Whereof the Seal of the College and the Signature of the President thereof are hereunto affixed.

President of the College

Dean of the College

"YES, SHE WAS LITERATE…" *Sr. Wilhelmina humorously wrote on the envelope containing her certificates, transcripts, and licenses. She was an excellent student, pictured here the year after graduation.*

After tracing the sad patterns of oppression through history, she comes to her own era, the societal upheaval of the 1960s. Here is the age of civil rights, of the Black man's coming into his own and into society, but at the same time here is the cultural revolution and society's wholesale abandonment of moral law. Hence Sr. Wilhelmina concludes her thesis with the lament:

> Will the black man ever be really free? Is there no other freedom for the black man than the freedom which the devil offers? Freedom without God; freedom without integral family life; freedom without private ownership of property; freedom without freedom!

> You see, for so many centuries past, when our forebears were outcasts, the law stood pat. You know: 'Thou shalt do thus' and 'Thou shalt not do so.' But now that we

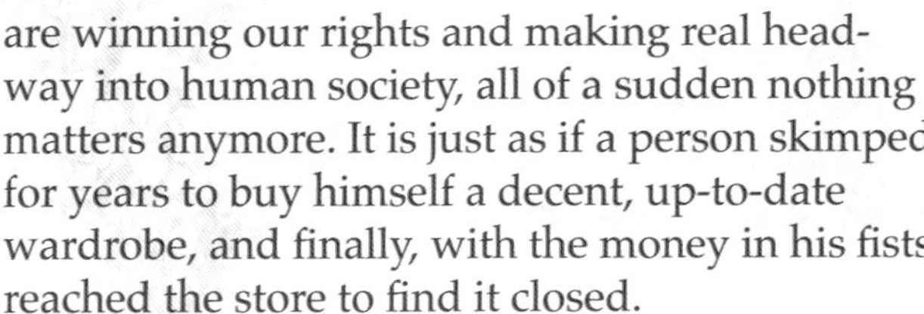

are winning our rights and making real headway into human society, all of a sudden nothing matters anymore. It is just as if a person skimped for years to buy himself a decent, up-to-date wardrobe, and finally, with the money in his fists, reached the store to find it closed.

> Come this way, Jesus Christ! Lord, stay with us, for our day is now just beginning. Others may be smart enough and self-sufficient enough to get along without you; but you must stay with us, for we will never let you go. We must keep you, because you're all we have; you are really *all* we have!"
>
> What a vast difference there is, between suffering alone in pagan bondage, and suffering as the beloved of Christ, sustained and refreshed by His hidden manna!

Despite the provocative title, "The Tragedy of Christianity," Sr. Wilhelmina did not consider the evil deeds of nominal Christians as cause for despair or for disillusionment with Holy Mother Church. Almost twenty years after submitting her thesis, Sr. Wilhelmina wrote an epilogue for it, entitled "The Glory of Christianity" and typed on a piece of stationery with a picture of Mother Mary Lange and the Oblates' motto, "Providence Will Provide." In this little essay, written on the feast of the Annunciation, March 25, 1985, she identified the paradoxical glory of the Catholic Faith:

> The glory of Christianity is that it requires all its adherents to be crucified along with their Master. 'God forbid that I should glory save in the cross of Our Lord Jesus Christ by Whom the world is crucified to me and I to the world.' Every man is born to live forever somewhere. Nobody wants to die, but die everyone must... The good news is that we have been redeemed from sin by the Lord Jesus Christ. Yet we are not saved against our free wills: we must go along with Christ's program of prayer and penance according to our state of life and to the authentic direction of the Holy Spirit. No two souls are exactly alike in all respects. There is but one human race; each member of it, nonetheless, is unique, loved by God with an everlasting love.

SISTER'S DEGREE *vas completed over twenty-year period, nostly in Summers when she was not eaching. She studied t Mt. St. Agnes College (top) and music Webster University bove) and Edinboro low) before complet- g at the University of tre Dame Maryland, esided by Sr. Marga- Mary, SNND (inset)*

Chapter 8

The Winds

The worst of today's persecution terrors:
The New Mass has many translation errors
That suit the heretic's unbalanced mind,
But how many bishops can anyone find
To outlaw the New Mass in their domain?
And to give their people the truth again!

I fear there may be martyrdom ahead;
The modernists want all traditionalists dead;
There's no coexistence of error with truth;
A person's the same, whether aged or youth.

Why don't bishops teach and
Defend well their flock
From those faithless creatures
Who blaspheme and mock?

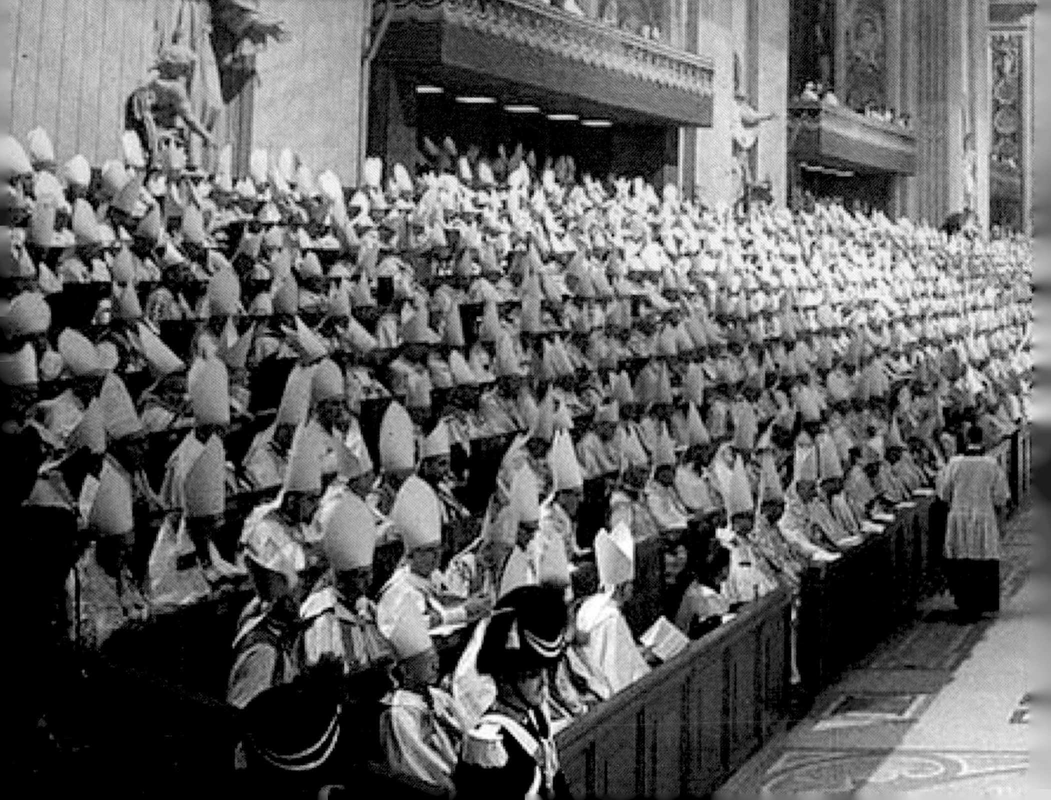

OF CHANGE

Disorientation

Not the music –
Not the dance –
Not the party –
Not the prance –
But the PRECIOUS BLOOD OF JESUS
Received in His Sacrament
Flows in all our veins and really
Makes us brothers true, content.
('Though Politician Caesar
Tries to ride on Christ's coat-tail,
His efforts to help govern Church
Will ultimately fail.)

THE SECOND VATICAN COUNCIL *(1962-1965) the Church's "French volution" according Cardinal Suenens, t in motion a series f changes touching every aspect of Catholic life.*

ARCHBISHOP ANNIBALE BUGNINI *took the reins on Liturgical Reform in Rome in 1948. Banished by John XXIII, he was reinstated by Paul VI, and is considered the architect of the New Mass. In 1974, he said the reconstructed liturgy proved a "major conquest of the Catholic Church." His request for the abrogation of the Latin Mass the same year was denied "as an odious act in the face of liturgical tradition." Paul VI sent him to Iran after credible evidence of Freemasonic ties were found in 1976.*

FOLK MUSIC *was introduced into Catholic Masses in 1965 through the Mass for Young Americans by Ray Repp, a former St. Louis Seminarian later turned gay rights advocate and conformist. Others followed suit in composing new music for the Mass, admittedly using popular music for inspiration, such as theme songs from television shows and from the Beatles.*

THE CLOSING OF THE COUNCIL *promised a reformed liturgy, but changes were anticipated even before the New Missal was released.*

The cultural revolution of the 1960s and 1970s had a great impact on her beloved community. They marked the most tumultuous epoch of Sr. Wilhelmina's life personally, professionally, ecclesially and in community. The changes in the Mass touched Sr. Wilhelmina first and most profoundly. At St. Frances in Normandy, Missouri, she saw devotion tapering off.

> Again, sitting behind rows of girls, I wondered why there was so much lethargy; they were almost literally lying down in the pews, as if they had been out all night. I worried much over their couldn't-care-less attitude. Eventually, a gentleman seeing my concern, said, "Give'em gospel." I hardly knew what "gospel" was then, and I was certain that it wasn't in the hymnbook we were using. For that matter, it wasn't in any of the music books that we were using. I soon learned that it was a style of music that didn't necessarily require adherence to written notes. One just sang or played the way one felt, the louder the better. I also experimented with the music of Ray Repp, writer of folk songs for the Mass, and tried to make the Mass more meaningful and appealing with: "Here we are! Altogether as we sing our song, Joyfully!" Neither "gospel" nor the songs of Ray Repp solved the problem of Mass attendance.

INITIAL ADAPTATION OF HEADGEAR *in 1962: four modest revisions were modeled for the Oblates, who voted for the version on the far left.*

After the promulgation of the *Novus Ordo Missae*, the New Missal of Paul VI on November 22, 1969, the Latin Mass known for centuries before was swept away with a pen stroke. Changes came with it: the addition of folk songs, the priest facing the people to say Mass in English, reception of Communion on the hand and the down playing of Our Lord's True Presence in the Blessed Sacrament to the rank of being a mere "symbol" of Christ for many Catholics. Observing all this, one elderly Sister commented to Sr. Wilhelmina, "Huh. I guess the Protestants were right!"

The sudden changes in the Oblate Sisters of Providence, beginning with the religious habit, deeply upset Sr. Wilhelmina. She tried to adapt to the initial stages of reform, but would return to the traditional habit a year after the Oblates had ceased using it altogether.

> Improvement on the OSP Habit that began in the fifties and was completed in August 1962 I was happy about; uniformity was desired by all the members of the community, and this was a beautiful uniformity. It lasted only five years. In January 1967 individual sisters were allowed to experiment with the headdress. Hair-showing had begun. Of course I was not for this at all. I had unfortunately gotten into that stupid hair-showing party; from June 1971 until Holy Saturday 1974 I was in it - to my great regret.

LEON-JOSEPH CARDINAL SUENENS *of Belgium encouraged a more radical updating of Religious life and habits to bring them "into harmony with the evolutionary state of the world and womankind," especially through his book published in 1962, The Nun in the World, and in lectures in America. At one such lecture, he told the religious there gathered: "I have not come here to preach peace, but to call for a revolution, a revolution in the life of active nuns." One of four moderators of Vatican II, he spoke at the Council in 1964 regarding habits: "these are a cause for ridicule for nuns in the street." The same year, he heralded the Charismatic Renewal on the Council floor, becoming a staunch supporter of it and enlisted the aid of the tragic "Singing Nun" (Jeannine Deckers) to compose music for the movement. Both also advocated ecclesiatical approval of contraception.*

On you I call
To help my Sisters,
each and all!
They need your work
Of wonder now
To help them keep
each holy vow.

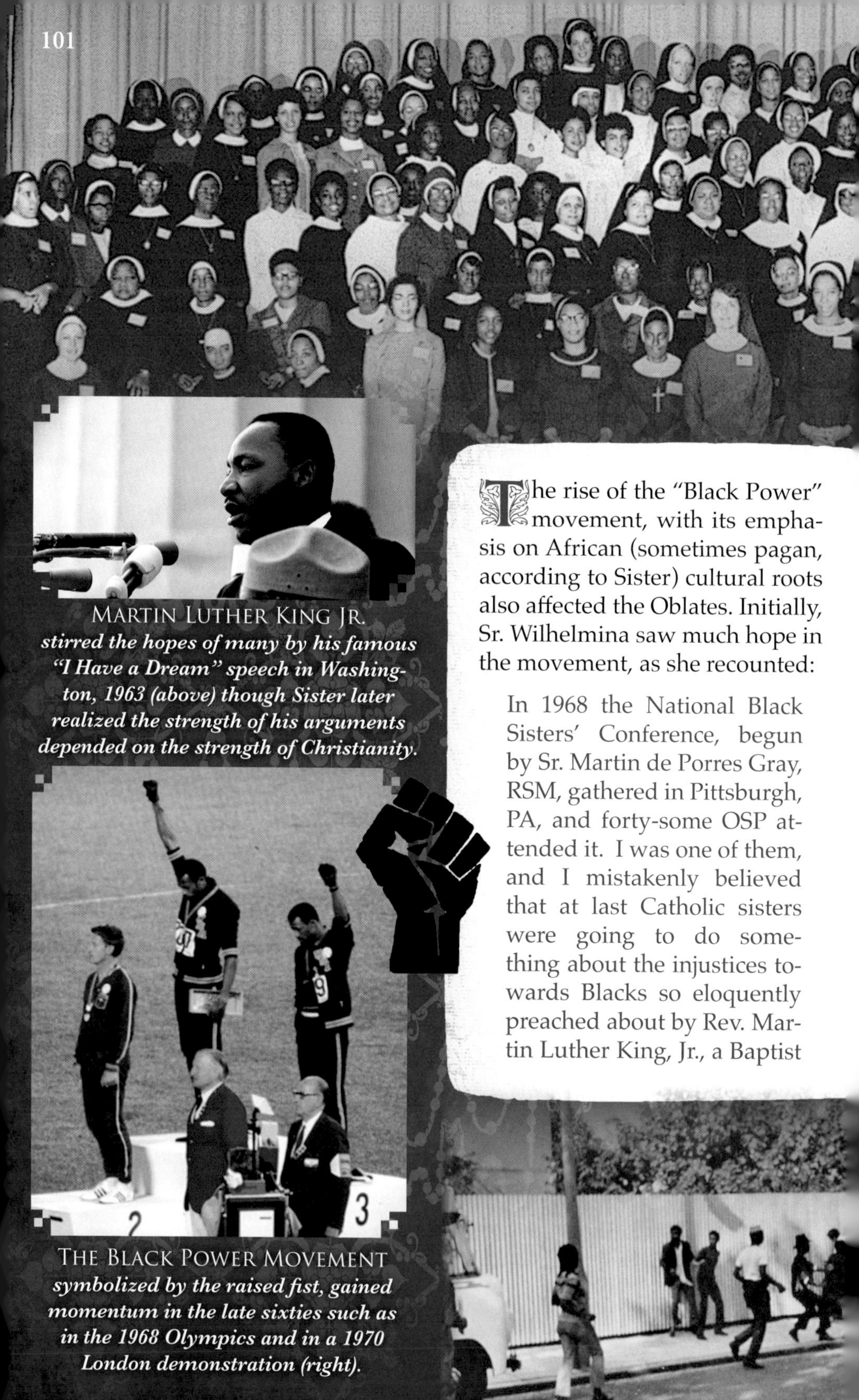

MARTIN LUTHER KING JR. *stirred the hopes of many by his famous "I Have a Dream" speech in Washington, 1963 (above) though Sister later realized the strength of his arguments depended on the strength of Christianity.*

THE BLACK POWER MOVEMENT *symbolized by the raised fist, gained momentum in the late sixties such as in the 1968 Olympics and in a 1970 London demonstration (right).*

The rise of the "Black Power" movement, with its emphasis on African (sometimes pagan, according to Sister) cultural roots also affected the Oblates. Initially, Sr. Wilhelmina saw much hope in the movement, as she recounted:

> In 1968 the National Black Sisters' Conference, begun by Sr. Martin de Porres Gray, RSM, gathered in Pittsburgh, PA, and forty-some OSP attended it. I was one of them, and I mistakenly believed that at last Catholic sisters were going to do something about the injustices towards Blacks so eloquently preached about by Rev. Martin Luther King, Jr., a Baptist

HE 1968 NBSC MEETING IN PITTSBURGH
attended by Sr. Wilhelmina.

Don't let me doubt Your mercy,
Sweet Lord, my Saviour dear!
I'll give no controversy
And trust without a fear.

minister. I disengaged myself from the NBSC in 1971 after their publication of "Celibate Black Commitment" in which they stated that Blacks couldn't or shouldn't be celibate.

As she had expressed in her bachelor's thesis, Sr. Wilhelmina understood that the true freedom and dignity of her race was the freedom and dignity of the children of God, the children of the Blessed Mother Mary, the children of Holy Mother Church. It is not the color of one's skin that matters, but the purity of one's soul, as she explains in the following essay, "Consider This," written November 2, 1979, with its imaginative and thought-provoking plays on the word "Black:"

"HOW I LOOKED IN THAT 'AGGIORNIAMENTO PERIOD' *June 13, 1971 to April 20, 1973," Sr. Wilhelmina wrote on the back of this photo, taken in October of 1972.*

SISTER'S FINAL TEACHING POSTS *were Holy Trinity in Orangeburg, South Carolina (1970-1971, above) and St. Francis Xavier in Miami, Florida (1971-1972, below.) The Oblates' first convent/ school in the former was burnt down soon after their arrival in 1930.*

A LIFE-LONG DEVOTEE, *Sister enrolled in the Archconfraternity of the Holy Face, and wrote the names of her last class on the back of its image.*

SR. MARY OF GOOD COUNSEL *the Superior who assigned Sister Wilhelmina to the archives.*

There are those who say that there is no connection whatsoever between the Black Madonna of Poland and the so-called black people of the United States of America and that black people look stupid venerating the Black Madonna of Poland as their Madonna.

I have news for them. Have you noticed the two scars on Our Lady's right cheek? Do you really know the story of how those scars got there? A Moorish soldier – yes, a colored man, one might say, from Northern Africa – slashed the picture twice with his sword, and dropped dead before he could land the third blow. He was angry because his side had lost the war against the Polish people, many years ago.

It is altogether fitting that descendants of Africans, that we, black or colored or Negro people as the world designates us, make up to the dear Mother of God and Mother of all men, as much as we can, with all possible love and devotion, for that insult offered to her so many years ago. It is true that Our Lady of Czestochowa is <u>not</u> black as we are; we are black, filthy sinners; but we love her just the same.

The 1970s were also a time of great change and transition in Sr. Wilhelmina's professional life. Her teaching career ended in February 1972, when Sr. Wilhelmina had disciplined a student too severely. She related:

I was brought back to the Motherhouse in Baltimore, now newly built on Gun Road. For the first time in my life, the superior general, Sister Mary of Good Counsel Baptiste, asked me, breathing in exasperation, what I wanted to do. I immediately replied that I would like to write a history of the Order. That is how I got to work on archival material.

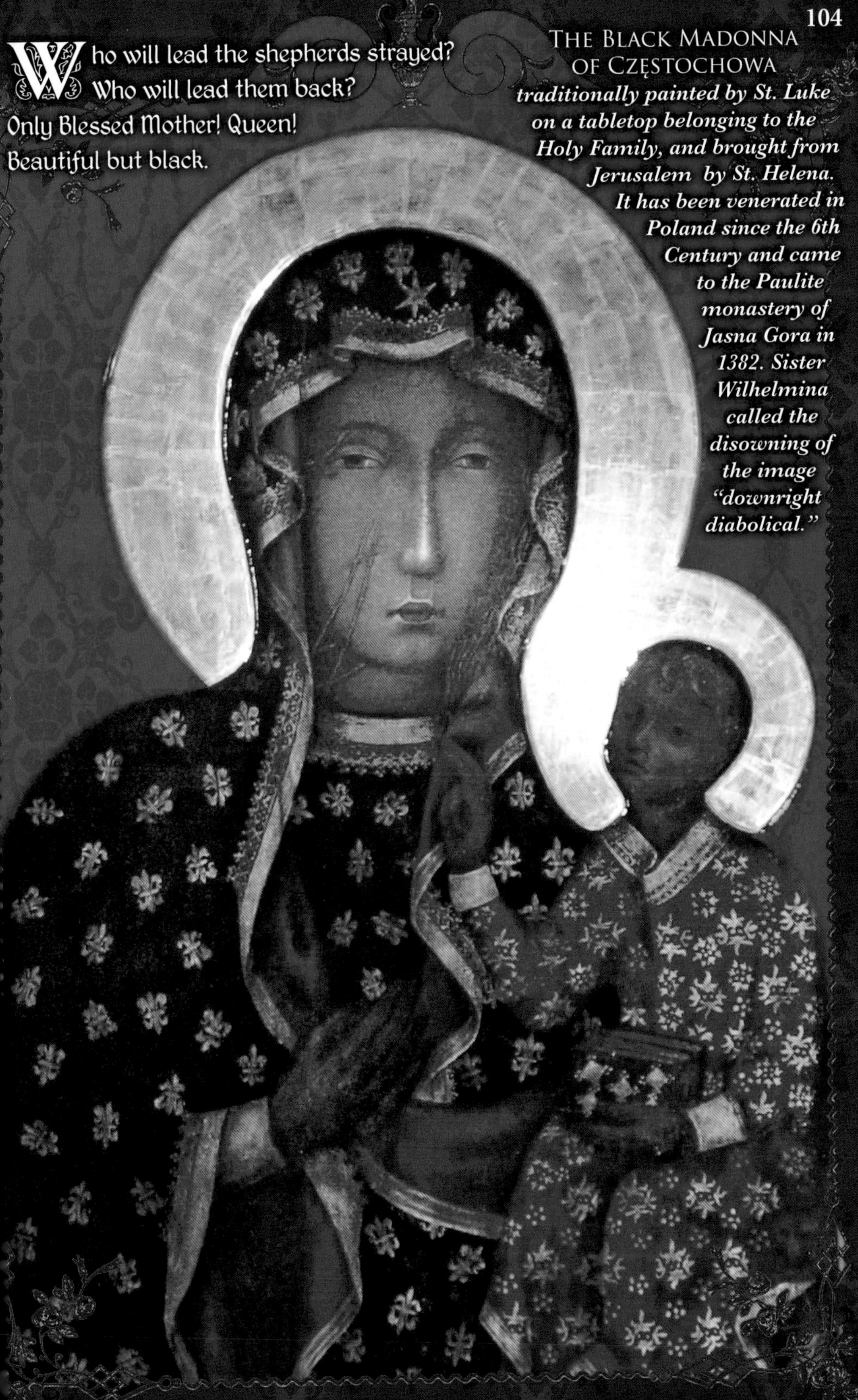
Who will lead the shepherds strayed?
Who will lead them back?
Only Blessed Mother! Queen!
Beautiful but black.
THE BLACK MADONNA OF CZĘSTOCHOWA
traditionally painted by St. Luke on a tabletop belonging to the Holy Family, and brought from Jerusalem by St. Helena. It has been venerated in Poland since the 6th Century and came to the Paulite monastery of Jasna Gora in 1382. Sister Wilhelmina called the disowning of the image "downright diabolical."

To be with Thee is my delight!
Lord Jesus, robed in red and white,
Scourged, mocked, derided, Thou alone
Art my Redeemer, on Thy throne,
Thy Holy Cross, Thy saving sign,
That Thou art mine and I am thine.

Sr. Wilhelmina was appointed archivist and also as extraordinary secretary to the General Chapter of 1973. She never did write a history of the Oblate Sisters of Providence, but she compiled valuable notes for such a document. Although she enjoyed her archival work, her transition from the classroom to the archives was not easy. She found her solace in submitting her writing talents to the service of her Beloved Lord:

> Around this time I became very despondent, feeling that I had failed as a teacher, that I could neither teach nor cook, and therefore why should I be alive. With my head on the desk in my cell, I was inspired with a poem honoring Our Lord in the Most Blessed Sacrament. When I finished writing it - and it came quite easily - I felt consoled and satisfied.
>
> I immediately took it to Sister Benigna who resided in the infirmary wing, but was still the community's topmost musician. She was not for any of the musical nonsense that was going on, and I knew that she would give my poem, "We Do Believe," quick shrift if that is what she thought it deserved. She read it, smiled, and then said, "I am going to write music for this." In a couple of weeks, it was done, and she was teaching it at choir practice. "We must not tell the sisters where this hymn comes from, for they will not sing it then," she warned me.

"We Do Believe"

placed in public domain.

We do believe, Lord Jesus Christ,
that Thou art present here.
Although but simple bread and wine
doth to our eyes appear.
Thy Body and Thy precious Blood,
Thou whole reality,
We do believe, Lord Jesus Christ,
we do believe in Thee.

The child once born in Bethlehem
and once to Egypt fled,
Doth dwell upon this altar
under forms of wine and bread;
Divinity is present here,
'Tis Jesus Christ Our Lord
Whom we adore! Whom we adore
as He should be adored.

True God-made-man is Jesus Christ,
yet on a cross He died.
All they who would salvation reap
must, too, be crucified.
We beg God's pardon for the sins
that caused Him so much pain,
O may we rather die than ever
disobey again.

Thou art the Living Bread Who com'st
to give us life today;
That we may rise in glory
at the end of time, we pray.
Without Thy wondrous gift of self
how hopeless we would be;
Lord, let us make return of love!
We give ourselves to Thee!

Thief Judas kept the common purse,
Ah! Dearly did he love it!
That purse held money: he did not
Think he had plenty of it.
He made a deal with Pharisees –
'Twas very bad behavior –
Just for a few old clinking coins
He sold his Lord and Savior.

O would that I could prudent be,
And fear no pain, no danger,
Except in my stupidity
To treat God as a stranger.

"Hosanna!" little children cried and watched Lord Jesus pass,
Majestically robed in red and seated on an ass;
And some of them did run before to throw palm branches down;
'Twas greatest demonstration ever held in that old town

Yet only five days later those boys were not to be seen;
Nor were their springtime branches waving, long and fresh and green,
But soldiers prodded One Who wore the mantle of His Blood,
With crossbeam on His shoulders He fell three times in the mud.

Final contributors to Sister Wilhelmina's angst in the early 1970s were personal changes, and much closer to home. These also brought Sister Wilhelmina to her "low point," when she had penned "We Do Believe." But Sister rallied again under the influence of Sr. Benigna, along with her devotion to her natural and supernatural mothers.

THE PILGRIM VIRGIN OF FATIMA *visited the Oblates' Motherhouse in 1942 (top.) The statue miraculously shed tears in New Orleans July 17-18 1972, one year and nine months before returning to the Motherhouse, when Sister Wilhelmina was inspired to resume the habit in 1974.*

Sister's parents endured a period of estrangement around this time, a pain Sr. Wilhelmina only referred to in the years preceding her death. Soon after this mysterious period, tragedy struck. Oscar suffered from heart failure, and passed away at a hospital in St. Louis. Sister Wilhelmina did not attend the funeral of her father, but visited her mother afterwards. When Ella saw her daughter in the modified habit, she scowled and said to her daughter, "it is a good thing your father is not here to see you like that." She was then resolved to resume the traditional habit, the same that Sr. Benigna had persevered in wearing. Sister Wilhelmina gave the final credit to her Beloved Blessed Virgin Mary:

> Our Blessed Mother helped me put the traditional habit back on when her Pilgrim Virgin Statue of Our Lady of Fatima came to visit our Mount, and the sisters went in procession to the gate to meet it. Needless to say, my return to the habit was not just for that occasion, but for the rest of my life.

Sister made the habit herself, which required some ingenuity, especially as the Oblates no longer made any of the parts. She ended up improvising the forehead piece of her wimple with a piece of plastic cut from a bleach bottle. A sister passing her in the hallway pointed at the traditional headdress and asked, "Are you going to wear that all the time?" "Yes!" Sr. Wilhelmina was determined. As she would later quip, "I am Sr. WIL-HEL-MINA – I've a HELL of a WILL and I MEAN it!"

Chapter 9

Music and

We must do penance for our sins
And never sin again;
While doing chores that we don't like
With truly joyful grin.

No frowning will I do, Lord,
But calmly face distress;
With all my trust in You, Lord!
Forever You will bless.

Unbelievers trample now
On those who do believe!
It seems these are to have no rights,
No matter how they grieve.
The cockle in the field has grown,
Is towering o'er the wheat;
'Tis time to rally 'round the King
Who's on His judgment seat.

In the Archives

Sister continued to work for fourteen years, diligently organizing historical documents and artifacts of her community's history, all the while conserving what Pope Benedict later called "a memory for the future."

MEMORIES

Back in the Habit

Man has time;
God has eternity!
God has nothing
To do with modernity.

God has no clocks, no calendars;
He lives in an eternal now.
He always was, will always be;
He, God alone, He hast my vow.
Let us in holy living then,
His Holy Spirit showing how –
Let us in fear and hope and love,
Let us in humble gratitude,
Let us with all our hearts and souls –
Adore His Sacred Majesty!

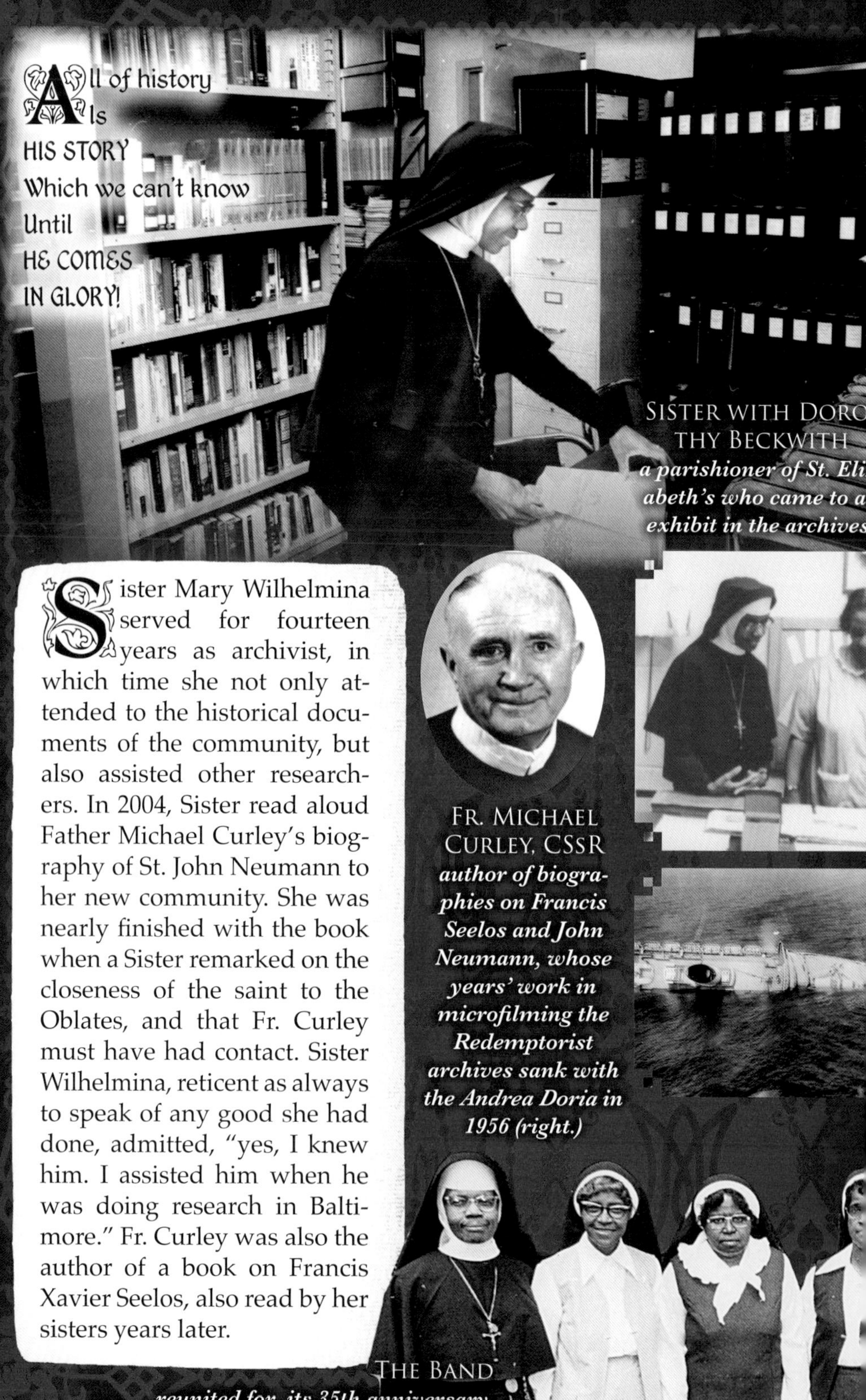

All of history
Is
HIS STORY
Which we can't know
Until
HE COMES
IN GLORY!

SISTER WITH DOROTHY BECKWITH
a parishioner of St. Elizabeth's who came to an exhibit in the archives

Sister Mary Wilhelmina served for fourteen years as archivist, in which time she not only attended to the historical documents of the community, but also assisted other researchers. In 2004, Sister read aloud Father Michael Curley's biography of St. John Neumann to her new community. She was nearly finished with the book when a Sister remarked on the closeness of the saint to the Oblates, and that Fr. Curley must have had contact. Sister Wilhelmina, reticent as always to speak of any good she had done, admitted, "yes, I knew him. I assisted him when he was doing research in Baltimore." Fr. Curley was also the author of a book on Francis Xavier Seelos, also read by her sisters years later.

FR. MICHAEL CURLEY, CSSR
author of biographies on Francis Seelos and John Neumann, whose years' work in microfilming the Redemptorist archives sank with the Andrea Doria in 1956 (right.)

THE BAND
reunited for its 35th anniversary.

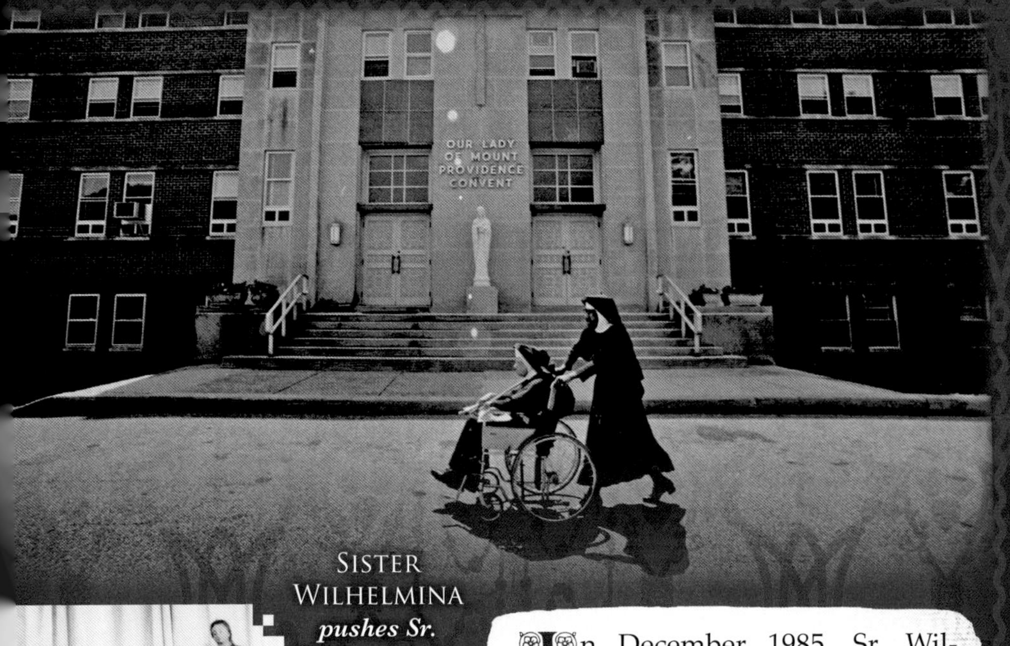

SISTER WILHELMINA *pushes Sr. Benigna in her wheelchair. (above)*

MARIAN ANDERSON *hough not Catholic, auded Sr. Benigna, ier accompanist since outh, (right) for her ntry into religious life n the threshold of fame. They remained life-long friends.*

In December 1985, Sr. Wilhelmina was appointed to assist Sr. Benigna Holland in the Mount Providence Center of Music and General Culture. This was a happy assignment for her, which she enjoyed right up until the day in May 1995 when she left the Oblate Sisters of Providence to found a new traditional community. The two teamed up to write other hymns after their first collaboration, "We Do Believe." Sister Wilhelmina was especially devoted to her friend:

Sr. Benigna was like a mother to me in many ways. She was one of the few Oblates who persevered in wearing the traditional habit; she taught me much by example in my young days, and even more after I became her assistant. A concert pianist (and accompanist to Marian Anderson) before

Jesus, King of Mercy!
Glory be to Thee!
All mankind is needful
Thy sweet Face to see!

Make believers trust Thee,
Trust! And love Thee more!
Serving Thee through Mary!
Never done before!

God is Beauty,
God is Good,
God for me has
Died on wood.
I, the sinner,
Now repent,
Making my life
One sweet Lent.
Now He reigns –
Eternal King!
Evermore His
Praise I sing.

entering the Oblates in 1930, she also had high musical standards. It was she, for instance, who taught me Gregorian chant and pointed out the value of the *Liber Usualis*.

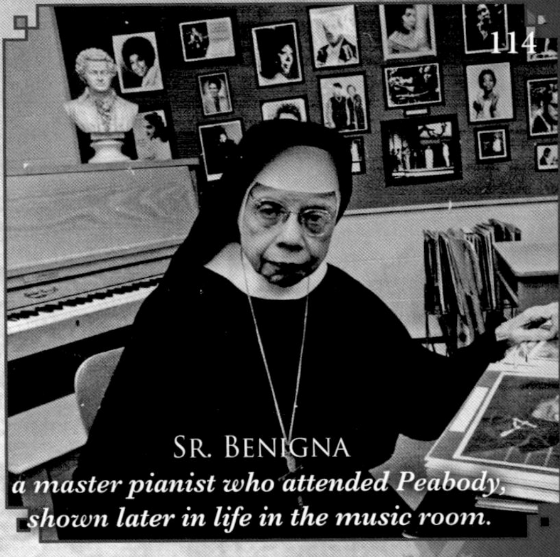

SR. BENIGNA
a master pianist who attended Peabody, shown later in life in the music room.

Under the tutelage of Sr. Benigna, she also gained a deep appreciation for the musical patrimony of the Church. She began to see Ray Repp's "catchy, not churchy" dictum as a repudiation of the centuries of tradition which had come before. Sister Wilhelmina reflected:

> In the old days the music was straightforward in style and dogmatic in substance. Hymns reinforced Church teachings. There was reverence, awe, majesty in them. Nowadays music is relaxed, formless, focused on self. I spent my youth studying diligently, striving to learn standard English as well as music, and now I am expected to be delighted with dialect and cornfield ditties. At Mass I want to give God my best, which broken or infantile English is not, just as various aberrations have been embraced in the name of "the spirit of Vatican II", so there have been numerous vitiations of the *Novus Ordo*. When the *Novus Ordo* began, with its choices of prefaces and Eucharistic acclamations, I had no idea that these would be bypassed for other expressions whenever there was felt to be a "need." I never dreamed that the beautiful Latin hymns and motets would be banned as "foreign to the culture" or "beyond the understanding" of the people.

In 2018, the last year of Sr. Wilhelmina's life, she received a letter of thanks from a former student from this period. He had pursued a musical career, becoming the director of music for a Catholic parish in Florida and was overjoyed to recognize Sr. Wilhelmina's name in a community newsletter:

> So often I look back on my musical studies with Sr. Benigna and yourself at the Mt. Providence motherhouse so many years ago… I thank God daily for having your influence in my life.

lost over 100 Sisters in the ten years following their 1965 peak membership of 337 Sisters serving 40 schools across the U.S. (Sr. Wilhelmina is toward the back left corner.)

Never cry,
never complain,
All about your
little pain!
Look at Jesus
hanging there:
Tell Him of your
love and care.

While Sr. Wilhelmina was going through these changes in her own life, her community continued to undergo experimentation, setting aside many traditional practices of religious life along with the habit. In response, Sr. Wilhelmina wrote an essay entitled, "Sister, Sister, Why Did You Enter?" It does not appear to have been published; perhaps she simply gave it to her fellow Oblates to read. This paper eloquently expresses Sr. Wilhelmina's understanding of her own vocation. She first identifies the purpose of religious life, in contrast to the notion in vogue that a religious was a social worker or a member of a sorority.

To be a religious means to consistently and openly express a total love for Jesus Christ in a particular intimacy which is neither expected nor required of the common Christian. A

I must be obedient no matter what the pain,
And imitating Christ Our Lord, a place in Heaven gain.

religious strives to be here on earth what all are destined to be in Heaven, totally engaged in Divine Union. The essence of religious living is neither apostolic concern nor the sharing of a common fellowship… the essential element of being a religious lies wholly in the realm of Divine grace obtained through assiduous prayer and the sacraments faithfully received.

Moreover, the total love for Jesus Christ is expressed in a certain poverty, a certain chastity, a certain obedience, and in the practice of all the Christian virtues. A religious is ever bent on getting to know Christ better through daily meditation on the Scriptures, and on empathizing with His every joy and pain.

Sister Wilhelmina encouraged her fellow religious to rise above the current class wars caused by discrimination and racism.

Anyone who would save his soul as a vowed religious of the Roman Catholic Church must, absolutely must, transcend all notions of class, caste and race, both from the "oppressor-superior" viewpoint as well as from the "victim-inferior" viewpoint. Both views are equally damaging to whoever harbors them.

My Love, my Lord, my Life, my Light!
Help me from now on do what's right!

Thank God, thank God,
For everything!
His Will is always done!
Although to us, things seem to be
Not quite our kind of fun.

She also addressed the prevalent prejudices against religious authority, in the face of a culture that would democratize the religious life, demanding independence, individual rights, self-determination and self-fulfillment, and casting suspicion and distrust between religious and their superiors.

> God is able to write straight with crooked lines… Observers should not mourn overmuch upon noticing inequities in the choice of superiors, although inequities in plenty there may be. Every religious in good spiritual health and in her right mind is truly happy to be obedient and subject, because the path of obedience is the safe and sure path; when one obeys, she is certain of doing God's will rather than her own.

She entertained no pretensions about the frailty and faults of religious, describing each as a weak and sinful soul who nevertheless "daily strives to cause joy among the angels of God in Heaven by the enactment of her <u>own</u> sincere conversion." For this, she must persevere in obedience to "the guidelines drawn up by ecclesial authority for the proper ordering of the religious Christian's life."

> Whenever a religious steps outside her cloister to fraternize with her brothers and sisters in the world, she is thereby presented with the odd and alluring opportunity of enjoying an extra, unscheduled, pizza and beer herself. Instead of criticizing religious as living in their ivory towers, insensitive to the world's needs, society really should be thankful that the bums are off the streets. The present-day demand that nuns come out of their cozy cloisters and socialize with the people has dubious origins. Part of the pressure might be the translation of a wonder how it is that religious can seemingly have such good times… and a desire to be invited to the conventual party as an observer of, and a partaker in, the <u>joy</u>.

> They who choose a sacrificial life for the love of God are often endowed by God with manna of such unspeakable sweetness that even unbelievers can perceive that something marvelous is sustaining them in spite of their deprivations. But this manna God gives to <u>all</u> who seek Him sincerely, as He promises: "Seek first the Kingdom of God and His justice and all other things will be given you besides." God simply cannot be outdone in generosity, especially to those who have been so generous as to surrender themselves entirely to Him.

O-be-di-ence!
The only fence
That keeps me
in God's garden!
All for the love
Of God above!
Let selfishness
not harden.

In the Music Room

Sister was visited by one of the Sisters in her community.

PRAYER FOR NIGHT-WORRIERS

Cause of our Joy,
help those
who weep,
Who toss and turn
and cannot sleep;
Souls who are over-
whelmed with grief:
Cause of our Joy,
give them relief.

My Mother has me
by the hand,
She brings me
to Thee now:
She's giving me
to understand
How I must keep
my vow.

For many years, Sr. Wilhelmina persistently petitioned her fellow Oblates to allow her to start a traditional branch of the community, adhering more to the old practices and habit which had been put aside.

I had no thought or desire of leaving my community in those days, but I was gung-ho for seeing it reformed. We had made a wrong turn, I said, and should go back. The rule of silence and monthly chapter were long gone. Sisters were invited—I was working in the archives then—to submit a replacement or improvement of Chapter. I wrote something and handed it in but never heard anything of it. Something else that I wrote in December 1972, "Is There Light at the End of the Tunnel?" was presented at a community meeting and caused a stir. It suggested that OSP recognize themselves as a three-pronged venture, one of which would be a contemplative unit. My suggestion nettled those who wanted to see us give up the habit completely and go into all the lovely colors. Others who were not as far out as this nonetheless saw the contemplative life as something medieval, dangerous and unjust.

The Chapter of 1973 was an education for me. Although not an elected delegate, I was appointed an extra secretary, and I witnessed all that happened without being able to open my mouth. All OSP had been allowed to submit proposals to the Chapter, and I submitted mine that a contemplative unit be formed. In Chapter after Chapter - 1973, 1977, 1985, 1989, under some wording or another, I submitted this idea. At last in 1993 I thought I had the perfect wording "traditional house be established" and this passed. It was hamstrung from the very beginning.

Sr. Wilhelmina's proposal follows:

I, Sr. Mary Wilhelmina Lancaster, O.S.P, remembering my initial formation and early training as an Oblate Sister of Providence, desire to bolster the infrastructure of the practices of genuine religious life. I desire to pass on to others the traditional practices which formed the infrastructure:

THE WEARING OF A UNIFORM HABIT,
THE SURRENDERING OF ALL MONIES TO A COMMON BURSAR,
THE OBEYING OF LAWFUL AUTHORITY IN ALL DEPARTMENTS,
THE GUARDING OF ENCLOSURE AND OF TIMES AND PLACES OF SILENCE,
and THE LIVING TOGETHER AN AUTHENTIC FRATERNAL LIFE.

She then submitted the name of the only sister willing to embark on such a project:

Sister M. Wilhelmina Lancaster

Jesus,
I trust
in Thee!
Jesus,
I trust in Thee!
I thank Thee, Lord,
for helping me live
And bear wrongs
patiently;
Jesus,
I trust in Thee!
Jesus,
in Thee, I trust!
Thou hast borne
me for many years
And wiped away
my foolish tears,
I trust in Thee,
I trust in Thee,
Jesus,
I trust in Thee!

Outward observances are NOT
What God desires; the inward rot
Of pride and self-love kill the soul!
God wants to see Christ in control.

A BRIGHT SPOT
in the difficult decade of the 1980s was Sr. Wilhelmina's final visit to her mother in St. Louis.

'Twas Gabriel who came, I think,
To Jesus in Gethsemane,
Prostrate with sorrow and the drink
Of bitterest of heminae.

The angel showed Him all the good
That would be His in Heav'n forever
And strengthened Him to shed more blood
In pains that life below would sever.

St. Gabriel, please help us comfort Christ,
As He for our salvation sacrificed
His Life, His Blood, His Body and His Soul;
Help us cooperate and reach the Goal!

The Will of God
Almighty,
My Creator,
Whom I love,
This suffering
does glorify,
And leads
to Life above.

Jesus,
King of
Martyrs,
Glory be to Thee!
Thou hast
suffered tortures,
Thou hast died for me!
Thou has risen from the dead!
Now Thou reign'st in Heaven!
To Thee and the Father
Be all glory given!

Glory to the Spirit
Who helps us endure
All our earthly trials
In the faith secure.
We rejoice that we shall rise

We shall go to Heaven
There the Spirit's welcome
To us will be given.

With the
Rosary of the day
And Novena
of the night
So my time in the world
passes by;
As I struggle
to obtain
That supreme
eternal gain
Of a home with my
Lord God
on high.

Since sin alone
keeps me out
I must fight
bout after bout
Against temptings
in thought,
word and deed;

Yet my good Lord
overlooks
All my craziness
and crooks
And supplies me
with everything
I need.

So with charity
my chore
I must tell Him
o'er and o'er
How I adore
His sweet infinity;
While I do not
hear reply
I am certain:
ne'er runs dry
The wondrous well
that is Divinity.

Sister Wilhelmina had not been entirely bereft of support. Many Sisters, especially from among the thirty-three community members who wore the traditional habit, expressed their personal backing for her initiative. But none felt that they could officially join her. Even Sr. Benigna, who loved Sr. Wilhelmina so much, sadly told her "I am too old." Sr. Wilhelmina described the disappointing conclusion to her initiative:

> Sr. Claudina Sanz, the superior general, announced to the whole community several months later, "We are the traditional house." Although humiliated, I was happy to be finished with the work of trying to reform the OSP. I saw nothing ahead of me but silent perseverance in the community until I died.

Squeeze the bead!
And do not plead
For change or rest;
God knows what's best.

SISTER CLAUDINA
superior general.

Chapter 10

Cries to

O Blessed Mother Mary!
Protect your Pope from harm!
His enemies are many
And they sound glad alarm
That he is old and dying
Will soon be off the scene
Then they'll return to lying
And being King and queen.
Help him proclaim the dogma
That you alone are queen,
That you alone are advocate
With Jesus, and serene
Protect our Holy Father,
He truly is your son!
Don't let his foes condemn him
Don't let him be undone!
A happy death awaits him
He surely cannot grieve
Who has proclaimed the dogma
That you are the New Eve.

Thank Thee, Lord, for every pain
All of them are my deserts.
Everlasting is Thy reign;
When Thou wilt, Thou'll heal my hurt

From 1979-1993
Sr. Wilhelmina appealed directly to the newly-elected John Paul II regarding the crisis in the church, the liturgy and her own community. The two met in 1998, on the occasion of the tenth anniversary of Ecclesia Dei.

PETER

Rome Bound Letters

hanks, for all that crosses me;
istractions... aridity...
Most of all, thank God for Thee!

During this troubling time of isolation within her own community, between 1979 and 1993, Sr. Wilhelmina had regular recourse to the Holy Father, Pope St. John Paul II. She first opened her heart to her Father in Rome in 1979, sending him her essays "Consider This" and "A Sesquicentennial Salute," sharing with him her love of her race and of her religious community, both of which she saw as needing true conversion and authentic reform. She wrote him several times subsequently, encouraging him and thanking him for his apostolic labors and sharing with him her own efforts to remain faithful to the Apostolic tradition.

As experimentation within the Oblates' community reached the liturgy, Sr. Wilhelmina wrote, protesting the introduction of African-American rites and begging for a traditional ordinariate, as requested by *Una Voce*, a coalition for preserving the Latin Mass:

> January 19, 1991
>
> Most Holy Father:
>
> I see no need for an African rite.
> I see no need for an American rite.
> I see no need for an African-American rite.
> I adhere to the Roman rite. Latin is the official language of the Roman rite. Gregorian chant is the official music of the Roman rite.
>
> I am a subject of Christ's kingdom, which is not of this world.
>
> Our Lord Jesus Christ founded one Church for all men regardless of skin color, regardless of living conditions, regardless of mother tongue. Everyone must die to himself and put on Christ. "Forget your people and your father's house," the psalm says.
>
> Please, Holy Father, listen to the cry of UNA VOCE: Establish a Traditional Ordinariate Consecrated to the Immaculate Heart of Mary!

She followed this with a letter to Augustin Cardinal Mayer OSB dated January 25, 1991, containing a single, pithy statement: "I am determined to remain a strict Roman Catholic and to have nothing whatsoever to do with the so-called African-American Catholic Church."

LITURGICAL DANCE ***was pushed as being part of African worship. Cardinal Ratzinger denounced this as an attempt to "make the 'reasonable Sacrifice' attractive" and ending with applause. "It is a sure sign that the essence of liturgy has totally disappeared … None of the Christian rites includes dancing."***

ONE AFRICAN RITE MOVEMENT ***led to schism in the "African Catholic Church" Iman Temples beginning in Washington DC (above.) The first Bishop was ordained by the excommunicant Archbishop Emmanuel Milingo (below) and the group sharply deviated from the church's teaching and practice, even "ordaining" a one-time Oblate of Providence.***

In all my years
What have I done
but sin?
Now I must die!
Let me begin
To trust in Thee, my Lord
Who reign'st on high!
Though Mary's Heart
Immaculate
I breathe this little sigh.

UNA VOCE *was founded by Georges Cerbelaud-Salagnac in 1964 for the continuance of the Latin Mass. He was joined by eminent musicians like Maurice Duruflé (above left) and Welsh author Michael Davies (below left) who headed the organization from 1992-2004*

Sr. Wilhelmina also sent unauthorized translations of psalms and canticles to Rome, begging that the superiors not mandate these spurious versions for the community's usage: "May religious communities change the wording of psalms or of familiar prayers such as the doxology at their pleasure? Please respond." Cardinal Mayer responded in the negative. Sister Wilhelmina brought this document to the attention of the Oblate Chapter, proposing that all Oblate Sisters of Providence adhere to traditional prayer forms used by the rest of the Roman Catholic Church, as Cardinal Mayer's letter stipulated. Her proposal, however, was not seconded and thus died on the floor of the chapter.

Sr. Wilhelmina, however, endured and even embraced these frustrations and heartaches as a purification. She shared this growth of her soul with the Holy Father; the formulaic replies from the papal secretary never dampened her vibrant faith in the Pope's loving concern for her as his true spiritual daughter:

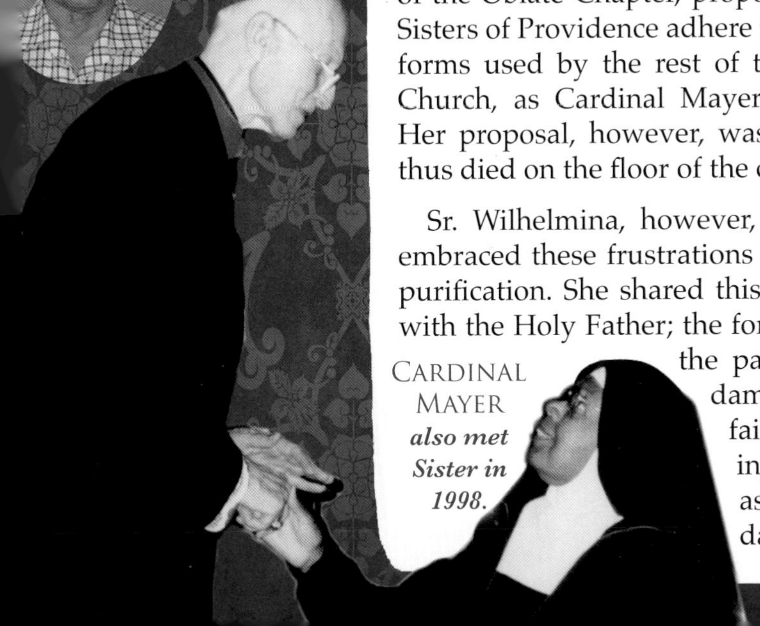

CARDINAL MAYER *also met Sister in 1998.*

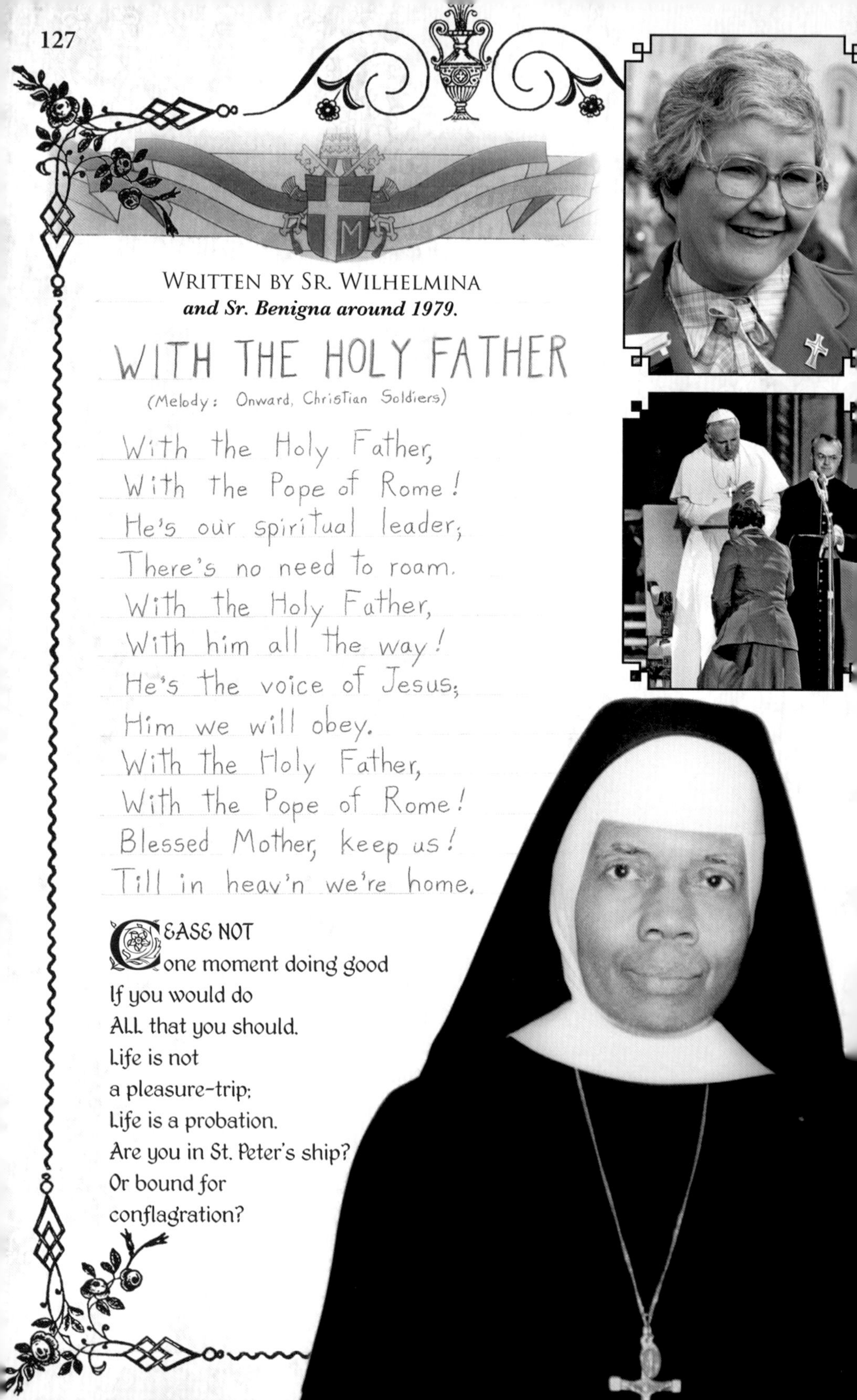

Written by Sr. Wilhelmina
and Sr. Benigna around 1979.

WITH THE HOLY FATHER

(Melody: Onward, Christian Soldiers)

With the Holy Father,
With the Pope of Rome!
He's our spiritual leader;
There's no need to roam.
With the Holy Father,
With him all the way!
He's the voice of Jesus;
Him we will obey.
With the Holy Father,
With the Pope of Rome!
Blessed Mother, keep us!
Till in heav'n we're home.

CEASE NOT
one moment doing good
If you would do
ALL that you should.
Life is not
a pleasure-trip;
Life is a probation.
Are you in St. Peter's ship?
Or bound for
conflagration?

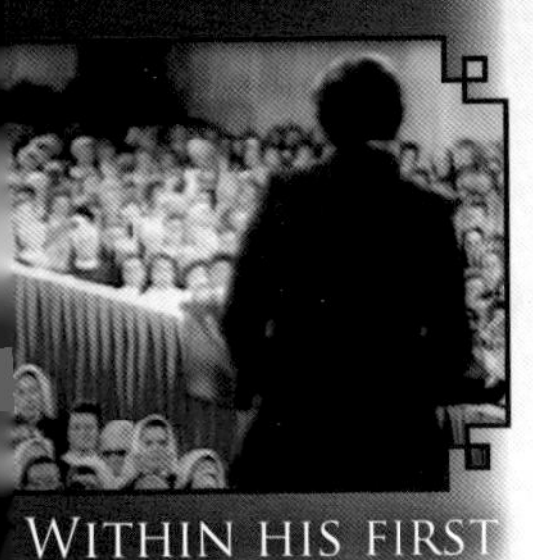

WITHIN HIS FIRST YEAR AS POPE, *John Paul II visited Washington DC, where he met religious at the National Shrine (below) Sr. Wilhelmina was appalled by Sr. Theresa Kane's address to him and attendees (above) calling for the ordination of women. Most of the nuns came in habit, and many refused to applaud. The Pope invoked Our Lady, Queen of Apostles and blessed Sr. Theresa (left.)*

Ascension Thursday, 1991

Most Holy Father:

Thank you for all your prayers and sacrifices for me! I have changed – my outlook has changed, become more Christian, more united with the Hearts of Jesus and Mary – since I first wrote you in 1979. You must have prayed for me!

I am sorry for any trouble that I caused you in 1979 with my ignorance and selfishness. Today I witness, even when I must stand alone: To be black is nothing! To be Catholic is everything!

Thank you again, my dear suffering, hard-working Holy Father! I will be remembering you in prayer on your birthday, Saturday, May 18, the vigil of Pentecost.

Your loving daughter in Christ,
Sr. M. Wilhelmina Lancaster, O.S.P.

Sr. Wilhelmina was able to see Pope St. John Paul II in person on the occasion of his visit to the Basilica of the National Shrine of the Immaculate Conception in Washington, DC, on October 7, 1979. The purpose of his visit was to deliver a major address to women religious, which Sr. Wilhelmina gladly attended. Sadly, at the conclusion of the Pope's address, a religious sister delivered her own remarks in which she admonished the Holy Father for upholding the Church's teaching that women cannot be ordained priests. Sister Wilhelmina was indignant and wrote a formal letter of apology on behalf of all the women religious in attendance, and received a reply from the Secretariat of State (excerpted):

Most Holy Father:

As one of the Sisters in the National Shrine of the Immaculate Conception on Sunday morning, October 7th, I thank you now for the encouragement and help that you gave in your address to women religious, and I am sorry about the remarks and demeanor of Sister Theresa Kane, R.S.M.

Dear Sister Wilhelmina,

The Holy Father has asked me to thank you for the message which you sent to him regarding his pastoral visit to the United States. He is grateful for the support of your prayers and for the devoted sentiments which prompted you to write.

His Holiness prays that the Holy Spirit will lead you to an ever deeper appreciation of the profound richness of your consecration in Christ and of your special mission in the life and holiness of the Church.

Most Holy Father:

For several years, it has seemed to me that an evil force in the world is trying to destroy the Catholic Church. Much that this evil force does is under the name "the Vatican," just as this news article uses the name, "the Vatican." Your name, too, "Pope John Paul II" is used, I cannot believe that Your Holiness has approved of female altar servers anywhere. The evil force has acted over your head, or behind your back, and of course, used your name. Please act for the good of the faithful and refute this lie.

Sr. M. Wilhelmina OSP
May 9, 1994

GIRL SERVERS

Coming soon to an altar near you

The Vatican has approved the use of female altar servers, subject to the pastoral needs of local churches.

In a letter to bishops' conferences around the world, the Vatican said that its interpretation of Church law on the subject had been confirmed by Pope John Paul II. The letter was signed by Cardinal Antonio Mariá Javierre Ortas, prefect of the Congregation for Divine Worship and the Sacraments.

Vatican spokesman Joaquin Navarro-Valls said that individual bishops would be free to permit or deny girls to serve. He also said that the decision has no connection with the debate over whether women should be ordained as priests. Service at the altar has a much different canonical and doctrinal nature, he said.

Archbishop William H. Keeler of Baltimore, president of the National Conference of Catholic Bishops, called the papal decision "a welcome one."

The letter advised bishops that any decision to use female altar servers should be explained well to the faithful. Pastors should note that women already perform such tasks during Mass as reading from Scripture and distributing Communion. The letter also said that lay ministries are temporary tasks subject to the bishop's judgment and do not imply "a right" held by either men or women. ❑

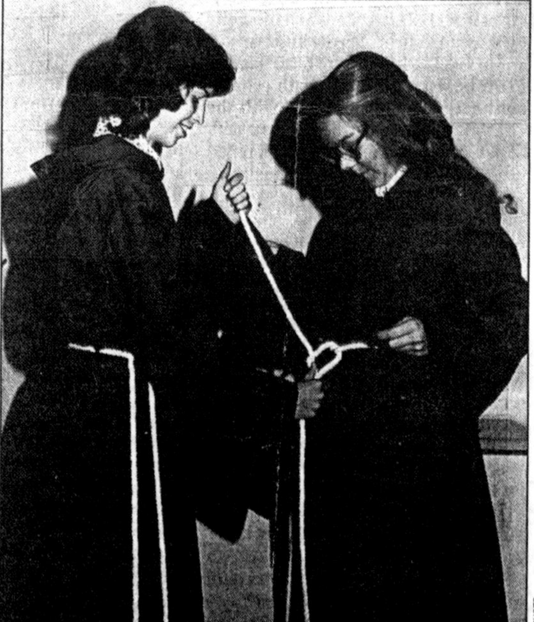
CNS PHOTO

"LEGIT" NOW: Altar girls

Our Sunday Visitor April 24, 1994

APPROVAL OF FEMALE SERVERS
prompted another letter to Rome from Sr. Wilhelmina.

THE GOLDEN JUBILEE
of Sister's band was celebrated with a Mass by William Cardinal Keeler.

MOTHER TERESA
who had also been dismayed by the approval of altar girls, visited Baltimore during Sister's last years there, welcomed by Cardinal Keeler and Oblates. Mother enlisted Sr. Wilhelmina as one of her "Veronicas," named for the Saint who consoled Christ (right.) The Veronicas prayed and sacrificed especially for priests.

For the conversion of bad priests I plead:
The irresponsible ones who feed
On lies; the scandal-givers who seek power;
The sexually-perverted in the hour
Of darkness; the cash-loving thieves;
The proud disobedient who no longer believes.

Thy yoke is sweet,
Thy burden, light;
Give Thy
poor priests,
Lord,
clearer
sight.

Lord,
save
Thy priest!
Don't let
him stray
No matter
what the pain!
But stay!

GOD LOVES HIS PRIESTS!
His chosen men!
And we should love them, too!
No matter what
their human faults,
No matter what they do!

Leave it to God to punish them
If they fall into sin;
We do our best to extricate them
From the mess they're in.

ON THE 1998 PILGRIMAGE *a Sister also snapped a photo of three speakers: Bishop Timlin, Michael Davies and Cardinal Ratzinger, Sr. Wilhelmina's other appellee.*

She also had a personal encounter with St. John Paul II some years later, after she had left the Oblates of Providence. In 1998, she had the opportunity to travel to Rome and attend a papal audience. Because her age required her to use a wheelchair during this pilgrimage, she was given a place in the front row and even brought forward to greet the Pope. She clasped his hand and exclaimed with joy, "Thank you, Holy Father, thank you, thank you for everything!" This encounter with Christ's representative remained one of her favorite memories.

Sr. Wilhelmina's last extant letter to Rome is addressed to Joseph Cardinal Ratzinger as Head of the Congregation for the Doctrine of the Faith, in which she shares with him another unauthorized paraliturgical rite used by the Oblates for the feast of the Immaculate Conception. She further shares with him seven points which she was resolved to follow in regard to her perseverance "as a Roman Catholic in sanctifying grace and as a true religious and child of the Blessed Virgin Mary." Her points are as follows:

Thank God
for working miracles
For all the faithful's good,
Converting sinners into saints,
Confounding those who stood
In pride and disobedience
Against His holy Church;
Assuring everyone who seeks
For Truth, 'though poor the search,
FOR HIS OWN GLORY
Rescuing
Those caught in evil lurch.

Lord, build us on the rock of Faith,
The rock of Faith in Thee!
No matter what the pain, the cross
Of tribulation be;
Help us believe, although this world
Sees us as fools quite lost.
Help us stay with Thee in the boat
Completely tempest-tossed.

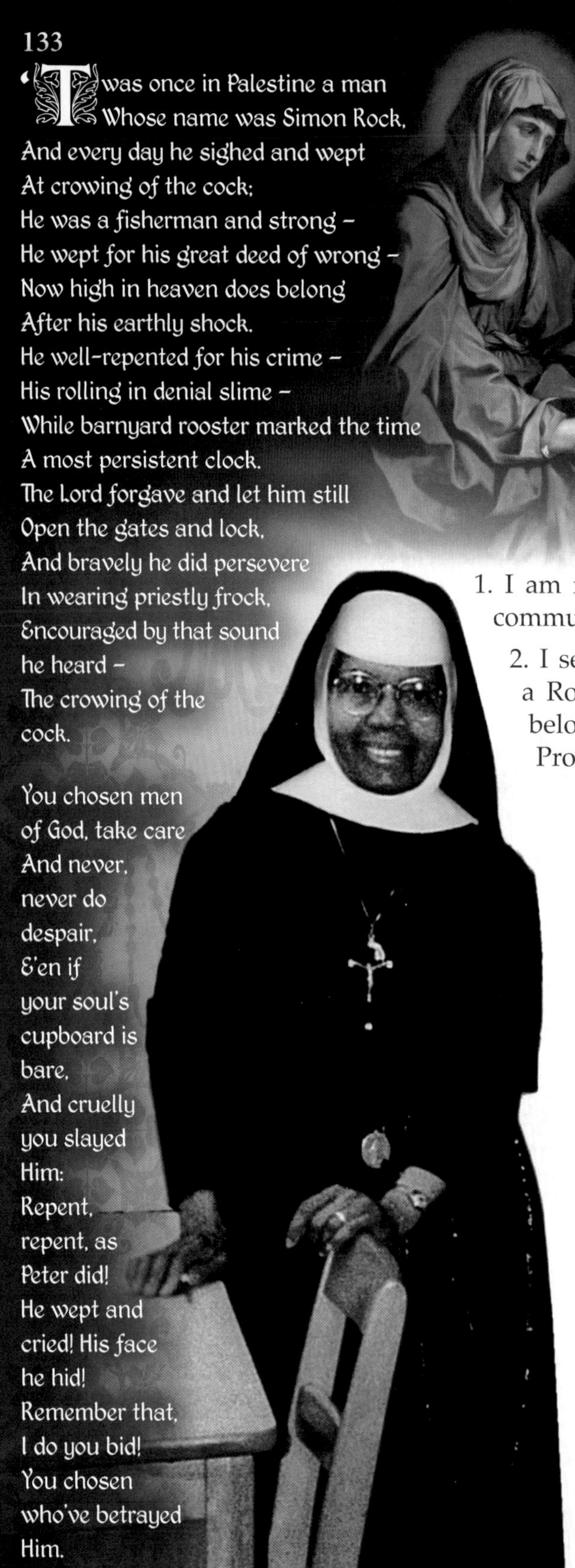

'Twas once in Palestine a man
Whose name was Simon Rock,
And every day he sighed and wept
At crowing of the cock;
He was a fisherman and strong –
He wept for his great deed of wrong –
Now high in heaven does belong
After his earthly shock.
He well-repented for his crime –
His rolling in denial slime –
While barnyard rooster marked the time
A most persistent clock.
The Lord forgave and let him still
Open the gates and lock,
And bravely he did persevere
In wearing priestly frock,
Encouraged by that sound
he heard –
The crowing of the
cock.

You chosen men
of God, take care
And never,
never do
despair,
E'en if
your soul's
cupboard is
bare,
And cruelly
you slayed
Him:
Repent,
repent, as
Peter did!
He wept and
cried! His face
he hid!
Remember that,
I do you bid!
You chosen
who've betrayed
Him.

1. I am not interested in leaving my community and founding another.

2. I see a rich spiritual patrimony, a Roman Catholic spirituality, as belonging to us Oblate Sisters of Providence.

3. Specifically, our Roman Catholic spirituality is Total Consecration to Jesus through Mary, and devotion to Our Lord Jesus Christ truly present in the Most Holy Sacrament of the Altar.

4. Social upheaval and misrepresentation of the Documents of Vatican II have obscured this, our patrimony, from us.

5. Consequently, I propose, I urge, the establishment of a traditional house: so that our spiritual patrimony may be secured and made to live again, unmolested by the spirit of this passing world.

6. The security of our traditional lifestyle must be guaranteed by persons of

SYNOD HALL CROSSFIRE *preceded John Paul II's 1994 promulgation of Vita Consecrata to address religious life. Bishop James Clifford Timlin of Scranton openly criticized the twenty-five post-conciliar years as "devastating to religious life." The most vocal of the American Bishops, he said "refounding and transformation" were now necessary, something he would literally fulfill in the founding of Sr. Wilhelmina's new order. "We have dialogued enough. We have experimented enough... The era of experimentaiton, or whatever we want to call it, has not been all that successful, and we should honestly and humbly admit it." His concluding intervention was a reaction to that of Joseph Cardinal Bernadin of Chicago, who called for a "broad scope of legitimate diversity" in religious reforms that the Bishops ought not criticize. Bernadin (below) was considered the arch-liberal leader of the American Bishops who illegitimately rammed the approval of Communion on the hand through the USCCB by amassing absentee votes according to Father John Hardon, SJ. Posthumous accusations of misconduct and anti-Catholic involvement have recently surrounded the influential Cardinal's legacy.*

like mind regarding the essentials of it coming together in one place, not merely talking about it, but actually living the traditional life.

7. Only if such agreement cannot be reached will it be necessary to appeal to the Pope for a new foundation.

She concluded, "Please, Your Eminence, help me to save my soul according to the Will of Almighty God." The moment for the new foundation was at hand.

CARDINAL RATZINGER
received Sister's letter, replying that her concerns would receive attention. Michael Davies placed much hope in Ratzinger as the future liberator of the ancient liturgy.

Chapter 11

O my Love,
High above,
I will let
And not fret,
You be God!
While I plod.

Make sure you sew and wash and iron,
Make sure you cook and clean!
But most of all be charitable –
Neither proud nor mean –
Remember you are being formed
By Mother Mary Queen!

Love! Love!
God is Love Eternal!
Love! Love!
Infinite and pure!
Love! Love!
Merciful Creator!
Love! Love!
Makes salvation sure.

Lady of Ephesus
Save all priests on earth!
Help them fight earth's battle
And come to heaven's birth!

Celebrating Mass each day –
Faithfully to fast and pray –
God's commands to obey
With true self-offering!

Following the Holy Way
Lord Jesus Christ, our King!

BAGGAGE

A New Calling

I arise in the morning when the bell rings,
I retire in the evening when I'm told;
And for all my obediences binding
God showers me with blessings manifold.

Thank You, Sweet Savior Jesus
Christ, for calling us to pray!
At Prime, at Terce, at Sext, at None!
Throughout the busy day.

The Mass is most important to us
Each and every day;
As we walk well with Mary
On the Dolorosa Way.
We do not fight among ourselves
About who will be boss;
We simply see our Savior
Suff'ring, dying on the Cross.

ON THE FEAST OF ST. BEDE

May 27, 1995, Sister Wilhelmina arrived at Elmhurst, Pennsylvania to begin a new religious order. She was greeted by Sr. Therese McNamara and Sr. Anna Marie McCormack.

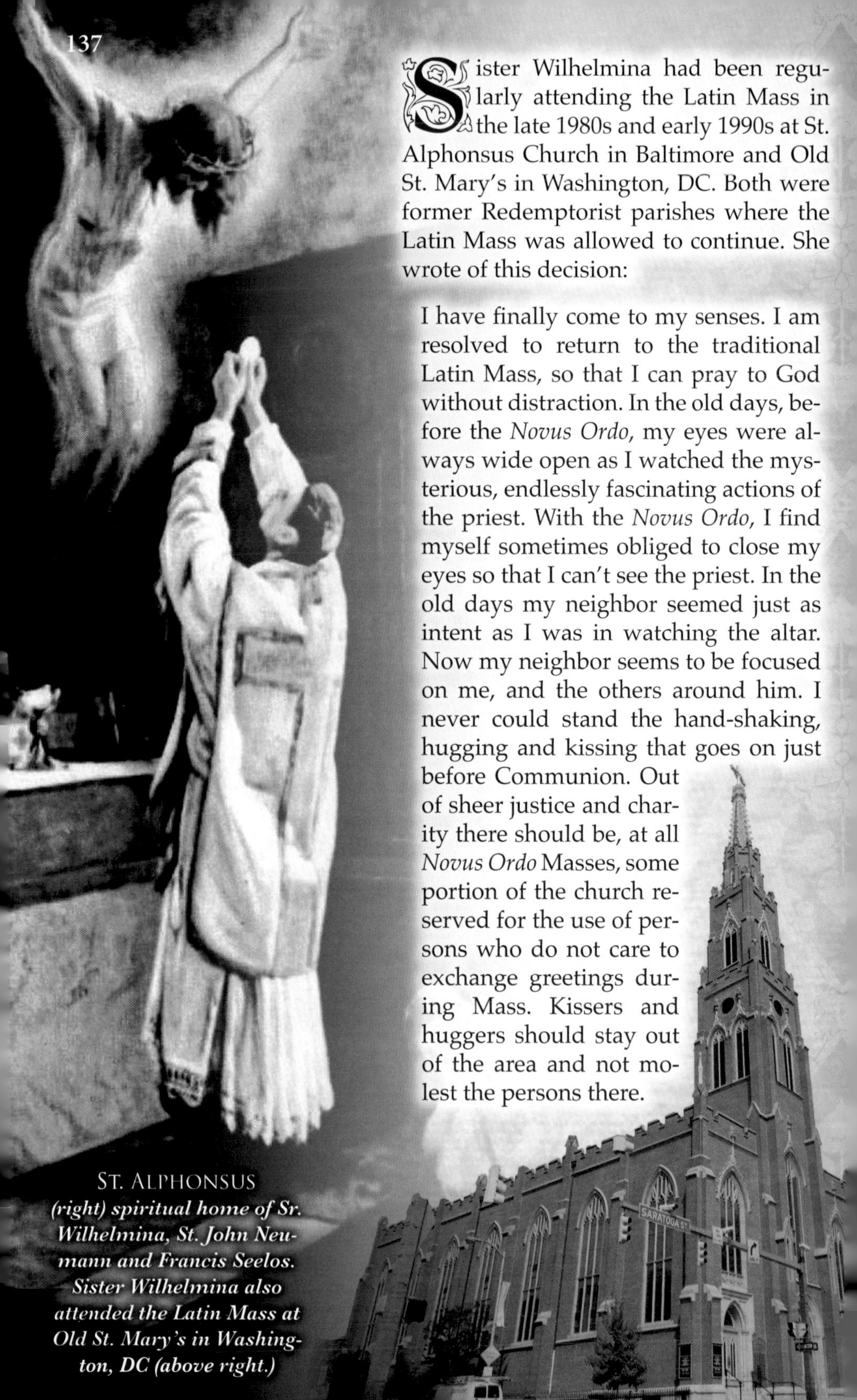

Sister Wilhelmina had been regularly attending the Latin Mass in the late 1980s and early 1990s at St. Alphonsus Church in Baltimore and Old St. Mary's in Washington, DC. Both were former Redemptorist parishes where the Latin Mass was allowed to continue. She wrote of this decision:

> I have finally come to my senses. I am resolved to return to the traditional Latin Mass, so that I can pray to God without distraction. In the old days, before the *Novus Ordo*, my eyes were always wide open as I watched the mysterious, endlessly fascinating actions of the priest. With the *Novus Ordo*, I find myself sometimes obliged to close my eyes so that I can't see the priest. In the old days my neighbor seemed just as intent as I was in watching the altar. Now my neighbor seems to be focused on me, and the others around him. I never could stand the hand-shaking, hugging and kissing that goes on just before Communion. Out of sheer justice and charity there should be, at all *Novus Ordo* Masses, some portion of the church reserved for the use of persons who do not care to exchange greetings during Mass. Kissers and huggers should stay out of the area and not molest the persons there.

ST. ALPHONSUS *(right) spiritual home of Sr. Wilhelmina, St. John Neumann and Francis Seelos. Sister Wilhelmina also attended the Latin Mass at Old St. Mary's in Washington, DC (above right.)*

Don't get me wrong. I have always been a supporter of active participation at Mass. For years before Vatican II, I did my utmost to promote the *Missa Recitata*. But I have also long appreciated the fact that the Mass is public, liturgical prayer, which differs from private, personal prayer. When one prays privately he can use any words, any books, any posture, any time. There are no rules, no rubrics. But for the Mass, everything is prescribed, because the liturgy is the prayer of not just the local community, but the entire Roman Catholic Church, the entire Mystical Body of Christ. That is why, for liturgy, the question of "approved texts" is fundamental. Liturgical norms allow—and even encourage— a priest

ARCHBISHOP MARCEL LEFEBVRE

long-time African missionary Bishop, Superior of the Holy Ghost Fathers and a leader of the conservative Bishops at Vatican II, proceeded with the consecration of four Bishops for his Society of St. Pius X in 1988 before Vatican authorization was officially granted. Pope John Paul II then issued Ecclesia Dei Adflicta in response. The ordeal indicated the ghetto-like existence forced upon adherents of the Latin Mass in this period. Like Fr. Hardon and Michael Davies, Sr. Wilhelmina was sympathetic with the views of Lefebvre while not actually approving of the Consecration.

> to vary the wording of greetings in the Mass, and to give explanations at certain fixed points. But the wording of the prayers, readings—and above all the Eucharistic prayers—is to be as set down in the approved texts only. So I'm frankly fed up with all the ad-libbing that goes on nowadays in the Mass. In my opinion, the worst confusion since the promulgation of the *Novus Ordo* has resulted from this substituting of personal prayer for the liturgy, which has literally driven some people out of the assembly. And now, as if things weren't already bad enough, a campaign is underway to change the existing English translations of both the *Novus Ordo* Mass as well as the Divine Office, to make them more "inclusive" of women. What nonsense. Anyone without sufficient grasp of our language to understand that women are, and always have been included in such terms as "mankind," has no business correcting third-grade English papers, much less the language of the liturgy. But enough—enough!—of these musical hacks, these illiterate improvisers, these tireless revisers, these liturgical lobbyist who treat the Mass as if it were their personal propaganda tool. At long last, I am going back to the tried and the true, to the set and unchanging—to the traditional Latin Mass.

Two days after the consecration of four bishops without ecclesiatical approbation, John Paul II released the Motu Proprio *Ecclesia Dei* in 1988. Along with the condemnation of the act, and excommunications (subsequently lifted by Pope Benedict) the letter went on to address the Bishops and the entire Church. It was this in particular that Sr. Wilhelmina declared to be "news that I latched onto as salvific. I was determined to return to and attend the Traditional Latin Mass as much as possible." The consecration had opened a deeper awareness of faithful souls like Sr. Wilhelmina who were longing for a return to tradition within the Church at large. The Motu Proprio stated:

> To all those Catholic faithful who feel attached to some previous liturgical and disciplinary forms of the Latin tradition I wish to manifest my will to facilitate their ecclesial communion by means of the necessary measures to guarantee respect for their

rightful aspirations. In this matter I ask for the support of the bishops and of all those engaged in the pastoral ministry in the Church…

Respect must everywhere be shown for the feelings of all those who are attached to the Latin liturgical tradition, by a wide and generous application of the directives already issued some time ago by the Apostolic See for the use of the Roman Missal according to the typical edition of 1962.

THE SISTERS OF CHARITY OF MARY, MOTHER OF THE CHURCH *in Baltic, Connecticut hosted Sr. Wilhelmina for a retreat in 1991. She seriously considered transferring to this community.*

Sister Wilhelmina made many friends among the traditional Catholics of Baltimore. They facilitated her annual retreats in 1991 with the Sisters of Charity of Mary Mother of the Church in Baltic Connecticut, and in 1992 with the Slaves of the Immaculate Heart of Mary in Still River, Massachusetts. In the course of this latter retreat, Sr. Wilhelmina happened to meet Sr. Therese McNamara. Sr. Therese was just about to leave the Slaves of the Immaculate Heart to join the traditional Benedictine community in Le Barroux in France.

Thou art my Love,
my only Love,
All glory be to Thee!
Preserve me from
my selfish shove,
Give me humility!

Sister Therese, born Deidre McNamara, entered the Slaves of the Immaculate Heart at only 14 years of age. She proceeded to make her novitiate with the Slaves, professing perpetual vows in 1981. Sister Wilhelmina remembered their first encounter:

Something told me then that the young Sister Therese who was directing the music at Mass that August 22 would be my superior some day. "See that sister down there?" I heard inside, "She's going to be your Superior some day." I rejected the idea as impossible and unreasonable. "That little thing? No way!" But the voice

THE CHAPEL AT STILL RIVER *where Sr. Therese's future leadership was foretold to Sr. Wilhelmina.*

If Only I Had Let Him Live

I came out of that
place
and closed the door,
And knew he wasn't
with me anymore.
It would be quick,
they said; they looked at
me and smiled;
They pierced my baby's
head! It was so painful
to my child!
Loud in my mind
I heard his muffled squall–
My baby could not
help himself at all –
The doctor seemed to
understand my case;
He even had a liking
for my race,
He smiled and said it
wouldn't take him long
But now I know –
I know I was so wrong –
I should at least have
let my baby live;
To see the sunset,
feel the summer breeze,
And walk beside me
under shady trees,
Able to love and laugh
and share and give;
Oh, if only, only,
I had let
my baby live.

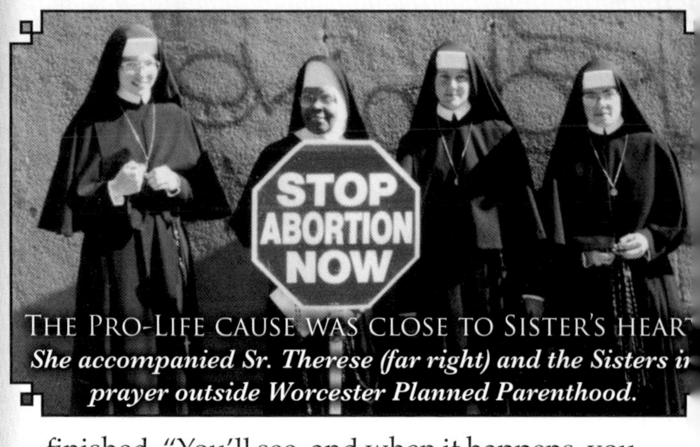

THE PRO-LIFE CAUSE WAS CLOSE TO SISTER'S HEAR
She accompanied Sr. Therese (far right) and the Sisters i prayer outside Worcester Planned Parenthood.

finished, "You'll see, and when it happens, you will know the truth of this."

Sister Wilhelmina finished her retreat and returned to the Oblate Sisters of Providence and her hoped-for renewal. She did, however, remain in contact with Sr. Therese, recognizing their shared aspirations for the resurgence of traditional religious life.

Sister Wilhelmina's personal notes during these years, 1993-1995, reveal the struggle in her soul as she sought to discern whether to persevere unto death in the Order to which she had been faithful for more than 50 years or to start anew. She had recourse, as always, to the Blessed Mother of God:

March 13, 1994

Because I want to persevere in the one true faith and witness for it, please help me to break whatever human ties I must in order to do so as a true religious and your most devoted child.

To kill that child
Is NOT the remedy!
Man must repent
And practice purity!

Unborn Child
Must be saved
Parents have
Misbehaved;
God forgives,
Died on cross
We must help
Prevent loss!

The following day, March 14, she drafted a letter to a priest of the newly formed Fraternity of St. Peter, whom she had heard was interested in forming a traditional group of religious sisters:

> Although I have been professed fifty years as an Oblate Sister of Providence, I am ready to begin anew serving Mother Church, having no desire whatsoever of being relieved of my perpetual vows but rather to persevere as a true religious and child of Mother Mary. Please let me know what is going on.

On March 18, she composed a prayer to the Holy Ghost:

> Lord Holy Spirit, Creator Blest, guide me in my quest for true religious life. For fifty years I have been an Oblate Sister of Providence. Help me to persevere as a Roman Catholic. The chapter approved the proposal "That at least one traditional house be established." Although no Oblate has been found to join me, help me to move out from among the Oblate Sisters as I should and work for the establishment of traditional sisters under the aegis of the Priestly Fraternity of Saint Peter.

BALTIMORE AND D.C. FRIENDS
especially from the Latin Mass circle included Mary Eloise Hopkins (top) Kelly and Christine Mucker (above) Rita Dent, John Ambs, Fr. William Define, FSSP, and Earl Swain (below.) John Paul II wrote to urge the Latin Mass Society of Baltimore, to which Sister belonged, to spread knowledge of the liturgy "from which source the whole community of the Church may draw spiritual profit."

THE 14 HOLY HELPERS

Saints Acathius,
Aegidius, Barbara
and Blaise –
To you
our anguished
hearts we raise –
Saints Catharine,
Christopher,
Cyriacus, Denis –
We're not playing
a game
of tennis –
Erasmus, Eustace,
George and
Margaret –
We are rather in a
very large fit –
Saints Pantaleon
and Vitus true,
We hope in heaven
to dance with you!

Heav'nly Father, let me love Thee
With my entire heart;
Even though I must endure of
Suffering a part.
Jesus, Jesus, let me love Thee
With my whole, whole soul!
Proving it by patient practice
Of true self-control.

Holy Spirit let me love Thee
With my entire mind,
Guarding it by thinking only
Thoughts pure and most kind.
Mighty Lord, please let me love Thee
With my entire strength,
Bring me, Lord, to live in heaven
With Thee, Lord, at length.

You must choose
from crosses three
On the hill of Calvary:
Praying for your own relief,
You can be repentant thief,
Or remain a selfish schemer
Crying out with the blasphemer,
Or embrace the cross of Christ,
Lovingly be sacrificed.

Three days later, March 21, saw the addition of a simple resolution: "I will willingly put beneath my feet all ethnic ties, and all self-aggrandizement, so as to be with You and Your Church totally, dying with You, so that I can rise again with You! While suffering here, I look forward to the joys of Heaven!" And two days later, she added the plea,

> Lord Jesus, help me as a true religious to surrender all attachment to my ethnic origin. You were rejected by your people, the Jews, and handed over to the Romans. Yet You loved your people dearly. Ridiculed as "King of the Jews," You became the Savior of the World. Help me to humbly follow You, the Good Samaritan, the Nazarene, my Beloved.

At the end of the summer of 1994, Sr. Wilhelmina wrote a poem reflecting on her fifty years in vows as an Oblate Sister of Providence. She borrowed an image from Pharoah's dream, which the patriarch Joseph interpreted to mean years of plenty followed by years of famine (Gen. 41), to express the changes that she underwent in her religious life. Her "temptations, attempts and failures," however, she recognized as part of the Lord's loving providence for her. Even amidst the anxiety and frustration, alluded to in "long, hot, sleepless nights," she recognized her trials as a purification for herself and ultimately a source of union with God in "deep delights of prayer."

1944-1994

Temptations
And attempts to change the scene
Of fat cows swallowed up
by years of lean!
All this has happened
as the Lord has willed;
I do believe, repentant,
having killed

Frustrations,
Failures, fits and deep delights
Of prayer on long, hot,
sleepless nights;
The sweat, the gall, the pain,
the purgatory;
God only knows
the entire golden story.

Around this time of interior struggle, Sr. Wilhelmina learned of the arrival of the Priestly Fraternity of St. Peter in Scranton, Pennsylvania, from Wigratzbad, Germany. She went with friends in a van to attend Fraternity events such as the solemn dedication of St. Gregory's Chapel in Elmhurst. John Ambs, the driver of the van on that trip, knew about the failure of Sr. Wilhelmina's 1993 proposal to the OSP Chapter. During the drive from Scranton, he informed Sr. Wilhelmina that Sr. Therese McNamara had come to Elmhurst. "Oh, no," Sr. Wilhelmina replied, "She has gone to join a traditional community in France." "But she is back!" John replied. He suggested that the two sisters spearhead a new traditional community. Sister Wilhelmina stated, "I did not hesitate." She wrote immediately to Sr. Therese:

April 27, 1995

> My last letter to you, Sr. Therese, was in June of last year, and in it I said that I had been strongly tempted to leave my community so as to join or form another, but that I had thought that temptation was over. Well, it's back, stronger than ever. Does God *really* want me to come to Scranton to join you? Such seems to be the case. I am actually praying now that God *will help me to leave* the Oblate Sisters of Providence of which I have been a professed member since 1944 and to join you in Scranton!
>
> Imagine! Lord, not my will but Thine be done… I'm praying the Miraculous Medal Novena not only for the needs of the Priestly Fraternity of St. Peter, but also the formation of – let us say – the Religious Sorority of St. Benedict. Ut in Omnia [sic] Deus glorificetur.

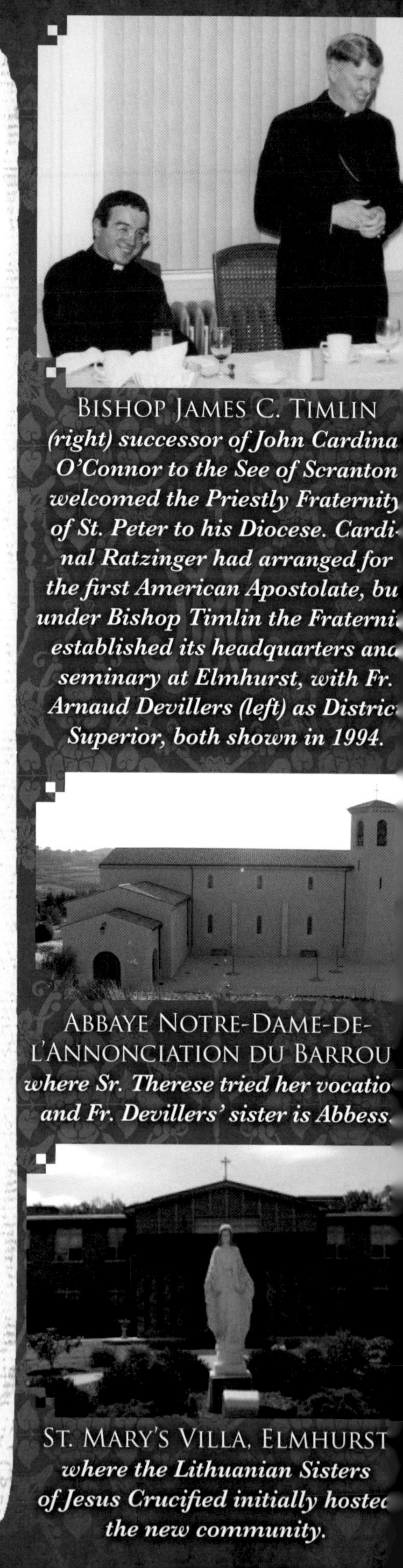

BISHOP JAMES C. TIMLIN *(right) successor of John Cardina[l] O'Connor to the See of Scranton welcomed the Priestly Fraternit[y] of St. Peter to his Diocese. Cardinal Ratzinger had arranged for the first American Apostolate, bu[t] under Bishop Timlin the Fraterni[ty] established its headquarters an[d] seminary at Elmhurst, with Fr. Arnaud Devillers (left) as Distric[t] Superior, both shown in 1994.*

ABBAYE NOTRE-DAME-DE-L'ANNONCIATION DU BARROU[X] *where Sr. Therese tried her vocatio[n] and Fr. Devillers' sister is Abbess.*

ST. MARY'S VILLA, ELMHURST *where the Lithuanian Sisters of Jesus Crucified initially hoste[d] the new community.*

Sister Anna Marie McCormack, a Benedictine of Corpus Christi Monastery in Michigan, had also come to Elmhurst with the blessing of her Superior. She had aided Sr. Therese upon her return to America, and had begun a proposal for a new community. Sister Wilhelmina also wrote to Sr. Anna Marie after Easter, asking if she would be the foundress, and emphasizing the need for clear authority from the start. Sister Wilhelmina summarized a future vision:

> You want independently governed sisters, yet sisters who walk parallel with the Priestly Fraternity of St. Peter, attending the traditional Latin Mass daily, and doing all in their power to spread it. This of course certainly means educating the young in Latin and Gregorian chant as well as praying in these ourselves We should teach our own membership before endeavoring to teach outsiders.

The letters addressed to Sr. Therese and Sr. Anna Marie were both shown to Fr. Devillers, who wrote to Sr. Wilhelmina on May 4, 1995. He invited her to come for a visit, proposed St. Gregory's Priory in Scranton as a possible first location of a new order of sisters, and told her of Bishop Timlin's approval of this new community. "I believe we might be able to begin this Summer or Fall," he wrote "with your assistance." In closing he said "We need your experience!"

She did indeed take the decisive step: exactly one month later, she left her beloved Oblates "bag and baggage" as she would frequentlly say later, setting off upon the new and mysterious path to which the Lord was calling her. With the blessing and permission of her Superiors, she bade farewell to her sisters. Most difficult was her good-bye to her beloved guide and mentor. She later wrote:

> Leaving Sr. Benigna, and all the rest of my fellow Oblates, was like leaving home a second time. They, like my parents and family, made me what I am today. I have many good memories of them, especially those early years when holy silence, much communal prayer, communal reading and wearing the habit were still important and practiced by all.

Sr. Wilhelmina *and Sr. Therese at Elmhurst.*

Sister Wilhemina recalled the remainder of that historic day:

> It was Mr. Ambs who collected the near one thousand dollars for my entry into the aegis of the FSSP and presented it, along with my arrival May 27, 1995 to Fr. Arnaud Devillers, FSSP.

Fr. Arnaud Devillers' intention in establishing the new community of Oblate Sisters was to answer the need for traditional active sisters to assist the Priestly Fraternity of St. Peter in their parish work. Several sisters from other communities had approached Fr. Devillers in the hope of founding such a community, but, as he recounted years later, "Sr. Wilhelmina impressed me the most – by far." He recognized her stable religious formation, her genuine humility and devotion, and also the experience that comes with age. Consequently, he judged her to be the ideal candidate to start "the Fraternity's sisters" in answer to "many requests in the past from girls and young ladies who were looking for a traditional and orthodox community of sisters." He appointed Sr. Wilhelmina as the superior of the fledgling community, and wrote:

> It's a question of finding the right people to begin with. And Sister Wilhelmina has been recommended to me for a long time…they're definitely going to base their spirituality and rule on the rule of St. Benedict. Of course, Benedictine sisters are usually contemplative, but they're going to try to combine contemplative and active…teaching catechism to the children, helping in the sacristy work, taking care of the girls… not necessarily hav[ing] to work with priests of the Fraternity."

Sister Wilhelmina formulated a checklist for future postulants:

"We need subjects who…

1. Will give themselves entirely to Jesus through Mary.
2. Are determined to live a more perfect life, to avoid all that displeases God and to do all that God desires of them.
3. Esteem and love obedience as an excellent, necessary and useful virtue, and zealously observe the stipulations of our constitution regarding it.
4. Esteem and love poverty as the bulwark of religious life, the foundation of perfection, and zeal-

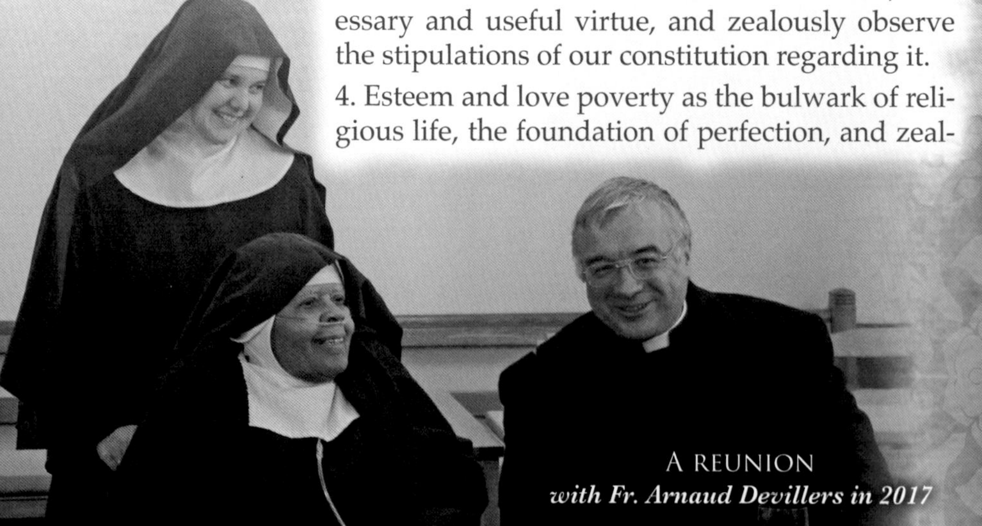

A REUNION
with Fr. Arnaud Devillers in 2017

Thou art blessed who didst believe;
As thy dear child, let me not grieve
O'er sufferings which annoy us.
Thanks be to God for all He's done!
Thou art the Mother of His Son!
In glory, please employ us!

God knows when
and God knows where,
God knows how and why!
Cast on God your
every care;
Look to God
on high.

ously observe the stipulations on our constitution regarding it.

5. Value and esteem the works of charity in which the community engages, and in regard to sisterly love strive to follow the example of Christ expressed: 'This is My commandment, that you love one another as I have loved you.'

6. Zealously strive for humility, the moral virtue without which no other can exist, and really believe that they will never attain the aim of their holy vocation if they do not do their best to destroy self-love.

7. Strive to imitate the meekness of Jesus, and esteem and love prayer as an essential obligation, a necessary means without which the graces needed to fulfill the duties of their vocation cannot be obtained.

8. Have a boundless trust in God, expecting all from Him for themselves as well as for others.

9. Consider silence as one of the important points of the constitution and uphold the having of a reserved area.

10. Read, meditate on and sincerely strive to live by the gospel of our Lord Jesus Christ and the community's constitution."

Sr. Wilhelmina had unwittingly described her own virtues, which she generously rendered to God in her "fiat" for a new foundation.

WEARING THE NEW HABIT
Sister retained her wedding ring. The white cap and guimpe were later joined.

Chapter 12

The Ship Leaves

The Promises of a Priest

Regarding his sheep
He makes promises three:
The first, that they come to the foot of the cross,
Confessing their sins with true sorrow and see
The blood and the water, Our Savior's great loss.

The second, that they to the Last Supper come
To eat with firm faith and love the Bread of Life;
Then finally hoping at sight of the tomb,
For grand resurrection to follow earth's strife.

Sr. Wilhelmina *and Sr. Therese in St. Gregory's Chapel, Elmhurst, Pennsylvania, surrounded by faculty and seminarians of Our Lady of Guadalupe.*

SHORE

Launching Into the Deep

O Mary, Queen of Apostles,
Convert the world
to Christ!
Don't let in vain
His Blood be spilled,
His Life be sacrificed!

O all ye holy Apostles,
We want to be like our Queen,
When she was living at Ephesus
In constant prayer serene.

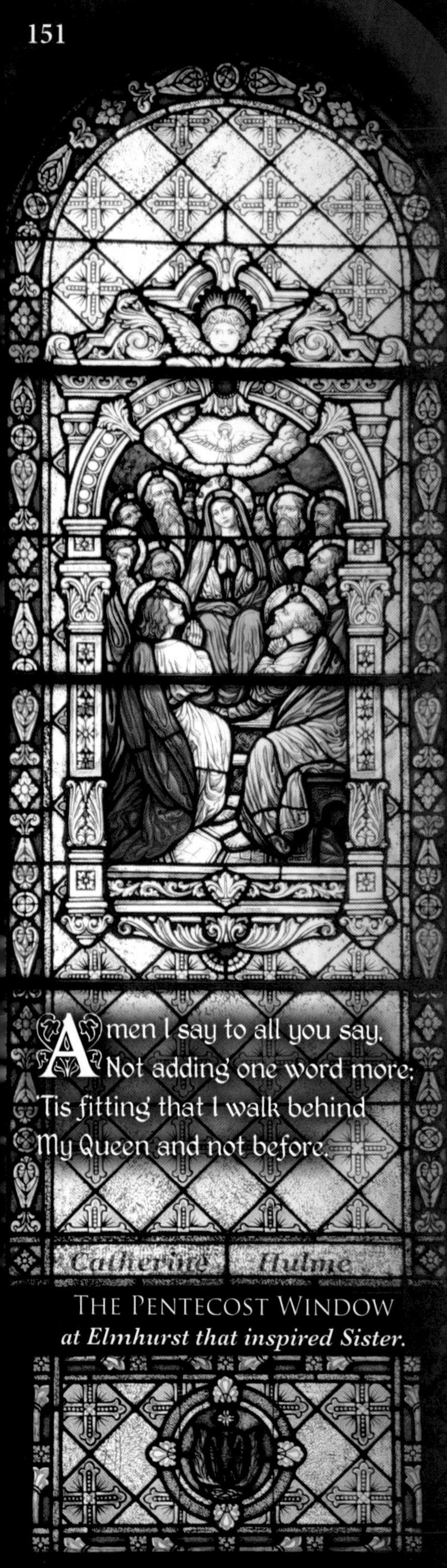

Amen I say to all you say,
Not adding one word more;
'Tis fitting that I walk behind
My Queen and not before.
Catherine Hulme

THE PENTECOST WINDOW
at Elmhurst that inspired Sister.

In an article entitled, "Starting Over," published in the spring 1996 issue of *Sursum Corda*, Sr. Wilhelmina described this turning point in her religious life:

> It would seem I've done a very foolish thing. After fifty years as an Oblate Sister of Providence I am starting the religious life anew – as foundress of a new community affiliated with the Priestly Fraternity of St. Peter. We will serve them in their own apostolate of offering Mass and the sacraments according to the traditional Latin rite, in conformity with the Holy Father's *motu proprio* "Ecclesia Dei." To those who say that my leaving my old community to found a new one doesn't make sense, I reply that it is understandable only in the light of faith.

She went on to describe the spiritual inspiration and the purpose that she envisioned for the new community: it would have a Marian character, seeking to be for the priests of our day what Our Lady was for the Apostles during her earthly life. Just as Our Lady supported the Apostles with her prayers and sacrifices and also with the work of her hands, making vestments and providing a home for them, so also these new Oblates would assist the present-day Apostles through their work and prayer.

> There is a window in St. Gregory's Chapel in Elmhurst [at the former Headquarters of the Priestly Fraternity] showing eleven apostles gathered around Our Blessed Mother during the nine days between Ascension Thursday and Pentecost Sunday. The Latin inscription on the wall around the picture reads: *Erant*

Discipuli Perseverantes Unanimiter In Oratione Cum Maria, Matre Jesus, Alleluia ("The disciples were persevering together in prayer with Mary the Mother of Jesus. Alleluia"). This is a perfect description of the religious sisterhood that is now forming. Only the Apostles and Mary are seen in the picture; but Scripture tells us that many more *persons – discipuli –* were gathered in that building waiting for the coming of the Holy Spirit. Likewise, we sisters work behind the scenes: through Mary, with Mary, in Mary, for Mary, trying to do for the Church today what she did during the years between the Ascension of her Son Jesus and her own Assumption. Mary helped the Apostles to live peacefully as brothers; she offered them the warmth and comfort of a place to stay and to offer the Holy Sacrifice; she gave them courage to go forth and teach all nations despite numerous obstacles. Like Mary, we sisters work and pray for priests. We are active-contemplative, doing all in our power to further the Faith, in obedience to the Pope. We are zealous that the Mass be celebrated worthily, in accordance with time-honored tradition, throughout the world, for all men of all time.

Over twenty years later, when this article had been long forgotten and Sr. Wilhelmina herself was too old to take part in the discussion, the sisters with one mind and heart chose this passage from the Acts of the Apostles, *Perseverantes Unanimiter In Oratione*, as the motto for their community, now an Abbey. A year after this choice, the sisters discovered the article with their beloved foundress' vision for their community, a providential confirmation of what her community had become.

SR. WILHELMINA AT ELMHURST *where the Basilian Sisters' former St. Nicholas Orphanage (background) served as Fraternity Headquarters, Our Lady of Guadalupe Seminary and St. Gregory's Academy (later independently refounded in 2012 at this location.) Sister smiles (at bottom) before the seminary's Pilgrim Virgin, below the later Abbatial coat of arms of Ephesus (adopted 2018.)*

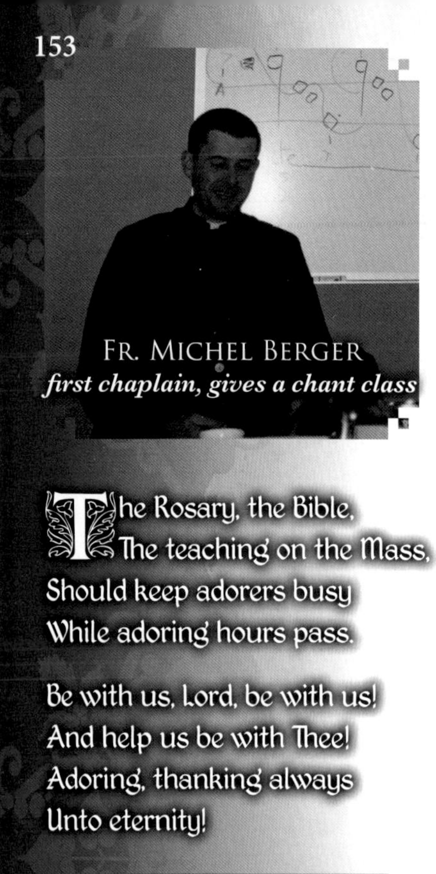

FR. MICHEL BERGER
first chaplain, gives a chant class

The Rosary, the Bible,
The teaching on the Mass,
Should keep adorers busy
While adoring hours pass.

Be with us, Lord, be with us!
And help us be with Thee!
Adoring, thanking always
Unto eternity!

COLONEL TIM GAHAN
(later Father Gahan) awards Sr. Wilhelmina the "prestigious" Green Horse Trophy at the end of the seminary's talent show.

Within a few days of the founding, Sr. Anna Marie could see that even with Sr. Wilhelmina's experience, there were incompatible characters and visions among her subjects. There had been unfortunate misunderstandings of Sr. Anna Marie's former commitments. She therefore took her leave of the new community, not without a valuable contribution to its beginning, and took up teaching at a Fraternity apostolate.

Sister Wilhelmina embraced the new challenge of starting a religious community with her customary determination and spirit of prayer. In a note dated, November 4, 1995, First Saturday, Sr. Wilhelmina expressed the pillars of prayer upon which she hoped to build the community:

> I strive to establish OBLATES OF MARY, QUEEN OF APOSTLES. Praying the Rosary and Way of the Cross together is a good practice for a day of recollection.

Upon this foundation of prayer, the Oblates based their active apostolate. An article entitled "What *Do* the Sisters Do All Day," published in the Fraternity's February 1996 newsletter, presents the way of life that Sr. Wilhelmina had established for the sisters in just nine months. The structured day, alternating between periods of prayer and manual work, already anticipated a Benedictine way of life. The holy silence and spirit of prayer and self-sacrifice which had formed Sr. Wilhelmina as a young Oblate of Providence now transformed the tediousness of the humble daily tasks of the new Oblates:

> The steps from the sisters' work room on the third floor to the laundry room in the basement are many and steep and the loads are heavy; the stains and wrinkles are stubborn and the starch messy; the sacristy supply ordering is

EVERY GIRL should
earn to sew,
To wash,
ron, cook
and clean!
She will
be able
to keep house
And have a home serene.

SR. WILHELMINA SUPERVISES *a young sacristy helper in the early days at Our Lady of Guadalupe. Sister always remained devoted to the seminary's patroness (below.)*

often quite hectic; the grinding of materials to make incense is noisy and monotonous; sewing with great precision for long periods on black fabric hurts the eyes. But there are holy priests to be formed here, a nation to be re-evangelized. There's a traditional and respectful liturgy to be restored, the Catholic Faith to be preserved, souls to be saved through the ministry of the priesthood. The spirit of silence in which we work permits us to ponder these things in our hearts, in union with Our Lady, who spent the last years of her earthly existence in the prayerful support and assistance of the first priests and apostles of the early Church.

One of Sr. Wilhelmina's poems from these early days of the Oblates of Mary, Queen of Apostles, expresses in verse the preeminence of the contemplative aspect of the sisters' way of life:

Love is the law, the law supreme,
Your inner principle of life;
Christ is your Spouse;
you are His wife.
The inner life
must be the soul
Of all your outward
self-control.

Dear Blessed
Mother,
Let me be
And do
All through,
all with,
All in, all for
Just you.

God is our Love,
our Life, our Light!
He makes us live
and do what's right.
He guides us safely
through the day;
With joy we look
to Him and pray.

Living

To live is to love
True God above.
To live is to pray
And God obey.
To live is to fight
To do what's right.
To live is to die,
Oneself deny.
To live is to see
And humble be.

Sweetest Jesus,
Thou'rt my Only Love,
I find Thee in Thy Mother's Heart,
And there we pray the Rosary,
Living together never part.

THE FIRST POSTULANTS *arrived in 1996, shown here with Sister at Elmhurst.*

Because of her own single-hearted fidelity to her vocation, Sr. Wilhelmina sought a similar dedication and determination from the sisters gathering around her. To one religious, who after much vacillation finally asked to enter the community, provided that the spirituality and way of life were not yet fixed, Sister Wilhelmina replied firmly, "The ship has left shore." She knew too well that a soul without a determined will could not make the commitment that religious consecration requires.

The task of leading a brand-new community, difficult for any person at any age, was particularly so for Sister Wilhelmina, who had never been in a leadership role in her previous community, and was also advanced in years.

Questionnaire

Can you sew, wash,
iron, cook and clean?
Can you keep house,
fit for king or queen?
Do you have
a woman's skills –
To alleviate
man's ills
And contribute to the
atmosphere serene?

Can you suffer?
Can you wait?
Do you care?
Contemplate?
Do you try to imitate
Our Blessed Mother?

You might give
our life a try –
Knowing that
each day you die
While you run
toward union
with Lord Jesus Christ
Our Elder Brother.

ST. GREGORY'S PRIORY
at 819 North Webster in Scranton, was home to the Sisters 1996-1999, with a brief interval down the street. A main room was converted into a chapel by the Fraternity for the Sisters' use.

As the first year of the Oblates progressed, she took an honest assessment of her limitations and her ability to continue to lead the Oblates as she approached the end of her own life. Perhaps swayed by Sr. Therese's energetic spirit, she humbly requested that Sr. Therese take responsibility as superior. She yielded also to Sr. Therese's suggestion that a younger superior might also attract other vocations. Fr. Devillers was extremely reluctant, but approved this change on March 2, 1996.

KINDERGARTEN MARCH

Love! Love!
God is Love forever!
Love! Love!
God is persons three!
Love! Love!
God had no beginning!
Father
And Son
And Holy Ghost!

AT ST. GREGORY'S CHAPEL
in Elmhurst (above) Sisters prayed their offices amidst seminary work. On Sundays, they taught catechism at St. Michael's parish in Scranton (left.)

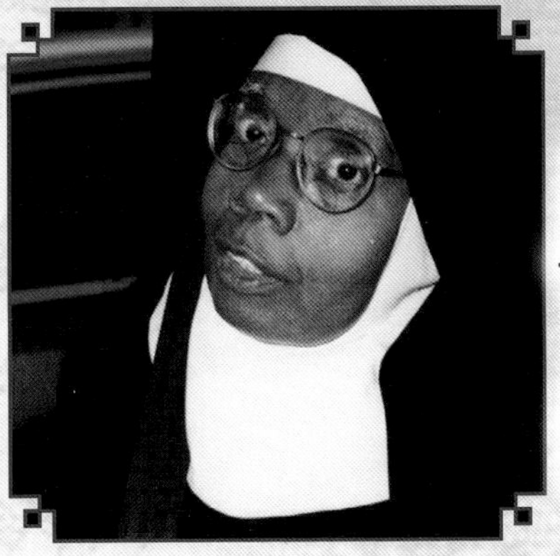

COMMUTING *to St. Michael's and Elmhurst was wearing, as was the juggling of the active and contemplative life. But the Sisters often packed picnic lunches to eat on the spacious grounds of Elmhurst (right.)*

Prayer is the power,
Given every hour
By our Heavenly Father;
Don't think it's a bother.

The change in leadership dramatically changed the course of the Oblates of Mary. Sister Wilhelmina had collaborated with Fr. Devillers to found a community of parish helpers to support the priests of the Fraternity, whereas Sr. Therese wished to follow both the contemplative life she had experienced at Le Barroux and the active life she knew with the Slaves of the Immaculate Heart. Fr. Devillers counselled her that she could not have both; one aspect, either contemplative or active, would have to predominate. Sister Therese persisted, however, in attempting to reconcile the two forms. By 1997, it was clear to all parties that the favoring of a more monastic expression of the spirituality would make cooperation between the Fraternity and the Oblates unrealistic. The following year, the Fraternity Seminary moved to Nebraska. The Oblates of Mary relocated to other areas of the Scranton diocese.

Don't play
When you
pray;
It's a fight!
Do it right.

OUR LADY OF GUADALUPE SEMINARY *envisioned by Thomas Gordon Smith. Fr. Devillers discouraged the Sisters from moving to Nebraska out of prudence and to give them the necessary space to develop their monastic vocation.*

THE SPIRITUAL ASPECT *of supporting priests flourished after the seminary's relocation. Thankfully, the balancing act began drawing to a close.*

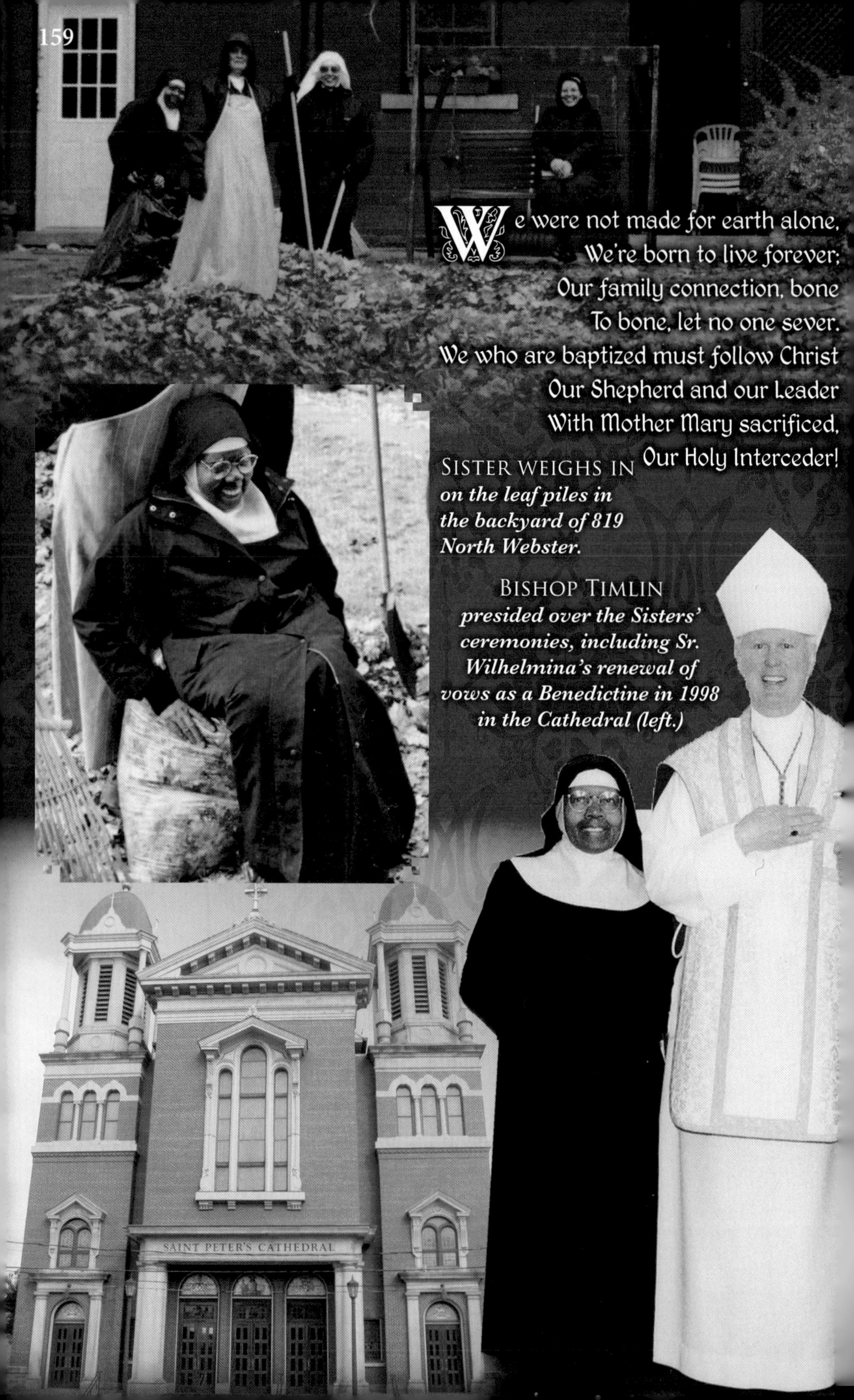

We were not made for earth alone,
We're born to live forever;
Our family connection, bone
To bone, let no one sever.
We who are baptized must follow Christ
Our Shepherd and our Leader
With Mother Mary sacrificed,
Our Holy Interceder!

SISTER WEIGHS IN *on the leaf piles in the backyard of 819 North Webster.*

BISHOP TIMLIN *presided over the Sisters' ceremonies, including Sr. Wilhelmina's renewal of vows as a Benedictine in 1998 in the Cathedral (left.)*

King of Mercy! King of Glory!
Mankind has a sinful story.
But we trust Thee, and we love Thee,
Every moment thinking of Thee.!

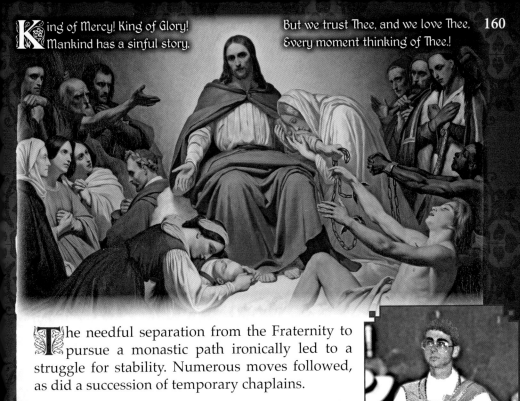

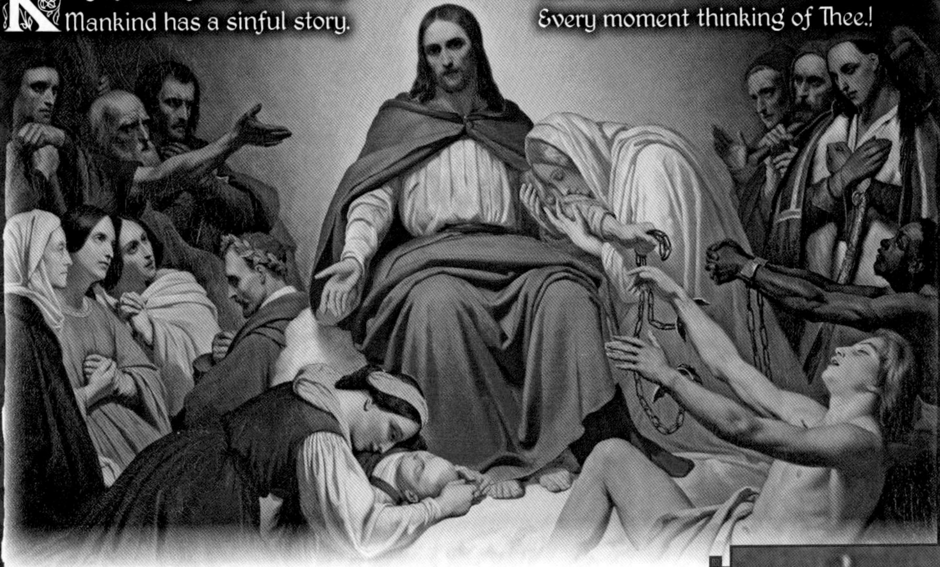

The needful separation from the Fraternity to pursue a monastic path ironically led to a struggle for stability. Numerous moves followed, as did a succession of temporary chaplains.

In 1998, Sr. Wilhelmina almost parted with the community as well, but for a different reason and destination. In early June, just as the community was finishing prayer, the sisters began to process out of their little chapel at St. Gregory's Priory. Sister Wilhelmina rose from her seat and collapsed in the aisle. She was hospitalized for ten days with pneumonia, complicated by her fall and yet another one at the hospital while she was unattended. It was believed that she would not recover, so the newly-ordained Fr. Joseph Portzer, FSSP was summoned to administer last rites. Sister Wilhelmina rallied immediately after the sacrament was conferred, and went on to live another twenty-one years.

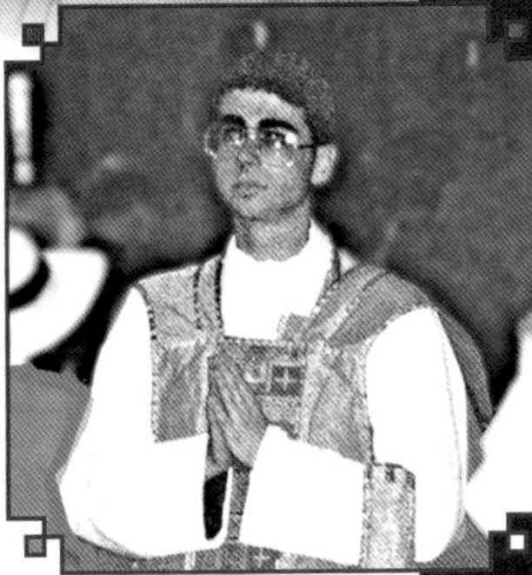

FR. JOSEPH PORTZER, FSSP ***at his ordination, days before he anointed Sr. Wilhelmina in 1998, initiating a miraculous recovery. Sister Wilhelmina thanked him again in 2007 (below).***

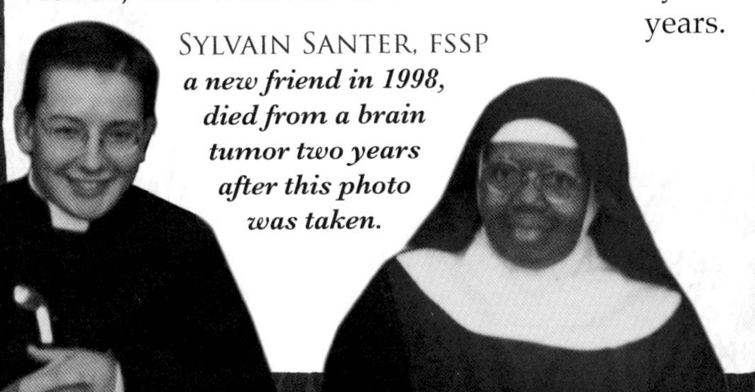

SYLVAIN SANTER, FSSP ***a new friend in 1998, died from a brain tumor two years after this photo was taken.***

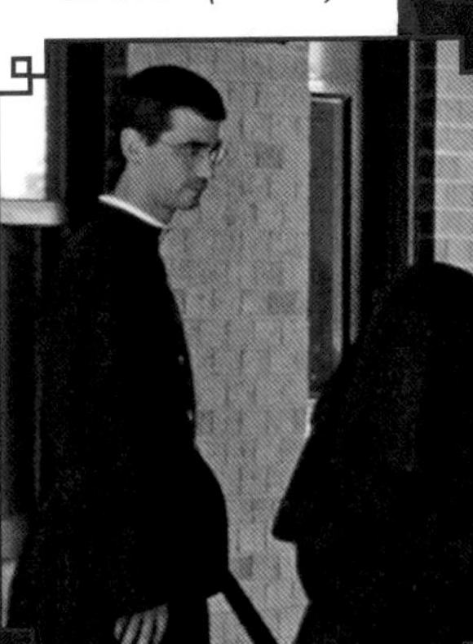

Chapter 13

Sisters on

Dear Lord, we need a place to live,
And work that good income does give;
We need to pray the Mass each day,
The holy traditional way.

You had no place to lay Your head,
Dear Lord, our true and living Bread:
How sweet it is, dear Lord, to be
With You in close intimacy.

(The above prayer was answered May 29, 2002.)

DEAR LOVE, Our Lord,
We're working hard
To do Thy Holy Will;
It is our fun
To get things done
Without a nasty spill.

Snowstorm Prayer

For all who travel in this storm,
I pray, Lord! Keep them safe and warm;
Help them to reach the destination
That Thou will'st! Each soul's salvation!

Snowdrops are like Hail Marys
Prayed constantly all day,
Oh, how they pile
To make her smile
Our Lady of the Way!

THE MOVE

Transitional Years

THE SNOW

Life smoke,
It flows down
From the roof,
Goes right,
Goes left,
Around and down;
Sometimes flakes blow up
From the ground
To mix with new flakes
Coming down.
In big
White puffs
It flows
And blows;
While colder grows
Someone not well-dressed
For this play,
Who dreams of
Long-gone
Summer's day.

We are Sisters on the move
Better you believe it!
Our experiences prove
Change, we can receive it!
Packed and stuffed we found it so,
In our motorola,
As to Greeley we did go,
Moving from Shohola.

Careful we packed and stored
Everything we're using
We had no time to be bored,
Not a second losing.
Sister needs a handkerchief
To catch her a-choo noise,
But they've all been packed quite stiff-
Tell this to the paid newsboys!

Sis Emmanuel unpacks
What's been packed already
Box is such a perfect match
Go some things and steady!
Troubles like this patience try,
Brave forbearance prove us-
And it's hard to say good-bye
To a cat named Rufus.

Finally when stools were gone,
And the pots and dishes
Floor was left for sitting on,
Pleasing to our wishes.
But we luckily had brought
Something to abide so,
Soon all of our hearts were caught
By a dog named FIDO

Sleeping on the floor we find
Firm, unique and restful.
Only spiderwebs combine
To make us distressful,
Setting up the kitchen we
choose the proper canister,
And we walk most carefully
Where there is no banister!

Now we hope to stay in place,
Far from being gypsy,
With no partying disgrace
Not becoming being tipsy.
Benedictines we are, true!
May God make us able
To be His in all we do-
Silently and stable!

THREE MOVES IN FIFTEEN MONTHS *brought the Sisters from Scranton to a cabin in Shohola where the dog FIDO was acquired (upper inset) in the midst of the move to an incomplete timberframe house in Greeley, then back to Scranton. The Sisters stayed at a house on St. Frances Cabrini Avenue named for Mother Cabrini (inset) who lived there and who had prayed at the St.Joseph Melkite Church on the other side of the street. The Sisters likewise daily crossed the street several times a day to pray the Divine Office in the little church.*

SWINGING HER CAN **Sr. Wilhelmina sings "Nothin' Could Be Finer" in a 2001 skit.**

The year 2000 was greeted amidst moving boxes, as the sisters had begun a chain of relocations in northeastern Pennsylvania. Sister Wilhelmina's writings and poetry of this time took all the inconveniences in stride, but heavily emphasized the need for future stability. Thankfully, the first persevering vocations entered in this year, both being admirers of monastic life. This was aided in part by the community's visits to Clear Creek in Oklahoma, toward which another move was contemplated. The documentation for possible relocation submitted to Bishop Edward Slattery was the fortuitous source of Sr. Wilhelmina's hidden short autobiography, from which many unknown details of her early life were later drawn. The Oklahoma plan did not materialize, as the Abbot of Fongombault anticipated hurdles at that particular time.

How blest you are!
You've been a priest
for almost sixty years!
This fact dispels and drives
away my Year 2000 fears;
I'll celebrate your holy state
throughout the Jubilee!
For only priests can consecrate
and bring Christ down to me.
I thank God for the Eucharist,
adoring Him each day;
Remembering your ordination,
the fourteenth of May.

FATHER WILLIAM JENNINGS ***was the recipient of this poem. A priest of Wilmington, Delaware, he was intrigued by Sr. Wilhelmina's article "Starting Over," and became a fast friend and generous benefactor of the new foundation. He died in 2014, at the age of 101.***

BISHOP EDWARD SLATTERY OF TULSA ***indirectly unearthed details of Sister's life.***

"GET GOIN' 'ROUND THE RING!" ***Sr. Wilhelmina obeys the recorded square dance caller at a 2001 recreation.***

KEEPING A PROMISE ***to the Fraternity, the Sisters hosted a girls' camp in Summer 2001. The girls decorated Sr. Wilhelmina's room for her feast day. She thanked them with a song and dance, (right) changing the words of "It Ain't Gonna Rain," to "Camp Kateri's the place, the place, the place for girls to go! You've gotta be quick and not too thick 'cause the pace goes fast, not slow!"***

THE TERRORIST ATTACKS *of 2001 prompted two poetic responses from Sr. Wilhelmina:*

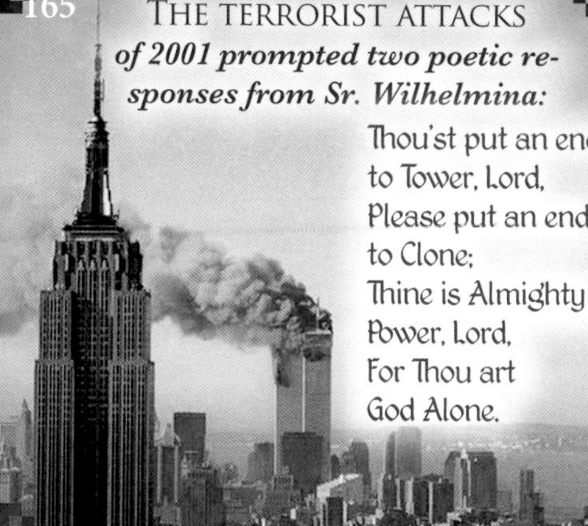

Thou'st put an end
to Tower, Lord,
Please put an end
to Clone;
Thine is Almighty
Power, Lord,
For Thou art
God Alone.

We must begin to truly love again,
Repent we must of every selfish sin.
God help us to be kind and to forgive!
And choose to love sincerely and to live!

Love means ability to freely choose;
And choose we must in order to be saved.
For centuries the Lord has plainly spoken;
We know quite well how we should have behaved.

Our free will gives us awesome, evil power!
We took God's gifts, but off to chaos ran!
But death was not in God's first loving plan;
The envy of the devil felled our tower.

Let us rejoice with the Eternal Victor!
Christ is our Love, the Truth, the Life, the Way!
In Him we see all men as needy brothers,
Needing our help to live and work and play.

Needing our love so they will not be lonely,
Needing food, clothing, shelter too!
But most of all, please help us understand, Lor
That most of all, all men on earth need You!
To live we must help others live as well,
And so escape the fiery pit of hell.

The kind Abbot had prudently foreseen that the clarity of vision and monastic maturity the community needed could not be supplied by the monks. It could only be achieved by a firm internal resolution to definitively and independently embark on a monastic course in a clear self-understanding, unhindered by another community's influence or the admixture of apostolic labors. The Abbot encouraged the sisters to find land and settle where they knew they were welcome: the Diocese of Scranton. The sisters settled on farmland just south of the New York border in Starrucca, Pennsylvania. The rural location and first semblance of stability brought great relief to the soul of Sr. Wilhelmina, as did five more persevering vocations that entered there.

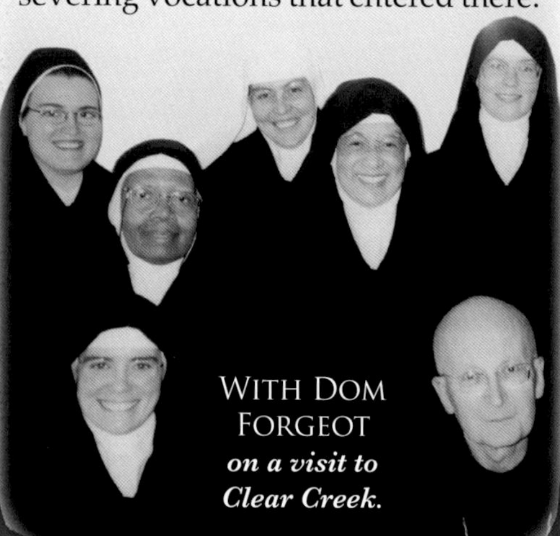

WITH DOM FORGEOT *on a visit to Clear Creek.*

THE "SOUL DOCTOR," FR. DAVID DELZELL ASKED OUR LADY TO OPEN THE DOO *"just a crack to saying Latin Mass again. She blew off the hinges" he said the day the Sisters asked him to be chaplain (below.) Sister wrote this to "the Farmer in the Dell:*

We've met Father Delzell!
We've met Father Delzell!
He doctors souls who are sick and sad
And makes them fine and well!

He took us all to lunch!
He took us all to lunch!
We ate him out of house and home
We're such a hungry bunch!

He promised to say Mass!
He promised to say Mass!
Whenever we have need of hin
So it will come to pass!

With Mary stand alone!
With Mary stand alone!
Believing that her Son will rise
With Ma-ry stand a-lone!

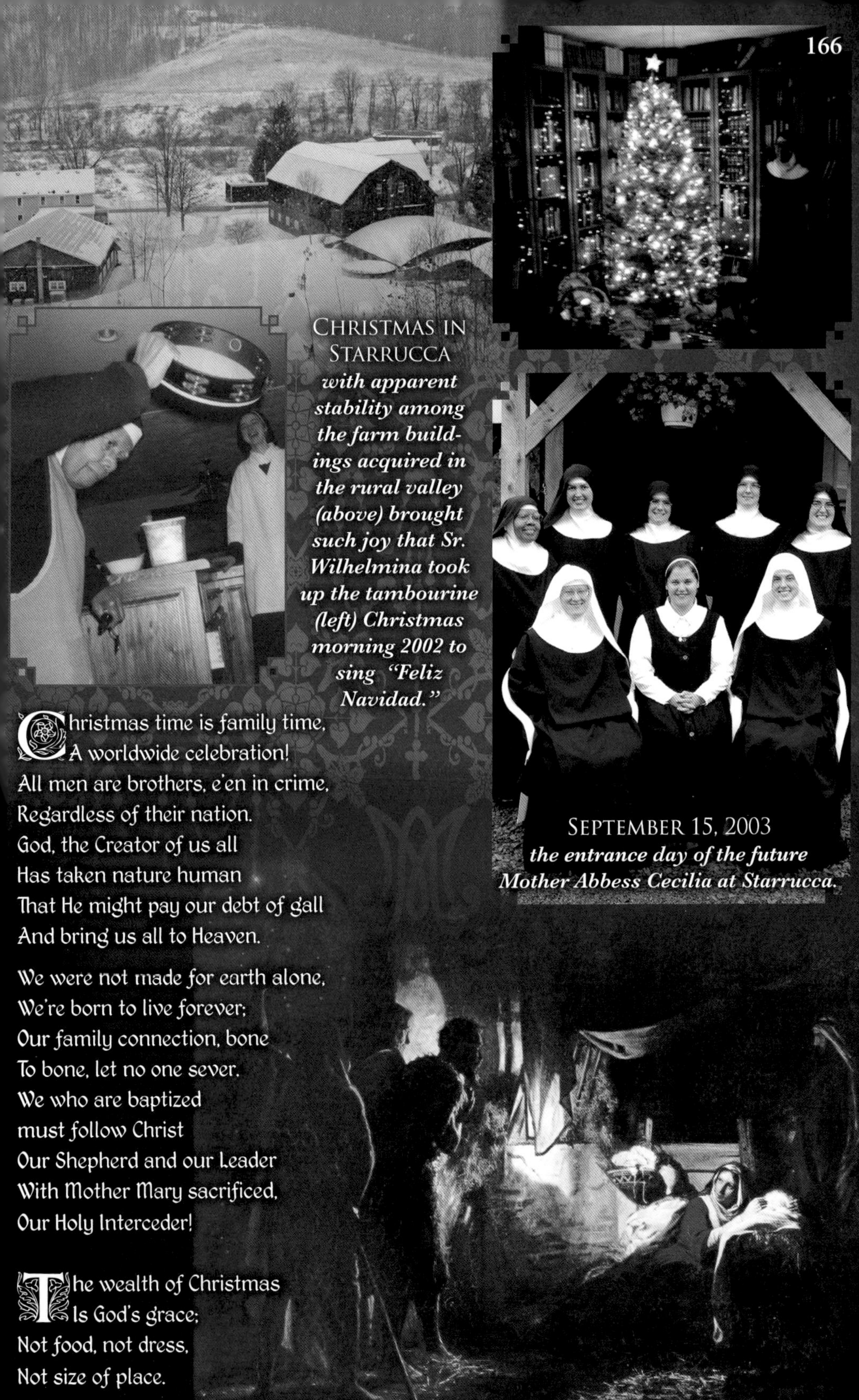

CHRISTMAS IN STARRUCCA
with apparent stability among the farm buildings acquired in the rural valley (above) brought such joy that Sr. Wilhelmina took up the tambourine (left) Christmas morning 2002 to sing "Feliz Navidad."

SEPTEMBER 15, 2003
the entrance day of the future Mother Abbess Cecilia at Starrucca.

Christmas time is family time,
A worldwide celebration!
All men are brothers, e'en in crime,
Regardless of their nation.
God, the Creator of us all
Has taken nature human
That He might pay our debt of gall
And bring us all to Heaven.

We were not made for earth alone,
We're born to live forever;
Our family connection, bone
To bone, let no one sever.
We who are baptized
must follow Christ
Our Shepherd and our Leader
With Mother Mary sacrificed,
Our Holy Interceder!

The wealth of Christmas
Is God's grace;
Not food, not dress,
Not size of place.

During this time, Sr. Wilhelmina had a crisis in her own religious life; in 2003, she was recalled to the Motherhouse of the Oblates of Providence. In June 1998, when her three-year exclaustration expired, she had written the Oblates, "I will no longer continue on as an Oblate Sister of Providence." She concluded, "They never answered that letter." Then in 2003, after five years on the new foundation, she wrote the Bishop of Scranton, requesting formally and with her customary sense of rhythm to make final vows in her new community:

> The best, and really only, reason that I can give for allowing me to make final, perpetual, Benedictine vows is to permit God to continue his multitudinous, marvelous miracles and mercies.

However, in September 2003, she received a letter from the Vatican sending her back to the Motherhouse in Baltimore to request dispensation from perpetual vows. She left the Oblates of Mary not knowing when or even if she would return.

It was bittersweet to see her Motherhouse and her sister Oblates after eight years. While she had many heartwarming reunions, she also could see clearly her inability to live according to the community's new ways: Sister Wilhelmina, holding fast to her initial formation, and the Oblates of Providence, continuing post-Vatican II experimentation, had grown in different directions. The emphasis on the community's African-American heritage led one Oblate to remark, "You're Black first, and Catholic second." To this, Sr. Wilhelmina declared what she had also written to the Holy Father: "To be black is nothing. To be Catholic is everything."

IN THE VESTIBULE *at Starrucca, Sister admired the Sacred Heart statue that followed the Sisters from early days.*

God loves me!
I love God!
Though He beats me
with a rod
Still I trust!
For I must!
With His shoes
I am shod
I love Him!
I love God!

TENEBRÆ *in Starrucca*

BENEATH THE OBLATES' WINDOW *at the St. John Neumann Shrine, 2003*

See our Mother,
Standing, weeping,
By the cross of her dear Son;
Here we have the
Frightful picture
Of all martyrdoms in one.

The Picture given
by Earl Swain
to the community in Starrucca.

MIDDAY

Twelve midday is the sacred hour
When Cross of Christ
was raised and dropped
Into its hole on Calvary:
Man was redeemed
with awesome power!
The lucid sun refused to shine
On this, Christ's gruesome agony.

Our Lord ascended into Heav'n
At twelve noon sharp from mountain height;
Disciples gazed in raptured awe
Until clouds hid Him from their sight.

The day of Pentecost at noon
Brought great rejoicing to each soul
When tongues of fire enlightened us
To clearly see our heav'nly goal.

OBEY

If you love Me,
Keep My commands.
Lord, please let me
Kiss Thy pierced hands!
None can be saved
Against his will;
Stand by Mary
On Calv'ry's hill.

"SWAMP" *an acronym for "St. William the Abbot Memorial Park" was "dedicated" by handyman Tom Schwerdt in honor of his "favorite Sister," who happily posed there for a photo on that day.*

All hail the world's best handyman!
Our Thomas Schwerdt, the gifted.
No trouble is without a plan,
from which we can't be lifted!

Thank you, Heav'nly Father!
For the bright, clear sky!
May I hug and kiss You
When I come to die?
Elmhurst boys are coming
Here to work the land;
May they give You glory!
Please give them a hand.

St. Isidore, the Farmer!
Please help men act like men!
In cleanliness and charity
And far away from sin!
Of God's Sweet Dove
Who leads us to our goal!

TO WELCOME GUESTS AS CHRIST *according to the Rule of St. Benedict, began in 2003 when Sister helped prepare priests' guestquarters (below) for their first retreatant, her good friend Fr. Neal Nichols, FSSP (right).*

TOM SHWERDT *would drive up to Scranton or Starrucca each Saturday from Philadelphia to volunteer his help in anything the Sisters needed including washing windows (above) He and Sr. Wilhelmina were particularly close. Tom was helped a few times by the "Elmhurst boys" of St. Gregory's, who came to Starrucca for manual labor, while the Sisters continued on in silence through their day.*

Sister continued to reflect at her Motherhouse:

What are Oblates witnessing? Is it wonderful blackness? Or the wonders of the Second Person of the Blessed Trinity, True God and True Man, Who said, "Without Me, you can do nothing." Oblates like to sing, "We've come this far by faith." This faith is in whom? And in what?

God is not impressed, nor influenced in any way, by either "blackness" or "whiteness." God is just. He became man in time, was born of the Virgin Mary, in order to suffer and die for every human being born on this earth.

Bless the guests
Who are ours
Ev'ry time they come!
Bring them all
For all time
To our heav'nly
home!

SISTER STARTLED GUESTS *when she presented a book saying, "no one leaves this house alive without signing our guest book!" None of the Sisters forgot August 23, 2003, as they pulled her in a wagon on a community walk, not wanting to leave her behind. She chanted the name of the saint of the day to encourage them uphill: "C'mon Sisters! For Saint Bartholomew, Saint Bartholomew!"*

Sister Wilhelmina especially missed the silence in which her new community was immersed. She wrote on her sojourn:

> … Last night at 9:45 since my next-door neighbors were still going strong in conversation, I got out of bed to sit at my desk and to begin writing what may be called a treatise on silence:
>
> "The most important thing in community living is the observance of holy silence. We are supposed to be living a life of prayer, and we need silence on our part so that God can get a word in.
>
> There are 24 hours in a day. For a religious, most of these hours must be hours of silence. During the night, they are hours of GRAND SILENCE, so that the soul can really hear what God has to say at the end of each day. Not everyone awakens on this side of eternity the next morning."

Sr. Wilhelmina understood that external practices such as wearing the habit and observing silence were not ends in themselves nor guarantees of salvation, but simply safeguards for her vocation, her intimate relationship with Christ. She also understood that without these safeguards, she could easily lose her awareness of this consecration. She consequently renewed her resolve to maintain traditional religious observance:

> I recognize that not all those who wear the habit persevere as religious, that the just man falls seven times a day, and that death is the end of all regardless of its manner. Perseverance in faith, hope and charity is important, and we must pray continually, asking for the salvation that Christ has won for us. Never, on this side of the grave, can we relax and say, "I need not fight any more."
>
> I testify here in answer to the question: "Sr. Wilhelmina, after fifty and more years with the Oblate Sisters of Providence, at your age, why are you leaving them now?"

DR. DENNIS Q. MCINERNY *(right) also much beloved by Sister, journeyed from the Seminary to give Philosophy classes to the Sisters, and in the Summers after the Nebraska move. She looked on as he was presented with a gift of thanks in 2004.*

How sweet it is
to be with Thee!
My Love, my Lord, my Light!
Please send me soon
a note from Rome
Directing me aright!
Thy Will be done,
no matter what
Thy Holy Will may be;
Thine is the Pow'r,
Thine is the fun!
O Lord, that I may see!
Console Thy priests
who suffer, Lord,
In Purgatory's fires;
Bring them to feasts
with Thee above
Where no more sin transpires.

"I am a weak, human being, one of the 'poor, banished children of Eve…' I need holy silence Oblate Sisters of Providence do not provide. We are too mixed up with the laity here. We seem to put man (whom we see) before God (Whom we do not see)..."

The distressing visit had an unexpectedly short duration: after just ten days, Sr. Wilhelmina was allowed to return to the Oblates of Mary, Queen of Apostles. Her faithful friends Kelly and Christine Mucker brought her to Starrucca, where her Sisters had prepared a fried chicken supper, Sr. Wilhelmina's favorite. When the Sisters asked if she wanted seconds, Sr. Wilhelmina bashfully confessed that the Muckers had likewise treated Sister to fried chicken for lunch. In November, the termination of her status with the Oblates of Providence was finalized, and she was able to renew her vows in her new community the following year, August 22, 2004.

Queen of Starrucca and Lady of Fatima,
Help us do penance and faithfully pray
Thy Holy Rosary, pondering mysteries,
Coming to heaven, forever to stay!

THE PILGRIM VIRGIN *came to Starrucca in 2004.*

RELEASED FROM HER VOWS *Sr. Wilhelmina renewed her private Benedictine vows August 22, 2004, where she began, at Elmhurst, and assisted in the investiture of Sr. Cecilia.*

St. John the Baptist, pray for the Baptists
And for the builders of this breezeway!
Pray for all God's priests on earth –
Especially Father Michel Berger.

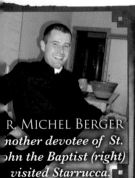

R. MICHEL BERGER *nother devotee of St. ohn the Baptist (right) visited Starrucca.*

THE COMMUNITY OUTSIDE THE BREEZEWAY, *with Fr. Lutz, Sr. Cecilia's former pastor, the day after her investiture. Sister Wilhelmina faithfully swept the breezeway connecting the chapel and farmhouse in Starrucca (left.)*

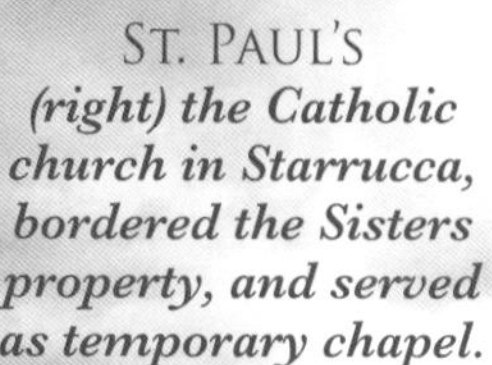

St. Paul's *(right) the Catholic church in Starrucca, bordered the Sisters property, and served as temporary chapel.*

The Four Seasons *at Starrucca were deeply appreciated by Sister. She loved "lifeguarding" (upper left) the sledding Sisters down the treacherous hills, and taking in the beautiful Springs.*

Guardian Angels of Starrucca!
Keep this borough free from harm
Save each fam'ly from disunion!
Prosper more the family farm!
Help us worship God forever!
Throughout day and throughout night
Lovingly and sinning never!
And to win earth's fearsome fight!

Jesus, make this borough Thine!
Change like water into wine
All the hearts that labor here –
Grant we labor all the year –
Loving Thee, the Lord of All,
Summer, winter, spring and fall!

In the ice and in the snow,
Make St. Paul's the place to go:
There, adore the Living Bread,
And remember all our dead.
Pray for us, sweet Oblate Grace,
That we come to see God's Face!

Present in Thy Sacrament
We adore Thee, quite content
Not to see Thee, but believe
Thou Who never does deceive
Ev'ry day and ev'ry night
We are with Thee in the fight!

Rule, Sweet Jesus, from Thy Throne!
Thou art God, and God alone
In Starrucca in adored,
Despite ev'ry pagan sword.
Constant are our prayers to Thee
Even to eternity!

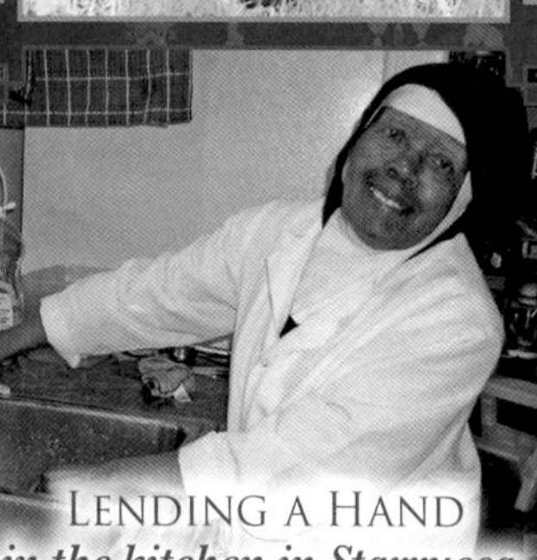

Lending a Hand *in the kitchen in Starrucca.*

Grace Radel *died nine days before her hopeful entrance date, and was buried at St. Paul's.*

The Farewell *to Fr. Delzell (left) and to Starrucca was a difficult one.*

The long-awaited stability found in Starrucca was also of unexpectedly short duration. Bishop Timlin had graciously initiated the Oblates of Mary, Queen of Apostles, but only as a "pious union." In 2005, his successor, Bishop Joseph Francis Martino, noted that the community had never been erected as a novitiate, and had therefore not received a canonical formation. Now that Sr. Wilhelmina had been released from her vows, formation had to be given by a non-member so that status of a public association could be granted. A long search followed, but all plans fell through. One superior general said of the situation, "you know what I call this? A sanctoral mess! You might be better off just starting over."

In the Diocese, the new Bishop began the work of merging parishes. Scranton was full of churches built closely together, each serving an ethnic group. Not only had faith decreased and ethnic ties fizzled, the population had almost halved in 75 years. Amidst the mergings, the Bishop's solution for the community ran along a similar vein: to be subsidiarized by another community. As this would have required the adoption of new usages and liturgy, the community appraised the earlier suggestion of the superior general, in light of a summons to Missouri.

'Twas sixty years ago, my God,
That I made vows to Thee;
I thank Thee
for the privilege
Of sweet intimacy!
Please help me
persevere in love,
Believing TRUTH
and free.

BISHOP MARTINO *at Starrucca.*

To Bishop Martino

You are
God's man
and we love you,
Trusting in
His mighty power;
We obey Him,
we obey you
In this testing
earthly hour.

God is One,
and we are with Him,
Let us then united be
In His love, His holy Victim,
and for all eternity.

A pro-life hero, the Bishop honored Sr. Wilhelmina's 60th Anniversary through a Mass at the Cathedral, and she wrote a poem in his honor just before leaving the Diocese. He resigned his See in 2009.

St. Joseph, help! Come to our aid!
Safe shelter for us must be made!
By no means can this be delayed.
With you the King
of Heaven stayed
When He our heavy
ransom paid.
Around your knees
He laughed
and played.
If He so will,
come to
our aid.

WEARING THE CORSAGE *made by the Diocese for Sister's 60th anniversary.*

Chapter 14

Back in

Lord make us strong, make us able,
Make us firm and make us STABLE.

St. Rita of Cascia,
Please help us in our plight:
We have no dwelling of our own
In which to spend the night;
We have no chapel of our own
Where we can sing and pray;
We need the most a tabernacle
Where Our Lord can stay.

A place to rent, a place to live
Is what we need to find;
A place where we can grow and where
The township doesn't mind;
A place where we can work and pray –
And walk around outside and play –
May God to this desire of ours
Be mercifully kind.

There really is
no end to prayer
Since God is infinite.
All they who say
there is no God
Are much
deprived of wit.

Missouri

With Wit & Wisdom

With Fellow Missourian
Sr. Tarcisia, Sister enjoyed a beautiful spring walk shortly after arriving.

Home is where you eat and drink and sleep;
Home is where you pray, and God's orders keep;
Where you live united and in love! Where you look to Heaven high above!

ARRIVING AT THE KANSAS CITY CONVENT
the Sisters were greeted by Bishop Finn. who blessed and exorcised it.

The Oblates of Mary received an invitation from Bishop Robert Finn to his diocese of Kansas City-St. Joseph, Missouri in early 2006. He had been praying to find a community of sisters who would pray and sacrifice for his priests. In March, he warmly welcomed the small community of fourteen sisters to his diocese.

Throughout all these transitions, beginning with the change in leadership in 1996 and culminating with a move halfway across the country, the sisters were struggling to understand their own charism and purpose and to realize Sr. Therese's vision of being all-contemplative and all-active at the same time and with the same intensity. As they realized more and more their Benedictine identity, they changed their name from the Oblates to the Benedictines of Mary, Queen of Apostles. Bishop Finn established them as a novitiate, receiving the necessary formation from Conception Abbey, a few hours north of Kansas City, supervised by the Abbey of Sainte-Marie des Deux-Montagnes in Canada, and renewed their vows as full-fledged Benedictines.

THE MAY 2007 PROFESSION AT CONCEPTION ABBEY WAS A "REUNION"
with many priest friends of the community, left to right: Fr. James Gordon Fr. Angel VanderPutten, Fr. Eric Flood, Fr. Christopher Henderson, Fr. Michel Berger, Fr. Phi Wolfe, Bishop James Timlin, Bishop Robert Finn, Fr. Paul Scalia, Abbot Gregory Polan, Fr. Paul Check, Fr. Dennis McManus, and Fr. (later Abbot) Benedict Neenan.

At the first Family Day *in Kansas City, Sister was visited by her beloved niece, Rebecca, the daughter of Sister's sister, Christine. To Becca, she dedicated this poem, harkening back to their own peaceful family life:*

The family must be restored,
With father its protector;
Immodesty must be deplored,
In every public sector.
To sew and cook women should learn
And keep the house in order,
While every man should take his turn
At filling up the larder.
Children must listen and obey
The orders given to them;
Although their main task is to play
Chastisement may be due them.
And when Grandpa is sick and old
And on his way to dying,
Please keep him sheltered from the cold
While on his bed he's lying.
Please give him food, please give him drink,
And call the priest to tend him!
Please bathe him so he does not stink,
But happily amend him.

Conflict persisted, however, between "being," as contemplative Benedictines, and "doing," as active religious sisters. Claiming and carrying responsibility for the community's foundation, Sr. Therese providentially commandeered toward the contemplative Benedictine life, corresponding with the graces God gave her. There was, nevertheless, a lack of internal stability in those days as a balance was still sought.

During these difficult years, Sister Wilhelmina's stability was the community's foundation. She had, thankfully, greatly underestimated her own strength when she had requested to be relieved of the burden of office; not only did she persevere for twenty-three more years of religious life, but she remained an inspiration to the far-younger women who joined the little community. One Sister recalled that when she doubted her own ability to persevere in the life, she looked to Sr. Wilhelmina, peacefully ironing corporals for the altar. She thought, "Yes, I can persevere in this life as she has."

Abbot Gregory Polan *of Conception welcomes Sr. Wilhemina. He was elected Abbot Primate in 2016.*

ɪe Former Convent *ere the Sisters lived 2006-2010. 's now owned by Catholic Radio.*

At Ste. Marie des Deux-Montagnes *the Sisters personally thanked the community that had overseen their canonical formation just after the 2007 professions.*

Another Sister, who was crying over a difficulty she faced in those early years, was discovered by Sr. Wilhelmina. She warmly embraced the Sister, saying soothingly, "Aw, baby doll!" Without another word, they returned to work. It was just enough for them both to take up their daily cross once more. For another novice, who was evidently also experiencing a trial, Sr. Wilhelmina left a tender poem that reflects her charity toward her sisters and also her lively faith in God's ability "to write straight with crooked lines:"

My little one,
God's will be done,
For both you and me.
You'll be a saint,
Without complaint,
Just you wait and see!

CONGRATULATING *her friend, Fr. John Berg, soon after his election as Superior General of the Fraternity.*

"HABEMUS PAPAM" *Sister chanted over and over with exceptional joy when Cardinal Ratzinger ascended the papal throne. Her joy was doubled in the promulgation of his Motu Proprio Summorum Pontificum one month after the professions at Conception, setting the Latin Mass free.*

RECREATIONS ON THE FRONT PORCH *or on the front walk of Kansas City included Sr. Wilhelmina's feast day celebration, in which a cupcake rosary was presented to her.*

This was the faith that Sr. Wilhelmina lived. When she herself received a harsh correction, she humbly composed a poem in response:

I want to do what God wants,
Please tell me what to do!
I'm sorry for my worrying –
My lack of trust in you.

Please give me one more chance to be
Your Oblate Sister true
In God I trust! In God I trust!
And so I trust in you.

In spite of her positive outlook, the strain of the foundational years began taking its toll on Sr. Wilhelmina. She began to have increasingly frequent seizures. She also grieved to see sisters leave, some after struggling for years to preserve their vocations. Sister admitted that after "someone I loved very much left," she realized how serious a crisis the community was suffering.

The long-term effects of the conflict of ideals became apparent, Sr. Therese resigned from her post and took leave of the community in July 2010. In her place, Bishop appointed Mother Cecilia Snell

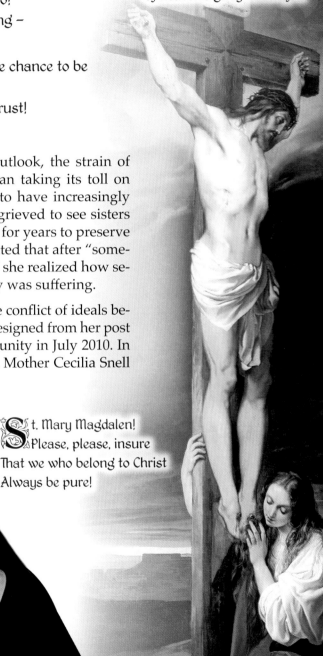

No man is saved
against his will,
But he must follow up the hill
Of Calvary! Believing still
All that his Savior says, until
Of Heaven's glory he has fill.

St. Mary Magdalen!
Please, please, insure
That we who belong to Christ
Always be pure!

It could be worse,
So please don't cry!
God loves you, and so do I!

Oh, the beauty of our God!
In His creatures, great and small!
In immortal human souls!
Soul of Mary most of all!

Jesus loves the Father!
I love the Father, too!
All by Mary, all with Mary!
Everything I do!
In, for, through!
In, for, through!
Jesus!
Mary!
I love You!

Mary is
Free from sin!
All Immaculate!
On her will
Ever still
We her children wait.

Mother Mary, I'm thy servant,
All I am and have is thine;
Help me to be persevering,
Eating Meat and drinking Wine.

I love you, Blessed Mother!
I'm fighting on your side!
Please help me to be humble
And not puffed up with pride!

as prioress. Mother Cecilia would lead the community to a lasting home in Gower, Missouri, where construction had already begun on a guest house that the Sisters were to live in temporarily. Later, prudence dictated that it become the monastery, made possible by future additions and the abbatial church.

Mother Cecilia and each of these sisters who entered before 2010 attest to the powerful example and influence of Sr. Wilhelmina's fidelity on their individual perseverance. Her poetry reflected not only her trusting serenity in the onset of old age, but also in her regard for the virtue of continuing obedience:

Getting older by the minute,
Trying not to die;
'Fraid of fire and being in it,
Trusting God Most High!

I must obey, do what I'm told
And not just what I like:
Especially now that I'm old
And to the grave must hike.

As the community gained stability both within and without, Sr. Wilhelmina began experiencing physical precariousness in things which were ordinarily easy, such as experiencing a good night's sleep:

Heavenly Father
Bless Mother Cecilia!
Make her strong in doing Thy will.
Help her in her daily duties,
Help her pay each awesome bill.

We cry to Thee, our Father dear,
All of Thy children gathered here;
Thank Thee for the sunny skies,
For ev'ry plant that lives or dies.
Help us fulfill our vows to Thee,
While we adore on bended knee.

Angels and archangels, Thrones
Guard you and your busy bones!
Help you in your working hours!
Dominations, Virtues, hymn
With Cherubim and Seraphim!

On this feast of St. Hedwig
May God give you your graces big,
Leading you to Heaven above,
Safe with everlasting love!

ST. HEDWIG'S DAY, 2010 *marked the appointment of Mother Cecilia as Sister Wilhelmina's second successor. She warmly embraced her new superior moments after the announcement (above.)*

Give me, Lord, the gift of sleep,
All my pride away to sweep,
No more piles of sin to heap,
Never looking at the cheap
Baubles that lead to the deep
Where the hellish sewers seep
And the smelly demons creep.

This converted poor black sheep
Would into Thine arms now leap
Safe with Thee, with Thee to weep,
And no longer evils reap,
Happy to Thy wishes keep,
With Thee on the mountain steep.
Give me, Lord, the gift of sleep.

On nights when attempts to sleep were futile, Sisters would still hear the movement of Sr. Wilhelmina's rosary beads in bed. She would sometimes awaken in the night, burning with some inspiration for a new poem, but would still obediently persist in the quest for sleep. Even when she was sleep deprived, nothing seemed to overcome Sr. Wilhelmina's characteristic wit and sense of humor. Poems, rhymes and ditties flowed from her pen, filling a sizeable stack of notebooks. She frequently re-wrote the lyrics of familiar songs to be performed at community recreations, with imaginative costumes and dramatic acting. She also composed rhymes to dramatize the little triumphs of daily life:

What joy to know the secret
of unplugging a clogged drain!
What joy no longer to endure
the "call the plumber" pain!
Just baking soda packed in well
and plenty vinegar dosed
Immediately loosens
what was keeping that drain closed.
Let sit for minutes, nine or ten,
then let the water run!
Use plunger to bring up
whatever keeps the job undone.

UNABLE TO SLEEP *in a Kansas City skit, Sister never needed coaching for acting. She always left everyone in stitches with her sense of humor.*

Let's all give God permission
To do with us what He likes,
To ride with us in our canoes,
To take us on long hikes;
To feed the hungry, heal the sick
And solace those who are crying;
But most of all we must be quick
To bring help to the dying.

ALWAYS A GOOD SPORT *amidst the many early outings, or even in an occasional game o[f] Bocce (below.)*

SR. WILHELMINA SANG TO RAISE FUNDS *in a mock "EWTN appearance" for one skit.*

Dear millionaire! I pray for you
That when you come to die,
Your soul may rise in joy and peace
To mansions great on high:
Partly because you always did
All that our Father willed,
Like giving us money
Sorely needed to build!
All saints in heaven have reached there
Because of Jesus Christ
Who mercifully, lovingly,
His body sacrificed.

Sister recognized everything as a gift from the Lord. When anyone asked how she was doing, she would customarily reply, "Grateful to God!" Evidence of this gratitude was her joy that overflowed one Easter morning as she was drying dishes in the kitchen. A sunbeam poured through the chapel window into the main room, prompting Sr. Wilhelmina to pause in her work and spontaneously perform a little tap dance routine, probably a remnant from her childhood, in the pool of sunlight, swinging her dishrag. This accomplished, she turned to find a delighted postulant watching her and giggled to see that her little demonstration of joy had been observed.

On one trip, the sisters pulled off at a rest stop at the same time as a busload of African-American women, beautifully dressed, and all wearing long skirts. Seeing them, Sr. Wilhelmina began an improvised song to her Sisters: "Hooray for the modest ladies, hooray for the modest ladies!" On her way back to the car, some of the group crossed paths with Sr. Wilhelmina. Facing the little figure in full habit, bent over her cane, one of the women loudly remarked to another, "Isn't she *cute?*" At the same volume, Sr. Wilhelmina replied earnestly, "I don't mean to be *cute!*" She turned and then glanced back at them over her shoulder with a smile, pointing her finger over her lifted cane: "I mean to be *good!*" Whereupon the women all cheered and laughed.

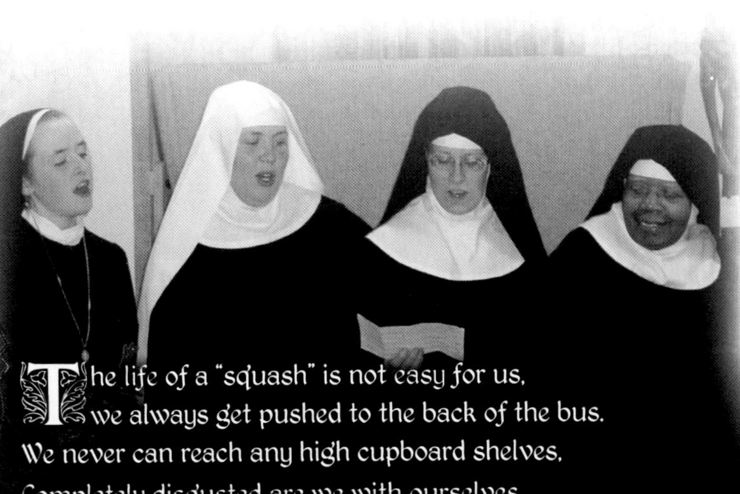

The life of a "squash" is not easy for us,
We always get pushed to the back of the bus.
We never can reach any high cupboard shelves,
Completely disgusted are we with ourselves.

"SQUASH" *a song written with Mother Cecilia for the shortest Sisters of the community.*

Evidence of the humorous but also meticulous way with which she approached her work is "The Boulaur Book," that she wrote by hand, "lovingly dedicated to the POSTULANTS" on how to iron the monastic wimple.

> Consider first what you are working with: an iron, a board and your two hands. The iron, usually held in the right hand, can do toe-dancing, drag back on its heel, and do side curving. Occasionally it stamps flat… First of all, there is the preliminary step. Never, never skip this preliminary step… look at the front of the boulaur to see if it is spotlessly clean. Don't bother to iron a stained boulaur. Why waste time? No Sister will wear a stained boulaur. Simply shove that boulaur under the bottom of the pile… I do not recommend leaving unattended boulaurs on any ironing boards, especially if there are worldly-wise wayfarers tramping through the area solely intent on their own concerns.

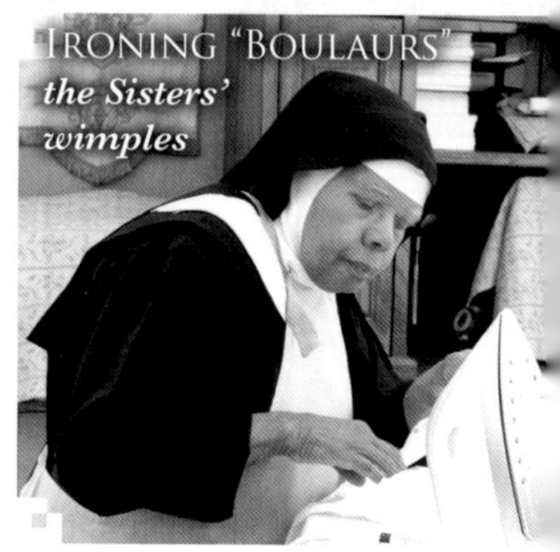
IRONING "BOULAURS" *the Sisters' wimples*

She continued to use her simple, monotonous tasks to fuel her spiritual apostolate of prayer, especially prayer for priests. It is evident what mundane chore inspired the following prayer for fallen priests:

Like wax stuck on a cassock, Lord,
Are priests in mortal sin!
Have mercy on them, Jesus!
Don't let the devil win!

He's making fun of them and pointing
At the Church's shame:
Have mercy, Lord! Convert them
For the glory of Thy NAME.

With her love of words, she pioneered the use of acrostics in prayer. The hidden word in the following acrostic illustrates the intensity and urgency that she brought to her spiritual apostolate:

Queen Mother Mary – stand with her beside the cross.
Unite with Mary's slaves, give yourself to her entirely.
I must be forgotten; exchange it for THOU.
Cross is temporary; eternity is forever.
King is Christ; reign with Him at the right hand of the Father.

God created
families,
The basic
government of man;
Each member
has a role to play
According to
God's holy plan.

In another way, as she reflected on the name of someone in need of prayer, she would use the letters of his name to spell out her own prayer. A classic case is her prayer for the conversion of President Barack Obama:

Obedience to God's law is not optional.
Be born! Believe and be baptized.
Advance and adore Our Lord in the Most Blessed Sacrament.
Meet Mary the Mother of God. Bring Muslims with you
to respond to the miracle she performs for you.
Admire all saints.

Again and again in her writing, Sr. Wilhelmina returned to the idea of the "All-or-Nothing Game." She played this game with many variations, sometimes considering God as "all" and she as "nothing:"

God always was,
Will always be,
Always remains the same;
He plays with us
Who live on earth
His All-or-Nothing game.

For God is All,
And we are naught
Except to pass the test:
Of choosing
Between God and men
Which of them is best.

For He is All,
And we are naught,
Him only we adore;
No greater good
Can e'er be sought;
Let's love Him more and more!

Another variation expresses the "all" that we must give to God and the "nothing" we must keep for ourselves:

We must give all we have and are,
With heart, soul, mind and strength;
Or selfishly live in our sins,
Until life ends, at length.

Once we have given all to Him,
God joins us to Himself;
If not, we burn for self alone,
On our own pantry shelf.

TRIPS TO GOWER ***to prepare the donated land for future building were always a joy to Sister, though she sometimes came home with chiggers and poison ivy, prompting the poem below:***

In Bed At Night

Thank You, Lord,
for every itch!
May I neither
scratch nor twitch,
But do penance
for my crimes,
Till I come
to cooler times.

Chapter 15

In Gower

Stability is what we need –
Stability of place –
In silent love, contemplative,
Before His Holy Face;
We pray to Him for needy priests,
For mercy and His grace;
Looking for Him, let us not join
In any worldly race.

Let us not long for worldly things –
Applause of men on earth –
Their money and approval are
To us of little worth;
We have been given by Our
Father supernatural birth;
He has reserved for us at
Home His everlasting mirth.

Beside the Cross, with Mother dear,
Lord! Thou hast set us free!
No matter how much blood flows down
Grant us stability.

Let us thank God for poverty!
Let us thank God for pain!
Let us thank God for joy and peace
In souls that Heaven gain!

O holy Guardian Angels please
Help us get settled in Gower!
Relying on Almighty God,
His Mercy, Love and Power!

Thou, Lord! Don't leave us in the lurc
Give us status in Thy Church!

For Good

Stability & Status

This is the land for which we've longed
For labor and for prayer!
Here we shall stand beside the wronged
Throughout this world of care.
This is the land where we shall love
With heart, mind, strength and soul!
Holding the hand of God's Sweet Dove
Who leads us to our goal!
Let us thank God for all His gifts!
For choosing us to be
Here on this sod until He lifts
Us to eternity!

The Lord is Master of this house,
Christ Jesus is His Name;
Good things alone our God allows,
No greed, no sin, no shame.

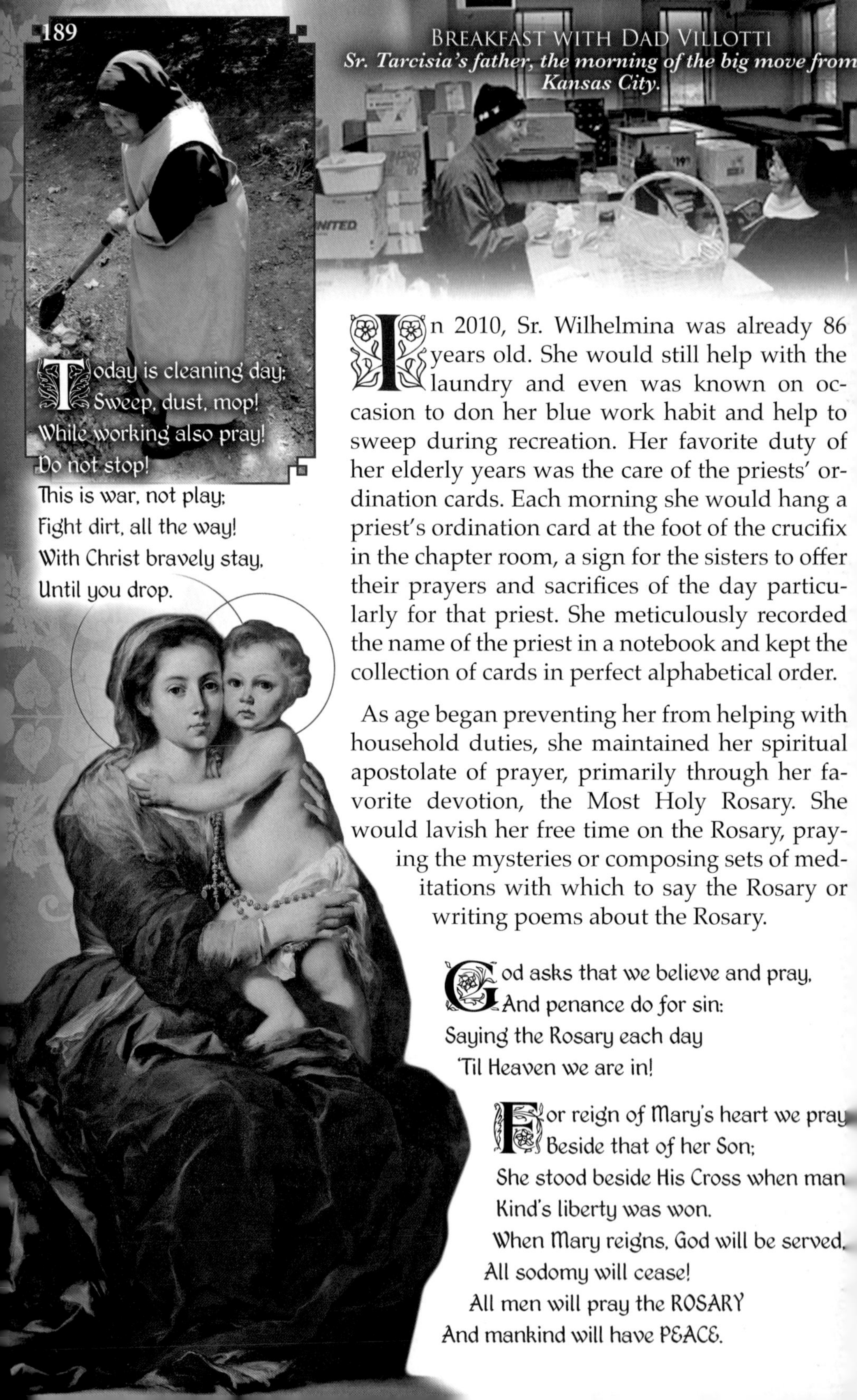

BREAKFAST WITH DAD VILLOTTI

Sr. Tarcisia's father, the morning of the big move from Kansas City.

Today is cleaning day;
Sweep, dust, mop!
While working also pray!
Do not stop!
This is war, not play;
Fight dirt, all the way!
With Christ bravely stay,
Until you drop.

In 2010, Sr. Wilhelmina was already 86 years old. She would still help with the laundry and even was known on occasion to don her blue work habit and help to sweep during recreation. Her favorite duty of her elderly years was the care of the priests' ordination cards. Each morning she would hang a priest's ordination card at the foot of the crucifix in the chapter room, a sign for the sisters to offer their prayers and sacrifices of the day particularly for that priest. She meticulously recorded the name of the priest in a notebook and kept the collection of cards in perfect alphabetical order.

As age began preventing her from helping with household duties, she maintained her spiritual apostolate of prayer, primarily through her favorite devotion, the Most Holy Rosary. She would lavish her free time on the Rosary, praying the mysteries or composing sets of meditations with which to say the Rosary or writing poems about the Rosary.

God asks that we believe and pray,
And penance do for sin:
Saying the Rosary each day
'Til Heaven we are in!

For reign of Mary's heart we pray
Beside that of her Son;
She stood beside His Cross when man
Kind's liberty was won.
When Mary reigns, God will be served,
All sodomy will cease!
All men will pray the ROSARY
And mankind will have PEACE.

R. Wilhelmina dutifully recorded *the priests whose ordination cards she had laced at the foot of the crucifix each day. She also kept a lively community chronicle.*

At the Priory's blessing
Sister met Mrs. Evelyn Quatman, whose father-in-law restored Mary's House in Ephesus, Turkey.

Little King, please help us build
On our high and spacious field!
So we faithfully may pray
As we should, both night and day.
Thy priests' house must soon be done,
For their rest and holy fun;
They're Thy soldiers in the fight!
Help them bravely do what's right!
Give us generosity
For true Holy Family.
Jesus, Mary, Joseph, save!
Now! Before we reach the grave.

Little King, Thou'rt building now!
Helping each one keep her vow!
To be childlike, to be humble,
And to never, never grumble!
Keeping silence and to pray
Every moment of the day,
As our Blessed Mother teaches
And our Pope John Paul II preaches.
Lord, each priest upon the earth
Let us bring to heav'nly birth!
Convert bad ones! Bless the good!
Make each behave as he should!

Little King, at Matins be
Light leading to Lauds and Prime;
Joyful Terce let us all see
In each daily morning time.
MARY's Rosary intertwined,
To no moment be confined.
LOVE, perpetually thought,
Be in all our actions caught.
Sext, then None, before the sun
Tells us that our day is done;
Vespers be our evening prayer;
Compline closes all with care.

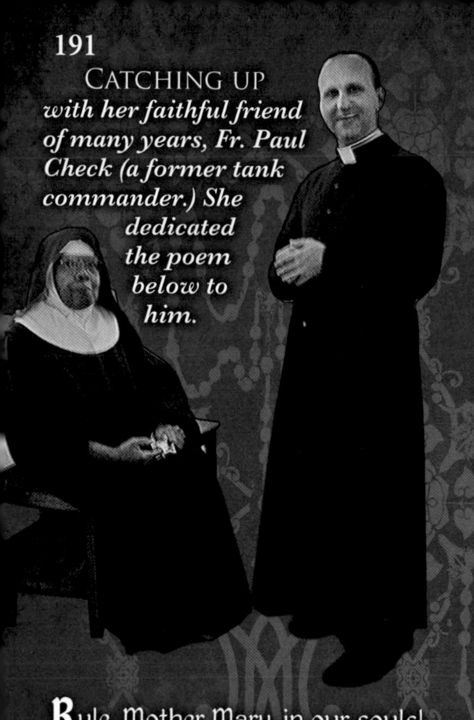

Catching up *with her faithful friend of many years, Fr. Paul Check (a former tank commander.) She dedicated the poem below to him.*

Rule, Mother Mary, in our souls!
Let us not work for worldly goals,
But practice proper self-controls,
Thy servants we, 'though in foxholes.

Educate all thy children here
That all may know thy Son most dear
Our God who shed a human tear
And suffered crucifixion drear.

Inspire us with sincerest thanks-
Money lies in celestial banks-
We pay no heed to Satan's pranks
But drive for thee, only thy tanks.

Gather us 'round thy radiant throne,
Make us belong to thee alone;
With loving hearts, not hearts of stone,
We love with love that is thine own.

Negroes are they - say NIGRA SUM!
Please lift to thine own GAUDIUM;
O, hear thou now this SUPLICUM,
Triumphant Heart! ROSARIUM!

Our Lady's House at Ephesus *discovered through the revelations of Anne Catherine Emmerich and restored in the mid-twentieth century by George B. Quatman, an Ohio native.*

The Priory of Our Lady of Ephesus *soon after its completion.*

Sr. Wilhelmina's fervent prayer for priests only increased as she entereed the most contemplative stage of her life. One Sister recounted that:

> Her deep love for priests was very evident, with her heart in her eyes! She was all attention to them when they spoke to her, and was deeply concerned about straying priests or struggling seminarians when such prayer requests were conveyed to her.

Her perception of priests seemed almost prophetic at times. In the early days, before the community had secured a regular chaplain, the Sisters occasionally went to a parish near their home for confession. Sister Wilhelmina came out of the church assisted by a Sister, where she encountered a young priest whom she had never met. She immediately went into something of a sermon to the priest there on the sidewalk, saying to him "I am telling you Father, you are *God's* man," and urged him to be very faithful to his calling. She spoke with such energy that her companion tried to quiet her. It turned out that the priest abandoned his vocation within the year.

Lady of Ephesus, Mother of God,
Drive all the devils from earth into Hell;
Make all creation God's great glory to tell –
Purity, chastity,
flourish and swell –
Happily, welcoming
Emmanuel!
Convert the Muslims
and convert the Jews!
All men believing
and sharing Good News.

Our Lady of Ephesus,
Please deliver
All of Us!
Put an end to
RACIAL STRIFE,
Stop
abortion,
SAVE
EACH
LIFE!

LADY OF EPHESUS,
save me from hell!
Save all the other
poor sinners as well;
Help us to know
and to love Jesus Christ,
And to live like Him
Who Self-sacrificed.

Daily your Rosary
help us to pray,
Making the Stations
with you every day;
Lady of Ephesus,
please make us saints!
Thanking God always
without sad complaints.

OUR LADY OF EPHESUS *or "little Mary" is a smaller replica of the Fourviére statue carved by Joseph Fabische, sculptor of the Madonna of Massabielle. The statue was also replicated on a large scale in white as Our Lady of Lebanon at Harissa.*

DEVOTION *to Our Lady of Ephesus deepened along with the realization of the contemplative vocation of the order, seeking the hidden monastic ideal of Our Lady over active assistance to priests. The stability attained after the move to the donated property at Gower both internally and financially allowed the Benedictines to construct a retreat house for priests.*

Jesus, my Love! Lord Jesus Christ!
For me, life Thou hast sacrificed!
With Thee I ever would keep tryst
And never shall my love be spliced,
But e'er in Mary's Heart be spiced!
Jesus, my Love! Lord Jesus Christ!

Crib, Cross and Altar,
Where we see Thee lying,
Heart of Jesus, loving sinners,
Thou art meekly dying.

Love, Love, Love!
Thou, my God Eternal!
Love, Love, Love!
Infinite and Pure!
Love, Love, Love!
Merciful Creator!
Love, Love, Love!
Makes salvation sure!

The Father, Word and Holy Ghost
From all eternity,
Have been in love, have been in love,
Have been in love with me.

It's now my turn to love God well
In faith and deepest trust,
Relying on His might and love,
Although I'm stinking dust.

Jesus Christ
God and Man
Glory be to Thee!
Save us from
All our sins
For eternity!

A TOAST!
Sister Wilhelmina raises her punch glass in honor of the Christ Child on Christmas Day, 2013. The community was joined by Fr. Check and Bishop Finn. She delivered a poem to the latter as a gift on Christmas Day 2012 (right.)

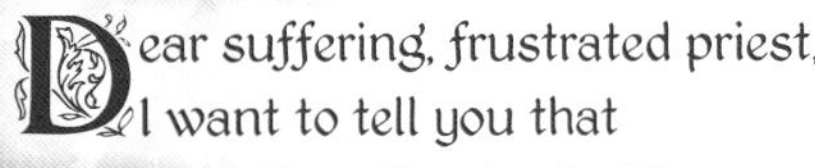

Dear suffering, frustrated priest,
I want to tell you that
Though mixed with
water, trodden on,
Salt never does
go flat;
Just as a city
on a hill
Cannot be hid at all,
The Word of God,
like thunder,
Must in every
valley fall.
Although the hearers
stop their ears
And much prefer to spat,
They can be positively sure
That salt does not go flat.

FR. SIMON ZURITA ***gives his first blessing.***

A CAKE AND A FLOWER ***presented by Sister to Fr. Mark Bachmann,*** OSB ***on his anniversary.***

Our Bishop Robert,
Our Bishop William,
Our Bishop Robert William Finn,

He's the man who's leading us to God
and true happiness,
true happiness,
forevermore.

He's leading us to God,
He's leading us to God,
Helping us receive the
sacraments and pray
well the Mass!

Sister loved receiving the first blessings of newly ordained priests in particular. It is an ancient custom to venerate the newly consecrated hands of a new priest by giving a "liturgical kiss" to each hand, a simple and silent gesture after the blessing. Sister Wilhelmina, on the other hand, would loudly give a smacking kiss to each of their hands and in a loud stage whisper say "God bless you!" to the young priest. She would then enthusiatically congratulate the new priest again outside the chapel. She was "all smiles and so full of love and attention to anything they might say," said one Sister.

Being elderly did not mean that Sr. Wilhelmina lost her sense of fun. She devised names and games for the most mundane of her geriatric equipment: her faithful walker was dubbed "Speedy." When a sister would come to escort her to Holy Mass, Sr. Wilhelmina would grab Speedy's handles and set off with the cry, "Run...! Run...! Run, to Heaven fun!" while the younger sister tried to check the energy of her elderly charge. When Sr. Wilhelmina's chronic lung problems required her to use oxygen, she named her portable oxygen tanks Snuff and Puff; and the series of air compressors to fill them were successively Father Air, Uncle Ben, Aunt Jemima and finally, Cousin Pete.

"BEAUTIFUL!!" EXCLAIMED SISTER ***upon seeing the completed priests' retreat house for the first time.***

What is the most
important spot
In sacrifices daily?
You sit and stand and genuflect
While turning pages gaily;
Please sing and keep the melody
United with the crew!
Remember you must harmonize –
Not be outstanding you –
United with OUR BLESSED LORD –
You thankfully receive.

SISTER PARODIED HER OWN DAY
in the video "Elderly" (scenes below.)

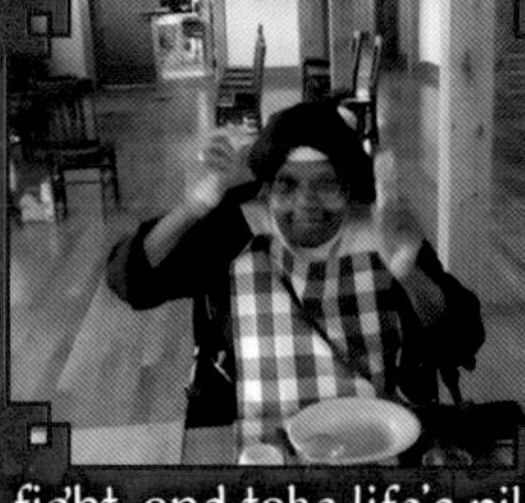

Why
eat
at all?
This is
God's Will:
To struggle, fight, and take life's pill.

Lord, help me
not to do it
any more:
Enter a room
with haste
and slam
the door!

Ye Seven Holy
Sleepers,
Please pray
for us who sleep
When we should be awake at prayer;
And holy vigil keep;
Don't let us be that lazy lout
Who didn't use his gift.
Please help us fight the winning bout
That souls to heaven lift.

Mornings are the hardest things
For us! Since no angel wings
Help us holily to live,
Certainly we must forgive!

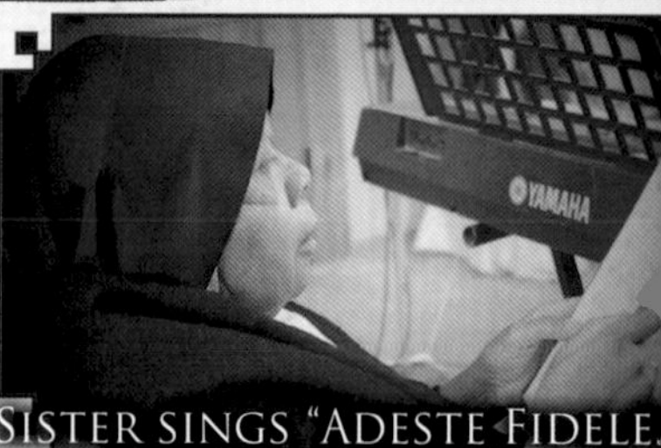

SISTER SINGS "ADESTE FIDELE...
on Caroling At Ephesus

The respiratory difficulties Sister suffered in later years often resulted in long coughing spells. It was for this reason that Sister was not included in the community's first CDs according to Sr. Therese's decision. This was upheld as future recording sessions became more taxing, due to a contract with Decca Records/de Montfort music. Distributing the music on a larger scale helped defray the construction debt Mother Cecilia had inherited, and went on to finance further construction projects. Eventually, the community returned to private productions, and Mother Cecilia saw no reason why Sr. Wilhelmina could not be included on at least one of the tracks. So Sr. Wilhelmina made her recording debut on *Caroling At Ephesus*, aiding the Sisters in recording the final track, "Adeste Fideles." In preparing the piece, her eyes were riveted on Mother Cecilia, who gave her instruction. This, as well as similar instances, reminded Mother Cecilia of the passage in the Psalm "As the eyes of the handmaid are upon the hand of her mistress, so are our eyes turned unto the Lord until He showeth us mercy." Her obedience to Mother Cecilia - fifty-four years her junior - was unwavering, believing she held Christ's place.

All the same, Sr. Wilhelmina loved to sing and never lost her strong singing voice. Her singing and acting came out uproariously well in a little homemade video, "Elderly," in which she and another Sister sang Lerner and Loewe's tune "Wouldn't It Be Loverly" with changed words adapted to describe Sr. Wilhelmina's daily life. She was a "ham" and brought much laughter to her Sisters, both in production and in the final product.

When her favorite hymns were sung at Mass, such as "O Sacrum Convivium," her dramatic and operatic tone would lead the soprano section, and very frequently completely drown them out, completely oblivious that all the Sisters had dissolved into smothered giggles. At recreation, she would regale the Sisters and also visitors with her "Negro spirituals."

Sister Wilhelmina also remained in touch with some of her siblings' children, and was always delighted by their visits. One year toward the end of Sr. Wilhelmina's life, she received a visit from three of her nieces, the daughters of her sister Christine. The spirituals came out again, and she entertained them with the collection of jokes that she had learned from the novices. "Why was six afraid of seven?" she asked her non-plussed listeners. "You don't know?" Then in triumph she gave the answer, "Because seven ate nine!"

"And how do you catch a unique rabbit?" Again, her question was met with mystified expressions. "You 'neak up on him!" When the laughter subsided, she had a quick follow-up, "And how do you catch a tame rabbit? The tame way!" Her deadpan delivery was also devastating. "I met a bum on the street who said to me, 'I haven't had a bite in weeks.'" "What did you do, Sr. Wilhelmina?" "I bit him."

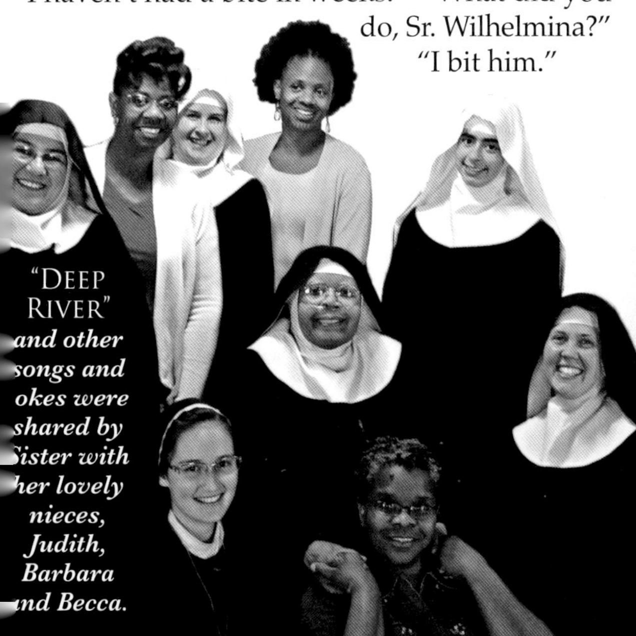

"DEEP RIVER" *and other songs and jokes were shared by Sister with her lovely nieces, Judith, Barbara and Becca.*

Jesus, Great
Miracle-Worker,
Do Your stuff!
Of our own badness,
We've had enough.

BAD WOMEN
GO TO HELL,
AND THERE
THEY HAVE
A SMELL
OF FILTHY,
STINKING
PRIDE!
THE DOORS
ARE OPEN
WIDE.

BOWLING OVER *the "seven capital sins" at an All Saints Day Party.*

Rosary! Rosary!
Rosary recall!
Purity! Purity!
Purity for all!
Treasure we family!
Its precious pieces!
Its uncles, cousins, aunts,
Nephews and nieces!
Mother Mary asks that we
Do our duty
Without looking for applause
Or some booty!
Rosary! Rosary!
Rosary recall!
Purity! Purity!
Purity for all!
Everyone must become
Saints in Heaven's hall!

SISTER'S 90TH BIRTHDAY
called for a party, with greetings sent from around the world.

SISTER INVENTED A GAME FOR RECREATION:

She wrote a poem on the whiteboard, leaving blanks for Sisters to guess words, e.g. "Mary is our mother, She works hard to save us, We must work hard with her, And ride on the same bus." Sisters "got her back" at her 70th anniversary party (below.)

The Rosary is a weapon That daily we must use
While travelling toward Heaven, Intent upon Good News

A ROSARY PROCESSION
on May 13, 2014 in honor of Our Lady of Fatima's first apparition and in thanksgiving for the cancellation of a public Black Mass.

Yet one more blessing came as the community approached its fourth anniversary in Gower. The Bendictines of Mary received approval of their Constitutions in Rome, thanks to Bishop Finn and through the instrumentality of Fr. John Berg. He had urged Mother Cecilia to go to Rome at the funeral of their late friend, Fr. Kenneth Walker. The community had been permitted to make Perpetual vows in 2010 so as not to be obliged to keep renewing their private vows, and it was at that ceremony that Sister Wilhelmina received her old ring again, newly plated in gold. But the vows were to remain private, and official recognition withheld, as authorities had foreseen an approaching change in community leadership.

Now that stability had been attained, the order she had founded was granted formal Ecclesiastical status. On December 8, 2014, Sr. Wilhelmina, who was beaming ear to ear, presented the chart solemnizing her vows to Mother Cecilia, in the presence of Bishop Finn. The religious vows she had been obliged to sacrifice in taking up private vows in her new community, were now fully and wholeheartedly recognized by her beloved Holy Mother the Church.

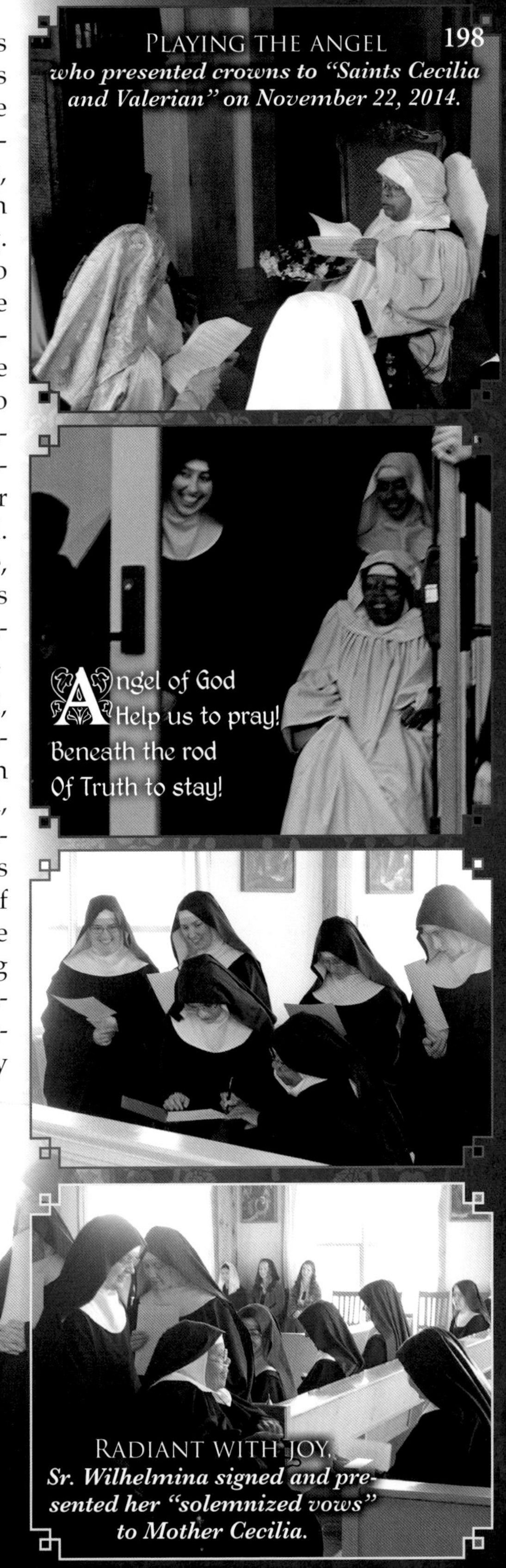

Angel of God
Help us to pray!
Beneath the rod
Of Truth to stay!

PLAYING THE ANGEL *who presented crowns to "Saints Cecilia and Valerian" on November 22, 2014.*

RADIANT WITH JOY, *Sr. Wilhelmina signed and presented her "solemnized vows" to Mother Cecilia.*

Chapter 16

Looking through

So many people I have known
Are now departed from this world;
Lord, grant them rest! I hope that they
Have not into the pit been hurled.

OLD AGE is the time God gives us,
To repent of the sins of youth;
To stop all stealing and lying,
To praise Him the Eternal Truth.

To learn to be meek and humble,
To learn to be humble and meek;
To learn to be meek and humble!
And God alone steadfastly seek.

The time has come for me to do
True penance for my sins;
Obedience to schedule is the place
Where it begins.
So rising with the rising bell
And not before the time
It is true penance for me now
To write this little rhyme

You old:
Please do remember that
You've one foot in the grave;
God has been patient many years!
When will you learn to behave?

You young:
Respect the old for they
Were once as young as you;
The young will die, the Old MUST die!
They've nothing else to do.

I want to be obedient
And do what I am told,
Thus penance do for all my sins
Now that I'm somewhat old.

Awake, old woman!
Penance do
For all your sins of youth!
Stop being fake!
Start being true!
Follow the Way,
the Truth!

Old age is a sickness
That always ends in death
I'll thank God for sickness
Unto my dying breath.

We love Our Father all the time,
When He says,
"Yes," or "No,"
He's taking us
to Heaven's clime –
That's where we want to go!

I would that every
beat of my heart
Were an act
of love for Thee!
Forever and
forever, Lord,
For all eternity!

THE LATTICES

Twilight Blessings

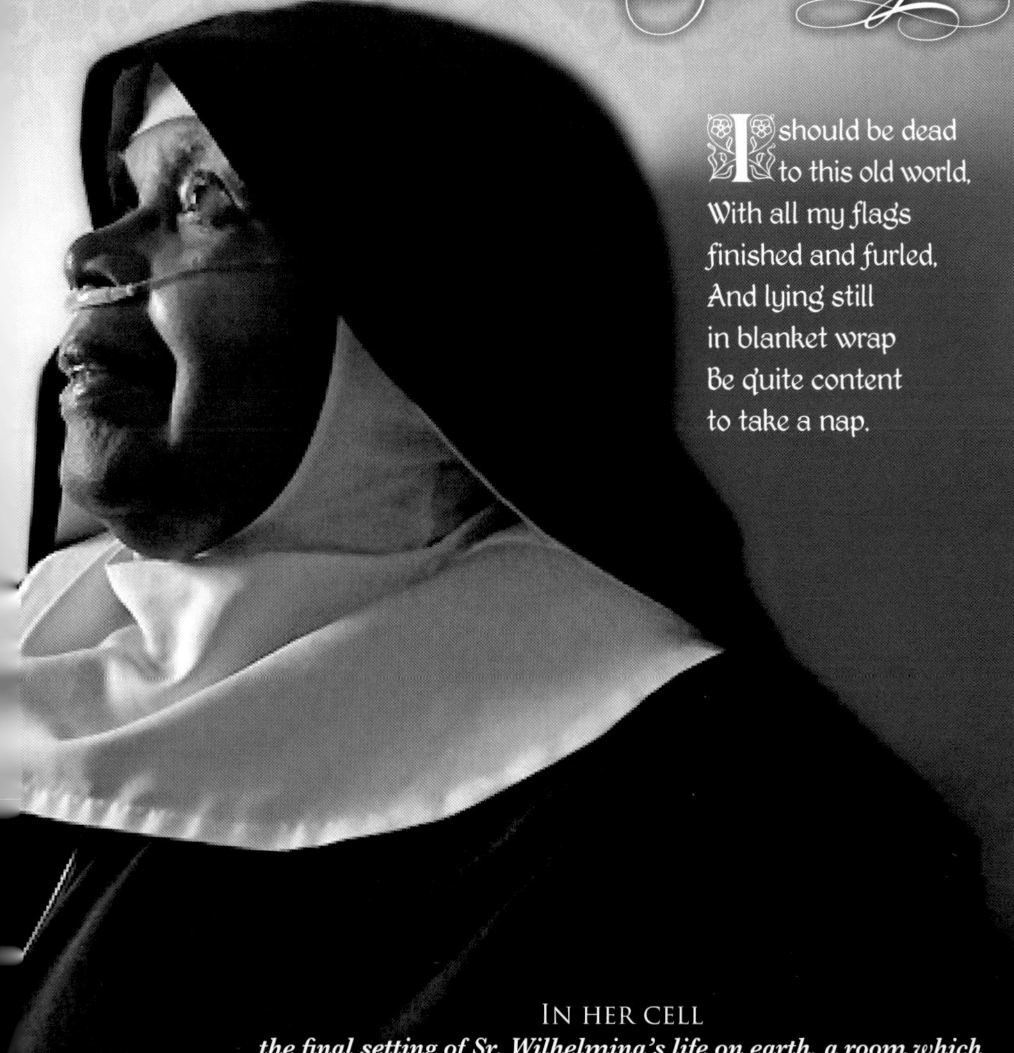

I should be dead
to this old world,
With all my flags
finished and furled,
And lying still
in blanket wrap
Be quite content
to take a nap.

IN HER CELL
the final setting of Sr. Wilhelmina's life on earth, a room which still holds memories for her community as the backdrop of spiritual victories won and glimpses of heaven caught

Angels and Archangels! Thrones! Holy Dominations!
Thanks for money! Large amounts! Thanks for large donations!
Help us beautify our land with no deprivations.
Powers! Virtues! Help each priest who fights this world's battle!
Never let him in the least sound the losing rattle!
Drive out snakes and ev'ry beast set to harm our cattle!
Principalities, insist that we love God truly !
Cherubim, help us resist all that is unruly!
Seraphim, help us raise fist faithfully and duly!
Take charge of our woods and land, Holy Angel Choirs!
Help us Heaven understand toward which each aspires.
Save our trees, both tall and grand, save us from bad fires!

ACTING ONCE MORE *in the life of her former patroness, Elizabeth of Hungary, early 2015.*

THIS IS A SONG ABOUT MY CHAIR, RUBY RED

Ruby Red, Ruby Red,
you lay down like a nice flat bed!
Ruby Red, Ruby Red:
I like resting in you!
You even put my feet up too!
Ruby Red, Ruby Red,
in you I like to rock!
When we start we just can't stop!

Ruby Red, Ruby Red, don't'cha know –
That you make me
so – happy!
Ruby Red, you like me most
When I stand up and you
keep me close!

Ruby Red, oh, Ruby Red!
Ruby Red! Ruby Red!
Ruby Red! ***(co-written with an angel to a snappy original tune about her napping recliner.)***

As the burdens of old age increased, Sr. Wilhelmina received the assistance of "angels," novitiate companions who would help her throughout the day. Paradoxically, the angels were the main beneficiaries of this arrangement, for they witnessed first-hand a faithful religious living her consecration unto the very end. One remarked, "Sr. Wilhelmina makes everything that she does a prayer." The novice mistress, Sister Scholastica, attested to Sr. Wilhelmina's fulfilling of the role as the "real novice mistress," as she taught the novices by example how to truly live the religious spirit with complete generosity of heart. One day, Sr. Scholastica went as a substitute angel for one of her charges who was called away. The last thing to be done in preparing Sister for bed was to administer eyedrops. "Now the trick is to get it in the eye, and *not* down the cheek," she would say to her angels. Sr. Scholastica looked for the eyedrop box on the shelf, but could not find it. Apologizing to Sr. Wilhelmina, Sister replied in her funniest tone "Oh, you're one of those *innocent* creatures that doesn't know! They put it in an *orange* bottle now," and there were the eyedrops out of sight, tucked inside of a prescription bottle.

All the "angels" testified to Sister Wilhelmina's ability to endure everything without complaint. She would make light of mishaps, a dropped item or something forgotten, with a little jingle

Dear Father Paul, please help us all –
Especially our sick –
For life is short, and Heaven's port
Is harbor we would pick:
Don't let us fall, dear Father Paul,
Into the devil's trick.

Dear Father Paul, please help us all–
Especially our old –
Lest stinking pride give them a ride
Outside monastic fold:
Where sunk in harm, although quite warm
They perish in the cold.

Dear Father Paul, please help us all –
Especially our young –
As they begin to Heaven win
And on the cross be hung:
That they be brave and not too grave,
Having their whole life flung.

All ye Benedictine blessed,
Help us! Holy Father Paul,
Thou hast worked so many wonders!
Help us, help us, help us all!

FATHER PAUL OF MOLL ***(above) a Flemish Benedictine and wonderworker of the 19th century had a very devout client in Sr. Wilhelmina. She addressed many prayers to him, and shared many of the same concerns as he did: fidelity of religious and priests, abortion, devotion to St. Benedict, and loving God in all things.***

like "whoopsie-doopsie-dumsy-dum!" She would even make the best of situations, such as when the water was shut off during construction. Going to the faucet and finding it did not work, she said to her companion with great joy: "Now we can be like the Christ Child and be really poor!"

Her efforts to hide her discomforts made "angeling" a difficult task at times. When Sr. Wilhelmina once winced in pain, a novice asked her what was wrong. "Well, I would really like my rosary." The novice persisted. She answered, "See my rosary over there? If I could just have it, I will be fine." "Sister, is it your stomach? I won't give you your rosary unless you tell me." "But if I just put my rosary on it, like this," and she spread her hands over her lap, "everything will be just fine." The novice relented, laughingly saying, "Sister, you are a stinker!" Sr. Wilhelmina laughed back and held her rosary close. "Hee-hee...yeah, a *stinker!*"

As surely as her complaining was absent, her compliments were frequent and sincere. "What a nice job you did making that bed!" she would exclaim with gratitude over deeds of service done.

Sr. Wilhelmina's strong will certainly found it difficult to be absent from more and more community exercises and to take additional exceptions required by her age. A note of exasperation is found in one of her copybooks, but sublimated into her longing for God and Heaven:

"Aren't you tired?" I'm continually asked. Here's my answer:

I never tire
Of loving God
Although I'm
Surely dying;

Now that I'm
Nearly under sod
It's home to heav'n
I'm flying.

Whatever it cost her, Sr. Wilhelmina resolutely set herself to accept all exceptions as God's will for her, and another means of offering Him her love and sacrifice. It was a particular cross for her to have to take a snack:

SNACK-TIME

For love of God
I eat this snack,
Although I'm old
And dumb and black.

My God is wise,
He lives in me,
He does devise
This poetry.

The daily nap was also difficult for her, but she always accepted it in the spirit of obedience:

OBEY AND NAP

May napping never interfere
With my persistent constant prayer!
I love Thee, Lord, for Thou art her[e]
Deep in my heart and ev'rywhere

To the directions of her novitiate angels, so many decades junior to her in both age and religious life, she would constantly reply, "Whatever you say, I will obey."

Old men remain
the little boys
That once they
used to be,
And no one ever
quite forgets
Life on his
mother's knee;
The longing cannot
be explained
That fills
the human heart
For Love! Let no one f[eel]
constrained
To give his little part.

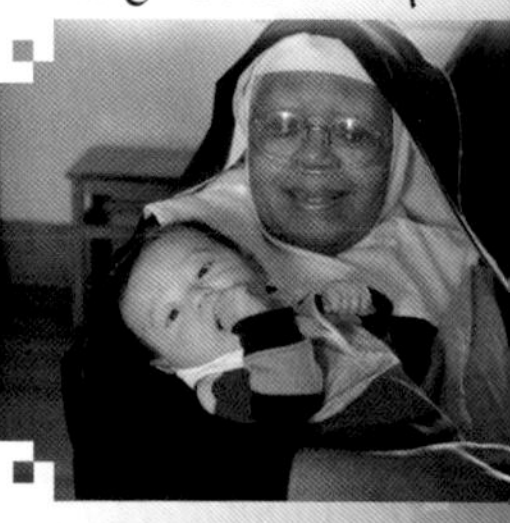

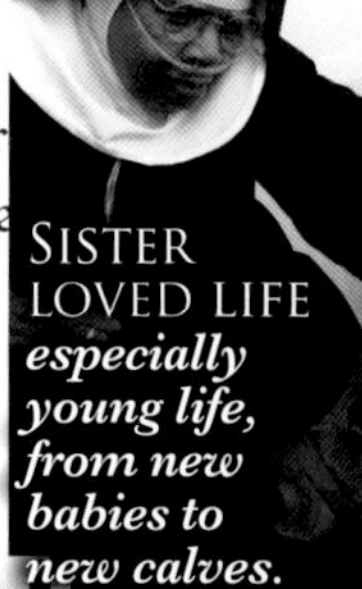

SISTER LOVED LIFE *especially young life, from new babies to new calves.*

DISTINGUISHED GUESTS OF 2016-17: ***Cardinal Burke and th[e] Pilgrim Virgin of Fatim[a]***

O dear St. Benedict,
Father of dear Father Paul,
Woes many now afflict
Us poor creatures, sinners all.

Pray that we turn and be
Full of faith and charity,
Ever seeking Jesus meek
And not straying from the way
Our loving God has picked!

O dear St. Benedict,
Help us enter
Heaven's hall!
Adam and Eve
were tricked
And we suffer
since
their
fall.

St. Benedict! St. Benedict!
Help persons who are dying!
So that repentant of their sins,
They're straight to heaven flying!

Being Benedictine
I must be obedient,
I must be humble,
And no matter what befalls,
I must never grumble.

Prayer first!
Prayer last!
Prayer at all times
in-between!
Sacrifice!
Please fast!
Be obedient
on the scene!

St. Benedict says,
"No grumbling!"
No matter
what transpires,
Since we belong
to God alone
We want
what God desires.

All ye Holy Benedictine Monks,
Help us poor sinners
who are struggling here
n poverty, and not with private trunks;
Help us to pray the Office and obey,
And keep the lily Chastity for aye
Sacrifice!
Please fast!

Dear Pope Francis,

The dogma yet to be proclaimed
  Tells of Our Mother Mary,
Tells of her spotless purity
  And all her many virtues
Beginning with humility,
  Her humility profound!
Her lively faith is next in line
  Followed by blind obedience,
And prayer unceasing,
constant prayer
  Mortification with it.
Adoration universal,
  Universal and constant!

Praying for sinners ev'rywhere,
  Praying for their conversion.
Standing beside her dying sons,
  Awaiting their repentance.
Awaiting with humility
  The news of their
homecoming.
The prodigals
must make return
  With heartfelt,
true contrition.

Then celebration will begin
  By angels high in heaven!
All brothers should take great delight
  And join the welcome party.
Giving great thanks for happiness
  And charity most ardent.
Patience heroic, patience
great
  And her angelic
sweetness.
Wisdom divine!
Wisdom divine!
  Upholding
all before her.

Jesus,
let us truly love Thee!
Let us love our Mother, too,
Sorrowful, Immac'late Lady,
No more sin, Lord, let us do!

THE PROCLAMATION OF THE DOGMA *of Our Lady as Mediatrix of all Grace, Advocate and Co-Redemptrix, an item of debate at Vatican II, was also a passion of Sr. Wilhelmina's, especially toward the end of her life, around the time when the above poem was written.*

EPIPHANY 2017
just after some Caroling.

We're in this school of St. Benedict,
We'd better obey
and be rather quick!
Let's never grumble as we silence keep
Meditating on our sins
that should make us weep.

We live together in charity,
Although we differ, we no fights see;
We trample on pride with humility
And manual labor keeps us busy.

Sometimes we gather and recreate;
Community life is our habitual state;
With Mother Mary we contemplate
The goodness of God which does not abate.

ONE OF SISTER'S JOYS
was to assist the youngest postulant in the May crowning of Our Lady.

A particular gift in the final years of Sr. Wilhelmina's life was the entrance of a young woman from Kenya. More than twenty years after she had "willingly put beneath her feet all ethnic ties," and "surrendered all attachment to her ethnic origin," her loving Lord gave her another black sister. On the day of the Kenyan sister's arrival, when she was introduced to Sr. Wilhelmina at recreation, Sr. Wilhelmina took the young, dark hand with both of hers and would not let it go, stroking it gently and observing now and then with gentle reproach, "Your hands are cold!"

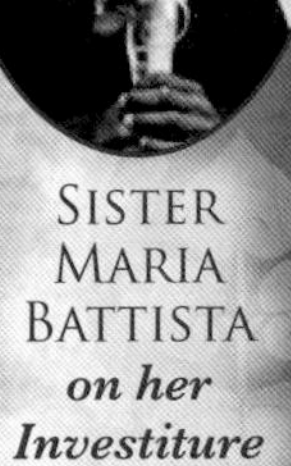

SISTER MARIA BATTISTA
on her Investiture day, 2017.

When this sister was preparing to receive the habit and her religious name the following year, Mother Cecilia remembered Sr. Wilhelmina's great desire to receive the name of the Precursor of Christ at her own investiture, and so asked Sr. Wilhelmina, "Don't you think we need a sister named after St. John the Baptist?" "Oh, yes!" was the enthusiastic reply. When the sister came to greet Sr. Wilhelmina after the ceremony, newly named for the Baptist, and with her black face beaming in radiant contrast to her bright new veil, Sr. Wilhelmina spread out her arms to embrace her, exclaiming, "I have been waiting for this hug all day!"

ON THE 4TH OF JULY *Sr. Wilhelmina energetically sang patriotic songs with the Sisters. Sister always said "I'm praying for the conversion of America!"*

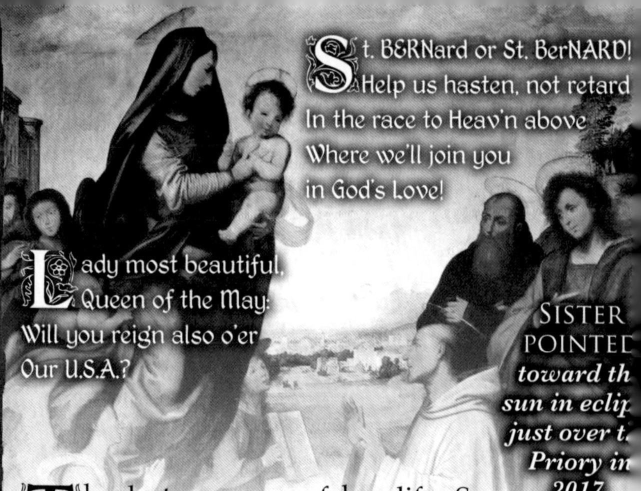

St. BERNard or St. BerNARD!
Help us hasten, not retard
In the race to Heav'n above
Where we'll join you
in God's Love!

Lady most beautiful,
Queen of the May:
Will you reign also o'er
Our U.S.A.?

SISTER POINTED *toward th[e] sun in eclip[se] just over t[he] Priory in 2017.*

America, so rich, secure,
warm and well-fed:
Yet ignorant of a true,
holy marriage bed!
Are you determined, still,
to kill that unborn boy?
Except repentance come,
for you there is no joy.
America, do penance
Before it is too late;
The Hell you're in will soon be sealed!
A most unhappy fate.

America immoral,
Except you soon repent:
You'll have to be in slavery
And hell-fire quite content.

America immoral!
Why don't you NOW BELIEVE?
In Jesus Christ? AND DO HIS WILL?
No longer His Heart grieve?

America immoral!
Don't be a Pharisee!
FORGIVE those who've offended you
As you would like to be.

We who call ourselves Christian,
Had better unite,
And living like Jesus lived,
For Jesus fight
Against our true enemies
Who make us sin,
Dragging us down until
Hell we are in.

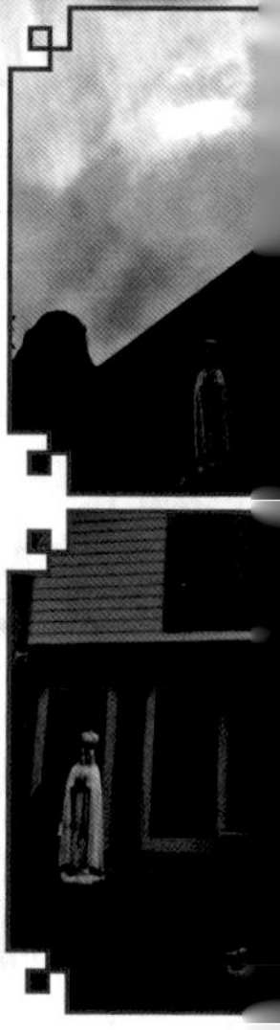

The last summer of her life, Sr. Wilhelmina was seated outside on the lawn after the first Masses of two newly ordained Fraternity priests, Fr. Martin Adams and Fr. Michael Cunningham. An impromptu concert began, with a couple of seminarians fiddling and strumming guitar and banjo. They started playing her favorites, "Deep River," "Swing Low, Sweet Chariot," and "Joshua Fit the Battle of Jericho" for everyone to sing along. After all had joined in for the rousing chorus of "Joshua," the accompanists subsided to simple strumming again, but Sr. Wilhelmina recognized her cue. With her unerring sense o[f] rhythm, she launched into a full-throated Gos[-] pel solo: "Well, you can talk about the people o[f] GIDEON, talk about a man named SAUL..." Sh[e] took down the house.

This same summer 2018, on the 4th of July, Th[e] community received news that Abbatial statu[s] was conferred upon them by Rome. Mother Ce[-] cilia would be the first Benedictine Abbess to re[-] ceive the traditional blessing in American histor[y]. The ceremony took place the day after the Conse[-] cration of th[e] newly-bui[lt] Abbati[al] churc[h].

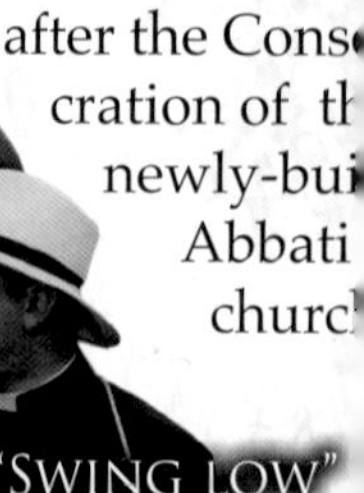

"SWING LOW" *with Fr. Zachary Ak*

Praying for you
dear Mother Cecilia
That both St. Cecilia
and St. Joseph
Rush to your aid
To help all souls
whom God
has made.

THE DEDICATION OF THE ABBEY CHURCH
a seven hour ceremony.

Remember your profession,
Remember what you've vowed.
Withdrawing from your abbess
Is by no means allowed.

SR. WILHELMINA PATIENTLY WAITED ***in her wheelchair until all the Sisters rendered their obedience to the new Abbess. Then a Sister wheeled her toward the center of the aisle, where she received Mother Abbess in a warm embrace, reminding Priscilla McCaffrey of Ella's words: "what does it matter whether you are first or last in line, you receive the Lord!" Afterwards, she greeted Bishop Robert C. Morlino like an old friend. The Bishop died $2^1/_2$ months after the ceremony.***

THE ABBATIAL BLESSING ***was attended also by Abbot Phillip Anderson of Clear Creek, the new Bishop of Kansas City-St. Joseph, James Vann Johnston, Fr. Devillers and many others.***

The winter of 2018-2019 saw increasing weakness in Sr. Wilhelmina. As the community watched her gradual decline, one of her angels from the novitiate prayed particularly for a preparatory grace before Sr. Wilhelmina's passing. The novice's prayer was answered, when, on the morning of January 10, she went into Sr. Wilhelmina's cell to find her smiling radiantly with "a very pure and innocent expression." "Jesus, Jesus!" Sr. Wilhelmina exclaimed, "He is the Good Shepherd. He wants everyone to go to heaven! He says everyone is supposed to go to heaven!"

When asked if she had seen the Lord, she answered, "Yes, I saw Jesus! Everyone in the world, everyone should go to heaven. Heaven, heaven, I want to go to heaven!" She looked up and smiled again, and then turned her eyes to her profession crucifix and gazed at it a long time. To the novice's query, Sr. Wilhelmina replied, "Yes, I look at the cross. We should meditate every day on the cross, every single day. We should meditate about His passion… He wants everyone to go to heaven, Oh, how I want to go to heaven!"

She continued to speak animatedly with the novice, in marked contrast to the preceding months in which she had shown increasing difficulty in speech. They spoke first about the necessity of the cross: "It is the right thing to do, you should embrace your cross," and then about consoling Our Lord: "That is right, it is like entering into eternity." She spoke with the voice of experience, having suffered so much in her religious life, but always embracing that suffering as a means of drawing closer to her beloved Jesus and relieving His thirst for love.

Always faithful to her spiritual motherhood, Sr. Wilhelmina promised to pray for the novice, marveling, "You are so young, and I am ancient in comparison to you. I wonder why God kept me so long on earth. Maybe that I tell you all this… We should always love our sisters…" She paused and then continued, "…And our priests. We should love, always love our holy sisters and our holy priests." She declared, "I want to thank God and praise Him for what He has done for me, I want to thank him for what he has done for you and I want to thank Him for all He has done for all my Sisters."

A few days after this conversation, these thoughts returned as Sr. Wilhelmina was again gazing at the cross: "I'm thinking how Our Lord suffered for us on this cross! I want to pray for the dying! Do you know when I will go to heaven? When will I go to heaven?" Then she exclaimed, "I really want to go to heaven!"

Like the flight of a bird past a window,
Is the longest life on earth;
Like the cry of a weak, helpless infant
At the moment of his birth.
To prepare for death is high wisdom
For we die at rapid rate;
Let us not run the risk of the horrors
Of repentance come too late.

God made the insects,
God made the birds,
God made the poets,
And gives them the words.

My God,
I love You!
I love you,
My God!
I want
What You want!
What You want,
I want!
Thank You
For all things!
For all things,
Thank You!
For You
I do hunt!
I do hunt
For You!

My arising and retiring
are the hardest,
The beginning and the ending
of each day,
But no matter what the pain
I am determined
To let Lord Jesus Christ
have His way!

Obedience! O-BE-DI-ENCE
Is my myrrh, gold and frankincense!

MOTHER ABBESS GREETS SISTER ***on Christmas morning, 2018. Years earlier, in a discussion about the necessary qualities of a Superior, Sr. Wilhelmina, who had noticed a fly in the room, blurted out "We need a superior who can do something about these flies!" She later wrote in light of the charge and blessing given to her successor:***

Fiat! Magnificat! Fiat! Magnificat!
It's not the many flies you swat,
But fiat! Magnificat!

Though this was the clearest and closest to her death, it was one of the final links in a chain of many other manifestations of the Divine in Sr. Wilhelmina's life. The most common seemed to be when she was awakening from sleep. One novice, who had had difficulty helping her into bed on account of Sr. Wilhelmina's back pain, returned to awaken her. Finding her particularly radiant, the novice said "Sister, did you see the Blessed Mother?" "Uh-huh!" "Did she speak to you?" "Uh-huh!" "What did she say?" "She said–" Sister Wilhelmina caught herself, and turned away smiling. When she was told it was time to prepare for Mass, "she ripped out of the chair," as though she were in no pain at all.

On another occasion close to Sister's death, a novice found her awakening very agitated, murmuring something to the effect that she had been witnessing a portion of Our Lord's Passion. "They hit Him! They hit Him!" but when fully awake, would not comment further.

To Mother Abbess Cecilia, again so many years younger in age and religious life, Sr. Wilhelmina gave a truly filial trust and obedience. One evening, when Sr. Wilhelmina was exhausted from the efforts to prepare for bed and struggling with mounting agitation, the novitiate angels called for Mother Abbess to calm her. As Mother Abbess bent over the elderly sister lying in bed, the abbatial cross around her neck swung forward, and Sr. Wilhelmina grasped it tightly in her hands. "Now do you know who I am?" Mother Abbess gently asked her spiritual daughter with a smile. "You're my mother!" came the immediate and happy reply.

Lord Jesus Christ, Eternal King,
In adoration let me bring
My heart with all its love!
Without Thee, I can nothing do.
Thou art my King, my King most True!
I am Thy little dove;
I have so much to thank Thee for!
Please let me love Thee more and more,
And come to Heav'n above!.

SISTER'S 75TH ANNIVERSARY *celebrated with her favorite: ice cream.*

In the next few months, Sister Wilhelmina celebrated two significant milestones: on March 9, seventy-five years in vows, and on April 13, ninety-five years of age. On the great occasion of her diamond jubilee, the sisters brought her into the choir before the sanctuary of the Abbey church; there she sat, with a gentle smile radiating from her face, while the entire community chanted the *Te Deum* in thanksgiving for the gift of Sr. Wilhelmina's religious life.

Difficult goodbyes followed that month as the first daughterhouse of the Abbey was made in Ava, Missouri. The founding group was led by Sr. Mary Josefa, for whom Sr. Wilhelmina had prayed especially since her entrance, and Sr. Maria Battista. As the foundresses bade farewell to their original foundress on Mercy Sunday, one of them noticed that Sister did not seem particularly sad. She acted as though she would see them again quite soon, and even said "I am going with you to Ava."

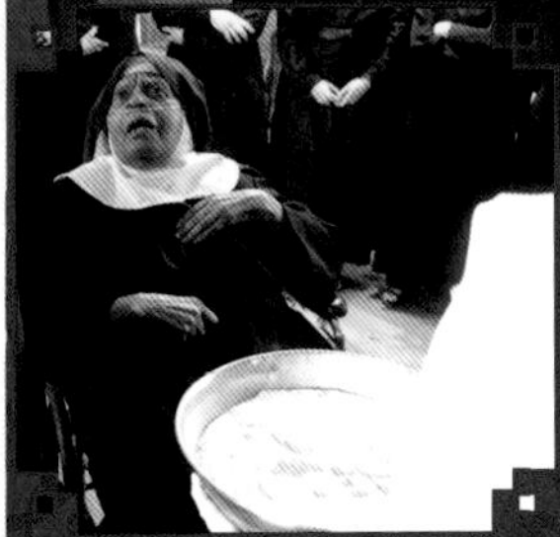

SISTER'S 95TH BIRTHDAY *led a novice to present Sister with a very large bowl of home-made ice cream.*

To eat or not to eat:
That is now the question!
Use your common sense, and
Don't get indigestion.

A BLESSING *for Sr. Maria Battista and the foundresses before departure.*

My Sister who has asked for prayers
I give, dear Lord, to Thee!
Please bring her although unawares
To GLAD ETERNITY.

Chapter 17
My Home Is

How sweet it is, to be with Thee, Lord Jesus!
How sweet it is, to be Thy Mother's slave!
Moment by moment loving Thee increases,
And so it will until I reach the grave.

I deserve to suffer;
I deserve to die;
Oh, how sweet it is with Jesus
In the grave to lie!

He's my Risen Savior!
I shall rise with Him!
When I'm in His company
Nothing can be grim.

Heavenly Father,
how You've loved us!
You gave us Your only Son!
To redeem us! Pay our ransom!
Bring us into Heavenly fun!
Thank You, thank You, Heavenly Father!
In our tribulations small
We hope for the final vict'ry
With You, safe in Heaven's hall!
Heavenly Father, let us love You
While we seek You night and day,
Loving You for Yourself only,
Not for Your reward or pay:
But we need You! How we need You!
Without You we cannot be.
As You've made us, so You'll keep us
With You, for eternity.

THE DAY OF HER BURIAL
Sister lay in state in the Chapter Room, with Sisters keeping vigil day and night. She wore a crown of flowers, and clasped her rosary and profession crucifix, with her profession candle tucked under her arm.

Over Jordan

Dying As She Lived

God is forever! So are we,
Although we have beginning.
We must obey! God knows the way,
God knows the final inning.
Humility from Christ we learn
If with Christ heaven winning.

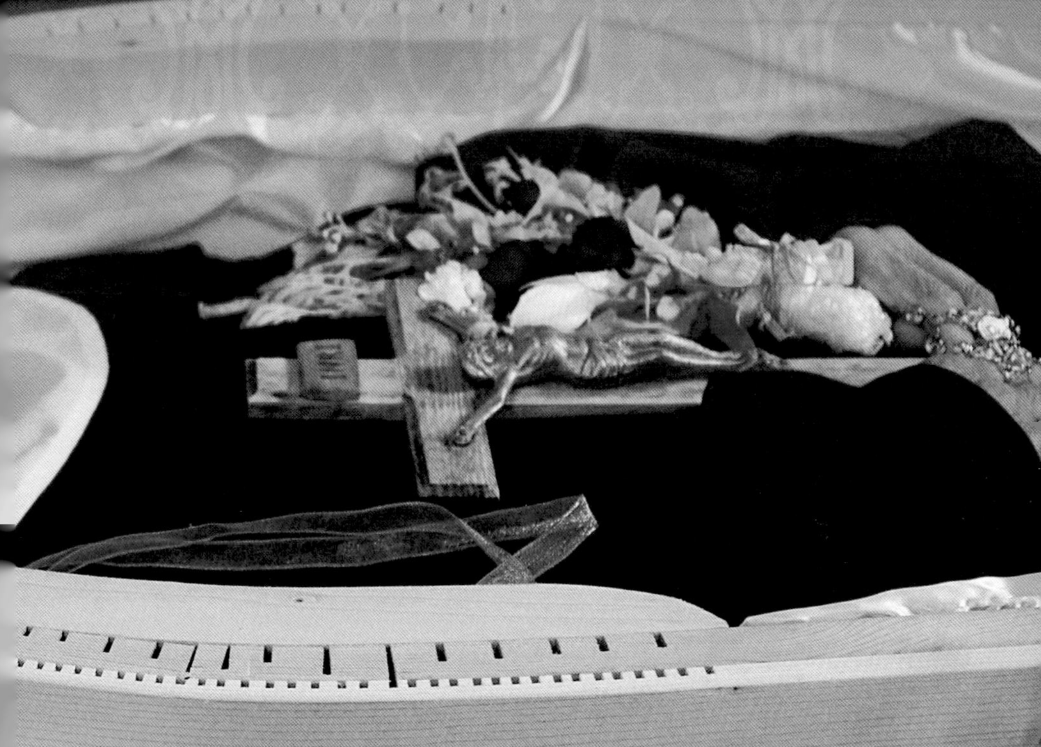

Deep river,
My home is over Jordan.
Deep river, Lord,
I want to cross over into campground.
Oh, don't you want to go,
To the Gospel feast;
That Promised Land,
Where all is peace? –Anonymous

O all ye Martyrs of our God!
You bravely suffered death!
Help us to love God, too, like you,
Unto our dying breath!

Everybody has a problem;
Everybody has a cross.
So I plead for each to Jesus:
"Save him from eternal loss!"

SISTER IN THE ABBEY CHURCH

a photo taken of Sister in the six months before her death. Her final struggle was emblematic of the spiritual martyrdom she had endured throughout her life, always bowing to the will of God, receiving His peace, and giving strength and joy to all around her.

All ye who were beheaded –
Or run through with a sword –
Or drowned – or stoned – or burnt alive
For Jesus Christ our Lord:
Or scourged – or tossed to savage beasts
Starved – crippled – crucified –
Oh, many are the painful ways
In which you martyrs died:

But now you live in joy and peace
In heaven high with Christ
And you are very glad that you
With Him were sacrificed:
O Martyrs! For poor sinners such as
I am, please do pray!
And for all persecuted Christians
In the world today.

The Provinces of Heaven:
How dare I write about
what eye has not seen nor ear heard?
I don't. I only look up and long.

During the spring months, Sr. Wilhelmina spoke very little and slept more and more. She became completely unresponsive in the afternoon of May 26, which was only the second day in all her elderly years that she was unable to get out of bed. Her last 'meal' was her favorite, a couple of spoonfuls of homemade vanilla ice cream. She then received the Last Rites in the morning before the community's Mass.

Her nurse came that evening to do a thorough examination, concluding that Sr. Wilhelmina had no more than twenty-four hours to live. Sisters stayed in turns at her bedside that night, beginning the prayers for the dying.

On Monday, May 27, Sr. Wilhelmina received not only the Apostolic Blessing, but also first blessings from two newly ordained priests. At one point, the community was gathered around her in prayer, when she held her rosary high, gently waving it. Mother Abbess enjoined that the rosary be begun again.

During the conventual Mass, Mother Abbess stayed with her, and just as the bells for the consecration rang, she witnessed Sr. Wilhelmina extend her arms and moan deeply, as though she, in her frail body, were participating in the Sacrifice of Our Lord on the Cross, taking place in the Abbey church just across the courtyard from her room.

Thy priests, dear Lord!
Lord, save Thy priests!
Don't let them join
The worldly beasts!
Whether
they're good,
Whether
they're ill,
Thy priests they are,
Forever, still!
Thou made
them all
Thy Mother's sons:
To fight for her
But not with guns.
Living for Thee
In faith and love,
Preparing for
Their home above.
Save them
from war,
Save them
from crime;
Bring them
into the Life
sublime.
Most
Precious
Blood
Of Jesus
Christ,
Thy priests
for souls
Are sacrificed!

NEW PRIESTS ***who blessed and assisted Sister in their first days of priesthood and her final days on earth: Fraternity priests Fr. Daniel Powers, Fr. John Killackey and Fr. Jesus Valenzuela.***

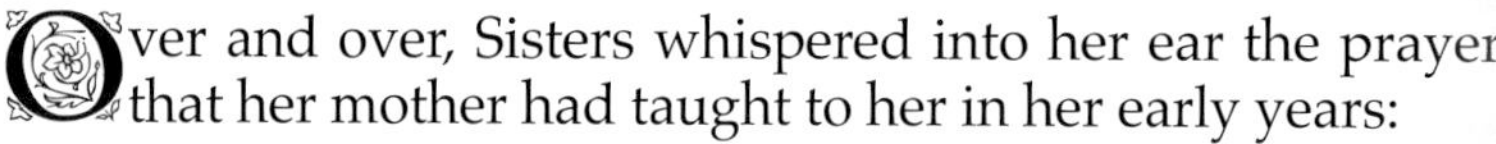

Over and over, Sisters whispered into her ear the prayer that her mother had taught to her in her early years:

> Jesus, Mary and Joseph I give you my heart and my soul;
> Jesus, Mary, and Joseph, assist me in my last agony.
> Jesus, Mary and Joseph may I breathe forth my spirit
> in peace with you. Amen.

Later that day, the founding Sisters arrived from Ava, Missouri, just one month after their sendoff. Consequently, all of the Benedictines of Mary were present that evening at Sr. Wilhelmina's bedside. They recited Matins together in her room before midnight. At least five or six Sisters remained praying at her bedside all night, with many others dozing off right in the room or nearby in the hallway outside. Sister Wilhelmina persevered through the entire night, though her breathing was becoming more labored.

On Tuesday morning, May 28, one of the newly ordained priests, Fr. Daniel Powers, FSSP, offered Mass in her room, the fourth Mass of his priesthood. He gave a brief, but meaningful sermon on the rewards of Heaven: the heavenly crown for which the faithful strive is a reward for charity and is itself an increased capacity for charity. Faithful love of God and neighbor practiced in this earthly life, persevering even until death, opens the soul to share more abundantly in God's life, which is love, in Heaven. The dying sister remained unresponsive during this Mass, simply maintaining her struggle to breathe, but the Holy Sacrifice offered next to her and these words about Heaven were surely a source of strength.

Sr. Wilhelmina continued to be unresponsive until after the conventual Mass, when all the sisters crowded into her cell once again and began singing all of her favorite hymns. Although she did not open her eyes, she obviously could hear the singing and even did her best to join in at certain points. Later, the nurse was astonished to hear that Sr. Wilhelmina had shown any signs of responsiveness, let alone her attempts to sing, since her blood pressure and oxygen levels normally would have precluded such exertion.

While the sisters were singing, Sr. Wilhelmina uttered, or rather sang, her final words, "O Maria," during one of her favorite hymns: "Hail, Holy Queen." During the singing, her eyes never opened, and her face remained expressionless as she struggled to breathe and even to sing. A few minutes after her final words, however, as the sisters sang "Jesus, My Lord, My God, My All," Sr. Wilhelmina's face changed dramatically. While her eyes remained closed, a heavenly smile passed over her face at the words, "Oh with what bursts of fervent praise, Thy goodness, Jesus, would I sing," as though she were granted a vision of the eternity awaiting her, where she would sing His praises forever. This radiant smile shown from her face for the rest of the verse. After about a half hour of singing, Sr. Wilhelmina returned to her unresponsive state and remained so until the next day.

SISTER'S SMIL
during the hym

The next day, Wednesday, May 29, the Vigil of the Ascension, after the morning hours of the Divine Office, the sisters gathered again in Sr. Wilhelmina's cell to pray the Rosary. The community's chaplain, Fr. Lawrence Carney, and Fr. Powers also came to recite the prayers for the dying over her. Because of her extremely labored breathing and low oxygen and blood pressure, everyone expected that she would not survive the morning, but little did anyone know that she was waiting to pass from this life in the same way as did her beloved St. Bede.

FATHER CARNEY
the Sisters' chaplain.

Years before, one of her novice angels had asked Sr. Wilhelmina who was her favorite Benedictine saint, expecting her to name her patron, St. William the Abbot. To the novice's surprise, however, Sr. Wilhelmina replied without hesitation, "St. Bede the Venerable! Because his feast was the day on which I became a Benedictine of Mary." Indeed, it was on the feast of St. Bede, May 27, 1995, that she came to Elmhurst, Pennsylvania, to begin the community. The Benedictines of Mary continue to celebrate this feast as their founding day.

Both Sisters and nurse expected that Sr. Wilhelmina would take her leave on the calendar date of St. Bede's feast, May 27. But the *liturgical* feast on which he died was Rogation Wednesday, the Vigil of the Ascension, when he expired peacefully as the evening Offices were being completed. He was consequently considered to have died on the feast of the Ascension, since First Vespers of the feast had been chanted, and it was an hour after sunset. Sister Wilhelmina would follow in her beloved saint's footsteps, not only in his love of the Divine Office and our Blessed Lady, but even in his manner of death.

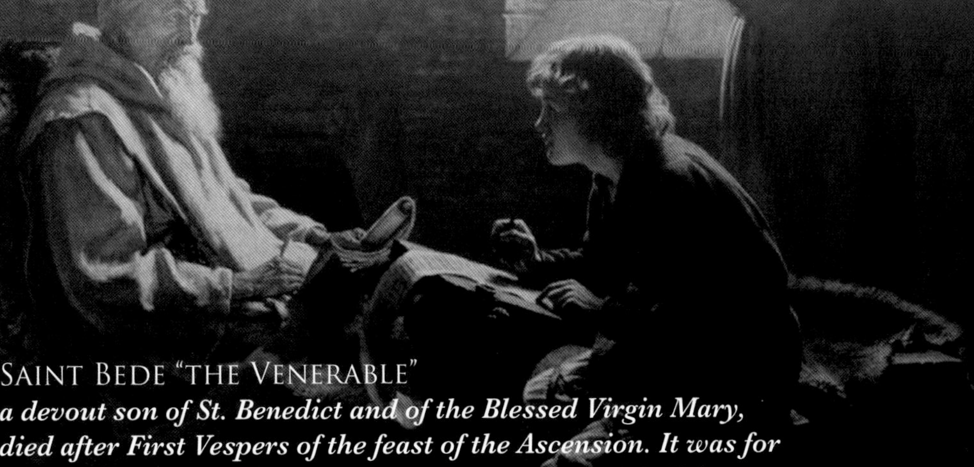

SAINT BEDE "THE VENERABLE"
a devout son of St. Benedict and of the Blessed Virgin Mary, died after First Vespers of the feast of the Ascension. It was for this feast that he wrote the beautiful hymn "Sing We Triumphant Hymns of Praise," a hymn well-loved by the Sisters.

The afternoon of May 29, just after a sister brought the Pilgrim Virgin statue from Fatima into Sr. Wilhelmina's cell, Mother Abbess was inspired to dress Sr. Wilhelmina in the habit once again as best as could be done, remembering how great was Sr. Wilhelmina's desire to die wearing it. Later, the sisters realized the uncanny parallel to the time when Sr. Wilhelmina had reassumed the traditional habit in 1974, on the occasion of the Pilgrim statue's visit to the Oblate Sisters of Providence.

The Feast of the Ascension had begun with First Vespers, and the whole community assembled at 7:00pm in Sr. Wilhelmina's cell where Mother Abbess read aloud numerous messages of assurance of prayers, along with prayer requests from family and friends. During the reading, Sr. Wilhelmina remained unresponsive, but there can be little doubt that she took everything to heart as she lay there, clutching her profession crucifix and her well-used rosary. The whole community experienced a tangible sense of joy and peace for the first time at these oft-repeated gatherings around her bed.

After singing some more of Sr. Wilhelmina's favorite hymns to Our Lady, the community chanted Compline together in her cell. Compline concludes with the ancient custom of the superior giving the community a blessing with holy water for the night. Mother Abbess intoned the customary antiphon for Paschaltide:

> Vidi aquam egredientem de templo, a
> latere dextro, alleluia:
> Et omnes ad quos pervenit aqua
> ista, salvi facti sunt, et dicent:
> alleluia, alleluia.

THE PILGRIM VIRGIN OF FATIMA ***seemed to accompany Sr. Wilhelmina all through her life. This large replica from Fatima was the one brought into her cell as she was dying, originally blessed by Bishop Athanasius Schneider.***

The sun had come out
after darkest night.
I came to move
the criminals from sight.
Their day of death
was ending with sunset;
Which I saw faintly
with a strong delight.

I took my lance
making transformation
And threw with a vim
into His side;
But did not see how it
then opened wide.
His gushing blood
was falling on my face
To wash me clean
of all my sad disgrace.
My eyes then opened,
as if struck by rod,
I cried then: "This man
was the Son of God!"

How else
could I explain
my eyesight clear?
The woman, standing, was
His Mother dear.

I saw water flowing out of the
Temple, from its right side,
Alleluia:
And all who came to this water were
saved, And they shall say:
Alleluia, Alleluia.

As the Sisters continued the antiphon, Mother Abbess froze, her eyes fixed upon Sr. Wilhelmina, who had suddenly taken on an air of profound peace. Intuitively, after Mother Abbess blessed herself with holy water, she sprinkled Sr. Wilhelmina's head, then sprinkled her again more copiously, signing a cross upon Sr. Wilhelmina's forehead with her thumb in the water, "as if she were baptizing her again," as one Sister later commented. Mother Abbess gently stroked her cheeks, and as she withdrew her hand (but not her gaze) to continue blessing the rest of the community, Sister Wilhelmina breathed her last, peacefully and without a struggle.

"THE TESTIMONY OF ST. LONGINUS" ***(left) was one of Sister's last poems, perhaps anticipating the mystery with which her life was finally taken up. Tradition holds that the centurion, St. Longinus, was purblind until the blood and water from Christ's' side cured him. The mercy of the Lord was opened to Sister Wilhelmina, on the very eve of her baptismal anniversary.***

The moment of Sr. Wilhelmina's death corresponded exactly with the antiphon, for she received holy water from the right hand of her successor, who had been blessed as the community's first Abbess less than nine months before, whom Sr. Wilhelmina ardently venerated as Christ Himself. Sister Wilhelmina received the water from the temple of the Lord's pierced Heart, which was symbolized by the Abbey church, and she died in the shadow of this edifice, which had also been consecrated less than nine months before. Ninety-five years after receiving the saving water of Baptism on May 30, 1924, Sr. Wilhelmina's passing on May 29, 2019, consummated her religious vows which were her "second Baptism." She took her flight to God, following the Lord in the mystery of His wonderful Ascension, as the community would sing in the Mass of the Ascension the following day. It was through the veil of this life that she was able to complete the antiphon and testify to the water through which she and the saints of Christ are saved, to sing "Alleluia" to her Bridegroom forever.

Spontaneously, Mother Abbess knelt at Sr. Wilhelmina's side after blessing the sisters, and all the sisters knelt also as Mother Abbess gently said, "She's gone." Mother Abbess began to weep, saying, "Oh, Sister, Sister, pray for us," as she kissed the limp hand and, in an eloquent gesture, took Sr. Wilhelmina's thumb to trace the sign of the cross upon her own forehead, receiving the blessing of her predecessor and foundress, even as Sr. Wilhelmina had not departed without receiving the blessing of her new Mother Abbess.

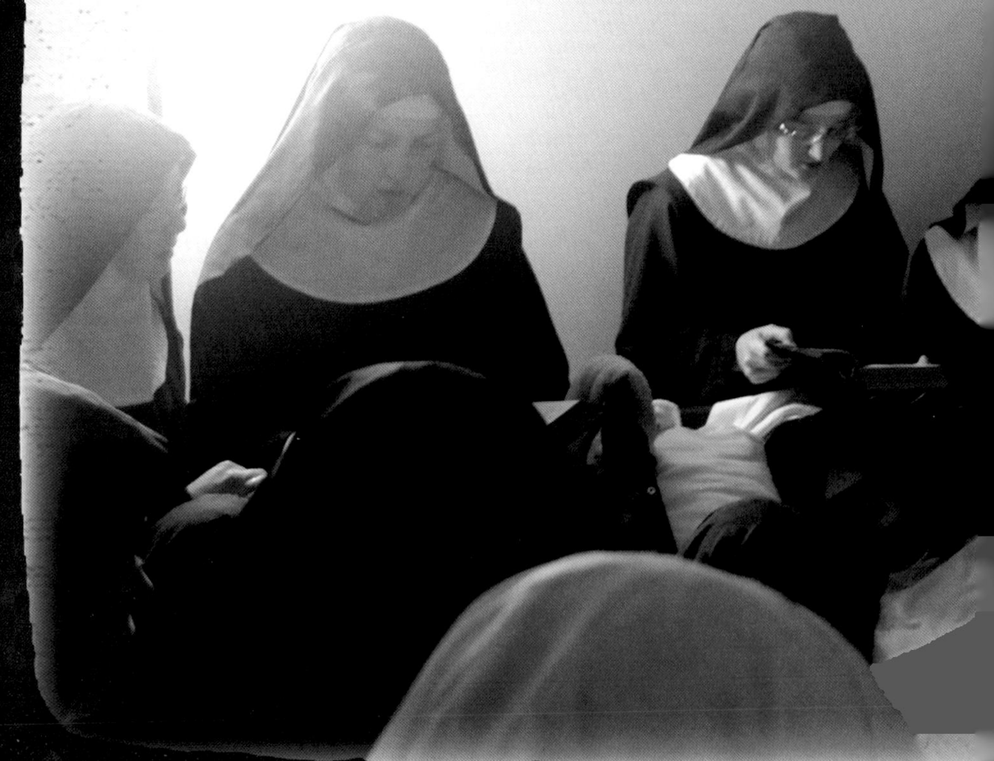

Mother Abbess wept again and, overwhelmed with gratitude that all the sisters had together witnessed such a grace, cried out, "How much God loves us! How much He loves our community!" Our Lord could not have chosen a more fitting nor consoling moment to withdraw the treasure of the community unto Himself. The sisters also wept, but the tears were more of joy than of grief. One Sister recalled seeing Sr. Scholastica, smiling through her tears just after the passing, whispering "well done, well done!" Yet another Sister, who tends to be more reserved, actually let out a chuckle, as she thought "You little stinker, slipping off to heaven just like that!" Sr. Wilhelmina would have undoubtably answered her, "Hee-hee...yeah, a *stinker!*" Sisters collected their rosaries they had twined around her hands, brushed away their tears, and lovingly took up their choir books to sing the "Subvenite," the song of departure. As the mellow tones of the traditional prayer for a deceased community member wafted heavenward, the church bell tolled ninety-five times, commemorating the many years of Sr. Wilhelmina's rich and holy life.

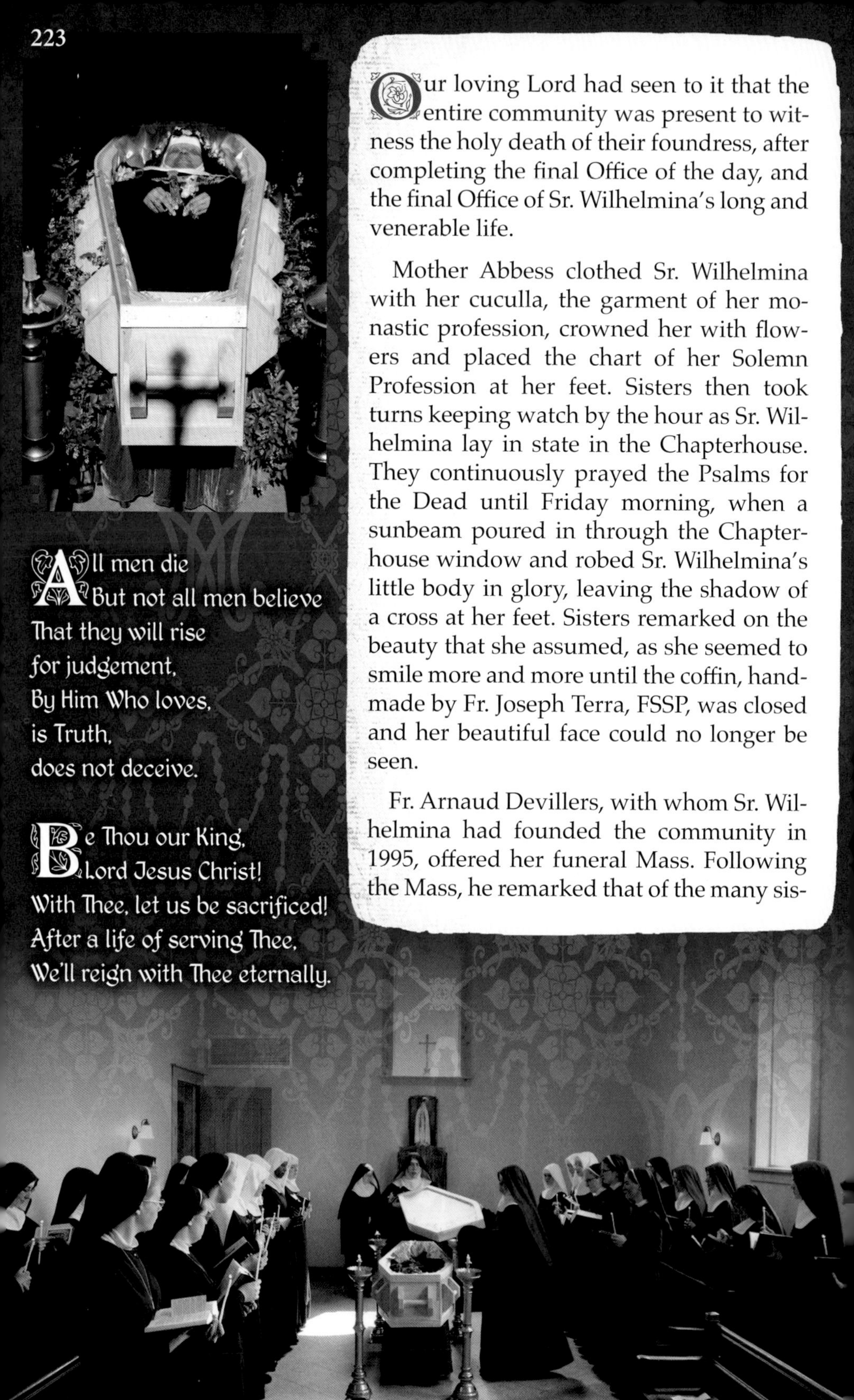

Our loving Lord had seen to it that the entire community was present to witness the holy death of their foundress, after completing the final Office of the day, and the final Office of Sr. Wilhelmina's long and venerable life.

Mother Abbess clothed Sr. Wilhelmina with her cuculla, the garment of her monastic profession, crowned her with flowers and placed the chart of her Solemn Profession at her feet. Sisters then took turns keeping watch by the hour as Sr. Wilhelmina lay in state in the Chapterhouse. They continuously prayed the Psalms for the Dead until Friday morning, when a sunbeam poured in through the Chapterhouse window and robed Sr. Wilhelmina's little body in glory, leaving the shadow of a cross at her feet. Sisters remarked on the beauty that she assumed, as she seemed to smile more and more until the coffin, handmade by Fr. Joseph Terra, FSSP, was closed and her beautiful face could no longer be seen.

Fr. Arnaud Devillers, with whom Sr. Wilhelmina had founded the community in 1995, offered her funeral Mass. Following the Mass, he remarked that of the many sis-

All men die
But not all men believe
That they will rise
for judgement,
By Him Who loves,
is Truth,
does not deceive.

Be Thou our King,
Lord Jesus Christ!
With Thee, let us be sacrificed!
After a life of serving Thee,
We'll reign with Thee eternally.

ters he had met, he had full confidence in Sr. Wilhelmina's genuineness, because of her humility. It was upon that foundation that a new community arose for the glory of God.

After the funeral Mass, the Sisters carried their beloved foundress to the Abbey cemetery, in which they had dug its first grave by hand earlier that morning. After the fathers and brothers of several of the Sisters lowered the coffin into the ground, the Sisters, relatives and friends of Sr. Wilhelmina passed one by one to place some earth into the grave. The sorrow of the parting made many tears flow, but all experienced a deep peace and hope. The well-worn body that had been laid to rest was like the husk of a precious seed that would continue to bear fruit unto eternal life.

Later at the reception, one of Sr. Wilhelmina's nieces commented in surprise at the number of people in attendance. She asked if Sr. Wilhelmina's funeral were coinciding with a family visit for some of the other Sisters. "Oh, no," the Sisters replied, "All these people came to pay their respects to Sr. Wilhelmina." "Well!" Sister Wilhelmina's niece remarked, "I didn't know her tribe was so big!"

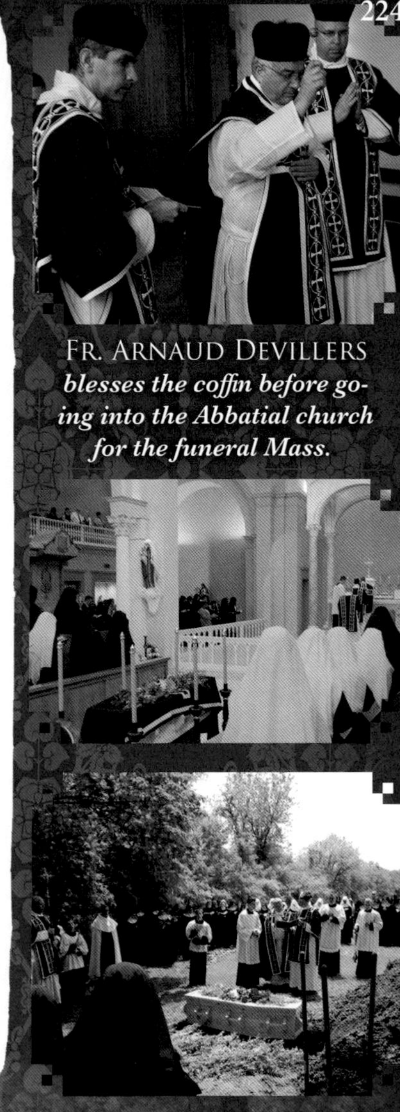

FR. ARNAUD DEVILLERS *blesses the coffin before going into the Abbatial church for the funeral Mass.*

MOTHER ABBESS CECILIA *and each of the Sisters took turns filling in the grave they had dug for their foundress in the cemetery blessed by Cardinal Burke the year before.*

EPILOGUE

GIVING

Thank Thee, Father
For Thy blessings,
Life and Holy Mary sweet;

Thank Thee Father,
For the Saviour
Who gives us Himself to eat;

Thank Thee, Father
For the Spirit
Who brings us to Love complete.

Thank Thee, Father
For Creation,
Work completed in six days!

Thank Thee, Father
For Redemption
And the gift of One who prays,

Thank Thee, Father
For Salvation
When upon Thy Face we gaze!

Thank Thee, Father!
Thank Thee, Father!
Thank Thee, Father, evermore!

Thank Thee, Father
For the mansion
Which I've never seen before!

Thank Thee, Father,
For Thy blessings;
Everlasting is Thy store!

Thy Will be done,
Lord! Thine be done!
For miracles
Are Thy great fun.

Thank you, dear Heavenly Father!
Thank you, Lord Jesus Christ!
For all You've been, for all You've done!
For all You've sacrificed!
For gift of faith, for gift of hope,
For gift of charity!
Thank you, dear Lord, for being God,
For all eternity!

Thank you, dear Blessed Mother
For the miracles so great
That you have worked for many years
In every town and state;
For bringing sinners to repent
In tears: abundant, tart!
But most of all we thank you for
The triumph of your Heart!

A ROSARY PROCESSION
in thanksgiving for a miracle.

THANKS

We believe in a God
Whom we do not see,
Yet we know quite well He's there;
St. Benedict gives Him His place
As being everywhere;
On every human head He keeps
Count of each human hair.
Love and adore, thank Him the more
For all His loving care!

All they who've asked us
for our prayers,
Lord, we hold up to Thee!
Entreating Thee to bless them now
And for eternity!

Our baby tried to help himself,
By crawling up the stairs;
And ev'ry step our baby took
Was free from selfish cares.

What God wants is what I want,
And nothing else besides!
God Almighty knows the end
Of all our earthly rides.

There's nothing that's
more wonderful
Than doing what God wants,
With smile and cheerful countenance,
No grumbles and no grunts.
You must obey no matter what
Misfortune then begin,
For no misfortune can compare
With a deliberate sin.

To love,
And to be loved,
Is everyone's desire;
To help,
And to be helped,
As to Heaven we aspire;
To live,
And never die,
Will be our great reward;
Always!
Let's try to live
In union with Our Lord!

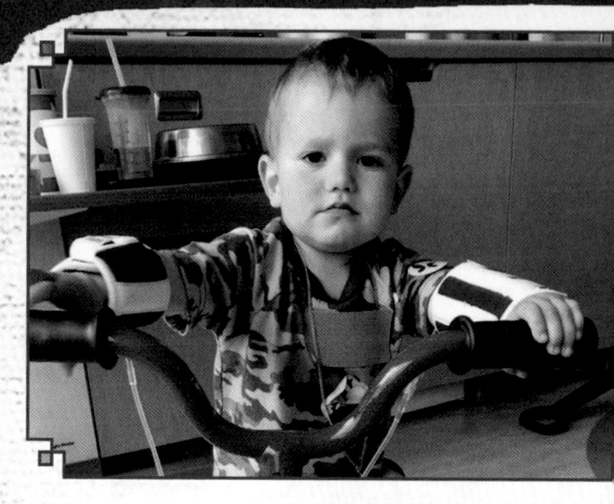

READY TO ROLL *a healthy two-year-old awaits his discharge from the hospital after a life-threatening emergency turned into a very brief stay. He thanked Sr. Wilhelmina at right.*

Indeed, Sister Wilhelmina's "tribe" is very big, and grows more so with each passing day. Sister Wilhelmina touched many lives in the course of her ninety-five years, and even now, her Sisters, relatives and friends continue to turn to her as a source of inspiration and even of intercessory prayer.

Soon after Sr. Wilhelmina's death, one of the Sisters' nephews, a two-year-old boy, had made his way into a bottle of Tylenol and had consumed most of it by the time he was discovered. His distraught mother brought him to the hospital, and feared him to be dying. The doctors concurred likewise, and life-flighted him to a larger hospital after administering emergency treatment. Liver failure was projected, and his chance of survival extremely slim. The Sister immediately enlisted Sr. Wilhelmina's help, and encouraged her other Benedictine Sisters to do likewise, asking for the nephew's cure and to avoid any medical measures against the Church's teaching on end-of-life issues. After a harrowing two days, the liver enzymes, which had risen to deadly levels, suddenly subsided, leaving no trace of damage. A family member pronounced it "nothing short of a miracle," and the boy was discharged after a few days. When paying a visit to the Abbey, the youngster was encouraged to thank Sr. Wilhelmina. He then knelt at her grave and gave her tombstone a big, smacking kiss. He remains a healthy little boy to this day.

THE ENTIRE COMMUNITY ***(left) of the Abbey and Ava foundation gathered less than two months after Sister's passing for Sr. Maria Battista's simple profession with her other classmates. All of these Sisters were present at Sr. Wilhelmina's bedside to witness her holy death.***

Lord, keep my Sisters beautiful and good;
Help them perform all the works that they should.
Make them give glory to Thee all their days.
And join the saints in their heavenly praise.

Reports of other miracles find their way to the Abbey. Some are, like Sister Wilhelmina's life, a drawn out blessing. A mother of a large family had been suffering terribly for years, with a strange reaction to a prescribed medicine. Invoking Sister Wilhelmina, she has found that her strength has gradually been increasing so that she can return to her maternal duties. The family found itself more unified and faith-filled, even though the physical improvement was slow.

Some of the miracles are also like Sister Wilhelmina's life, inconspicuous, but still wonderful. A benefactor who had a chronic ailment touched Sr. Wilhelmina's memorial card to herself before retiring, and awoke without pain.

Even as this book goes to print, a miracle is in progress. A Sister's blood sister was expecting her third child. She had consecrated her little one to the Blessed Mother in the womb and named him Emmanuel, and had a premonition of future danger. As it turned out, she contracted a very rare infection of the heart. An emergency C-section was done to save the child. The little one was unfortunately lost, but the family began invoking the intercession of Sr. Wilhelmina, as the young mother's life was gravely imperilled. Her heart stopped working, and dramatic measures were taken, though her life was still despaired of. Though the lack of circulation cost her her left hand, the young mother defied all expectations and began to rally, and is on the road to recovery.

THE TRUTH

Lord Jesus Christ
Was crucified;
Was sacrificed,
For us, He died.

The Rosary
Bring penitence,
Humility
Obedience.

Angel of God
Help us to pray!
Beneath the rod
Of Truth to stay!

On Easter morn
Our Lord arose;
'Til we are born,
To feed He chose.

In Mary's womb
We live and grow,
Escaping doom
That sinners know.

I want to keep my eyes on Thee, Lord Jesus!
At every moment of this passing day!
long, Thy shining beauteous face to see, Lord,
And tabernacle with Thee while we play.
No more sin!
No more sin!
Time to fight
For Heaven and win!
My King
WORD-CREATOR
Son of the Father,
From eternity Thou art;
MAN-GOD,
Born of Virgin Mary,
Let me have with Thee a part;
SAVIOR,
On the Cross expiring,
I love Thee
with all my heart.

All things are possible with Thee, my King!
Thy Will be done with those who are suffering.
Thou knowest when, Thou knowest where and why;
We only know that some day we must die.
We want to be with Thee, in Heaven high!
Raise us to life! Thy glory, Lord, to sing!

If you would go to Heaven
And not wander from the Way,
Thank God for graces given
And OBEY! OBEY! OBEY!

O you, of little faith, why
Did you doubt?
Of course I heard, and drove
The devils out.

God has been very good to me
In spite of all my badness,
He's working miracles galore –

Both day and night and o'er and o'er –
He even plans to bless me more
In an eternal gladness

SISTER WAS ONCE ASKED *by Fr. Michel Berger, the first chaplain: "Why did you become a religious?" Sister replied without hesitation, "because I was in love with Our Lord." She never fell out of love with Him.*

THE END OF THE ROSARY PROCESSION
in thanksgiving, August 30, 2019.

Around the time of Sr. Wilhelmina's passing, one of the Sisters herself became very ill. Mother Abbess prayed to Sr. Wilhelmina asking her, in the true spirit of obedience that she always rendered to her, to obtain the grace of this Sister's healing on August 29, the day marking three months since Sr. Wilhelmina's death. Mother Abbess also asked all the sisters to pray to Sr. Wilhelmina for a special grace without specifying her intention. August 29 came and the sister remained unwell.

Toward evening, around the same time as Sr. Wilhelmina had passed on May 29, the sister became violently ill, expelling the infection that had been menacing her for months. When that subsided, she went to the Abbey church to pray, asking Sister to ensure her healing in the name of holy obedience, the virtue that Sr. Wilhelmina exemplified. Just before she left the church at midnight, she felt a tingling sensation, not at all like the pain that she had been experiencing. She returned to her cell and fell into a deep sleep in which she dreamed that she was looking across the field where Sr. Wilhelmina was buried, and that it was full of beautiful flowers. While she could not actually see her, Sr. Wilhelmina stood next to her, and in a voice that "sounded younger," told the Sister that she was cured of her illness, but that she had to be careful of her diet lest she relapse: she must take baking soda for ten days, flax oil and lots of vegetables. The sister awoke, completely cured. Mother Abbess and all the Sisters rejoiced at the Sister's healing and that now, after so many years of obedience to infirmarian and novitiate angels' directions, Sr. Wilhelmina could now give instructions to her Sisters. Mother Abbess led the community in a Rosary procession of thanksgiving.

We're all in this together
Until God calls us home,
With lighted lamps and girded,
We'll cross the ocean foam.

COMPLINE BY SISTER'S GRAVE
May 29, 2020.

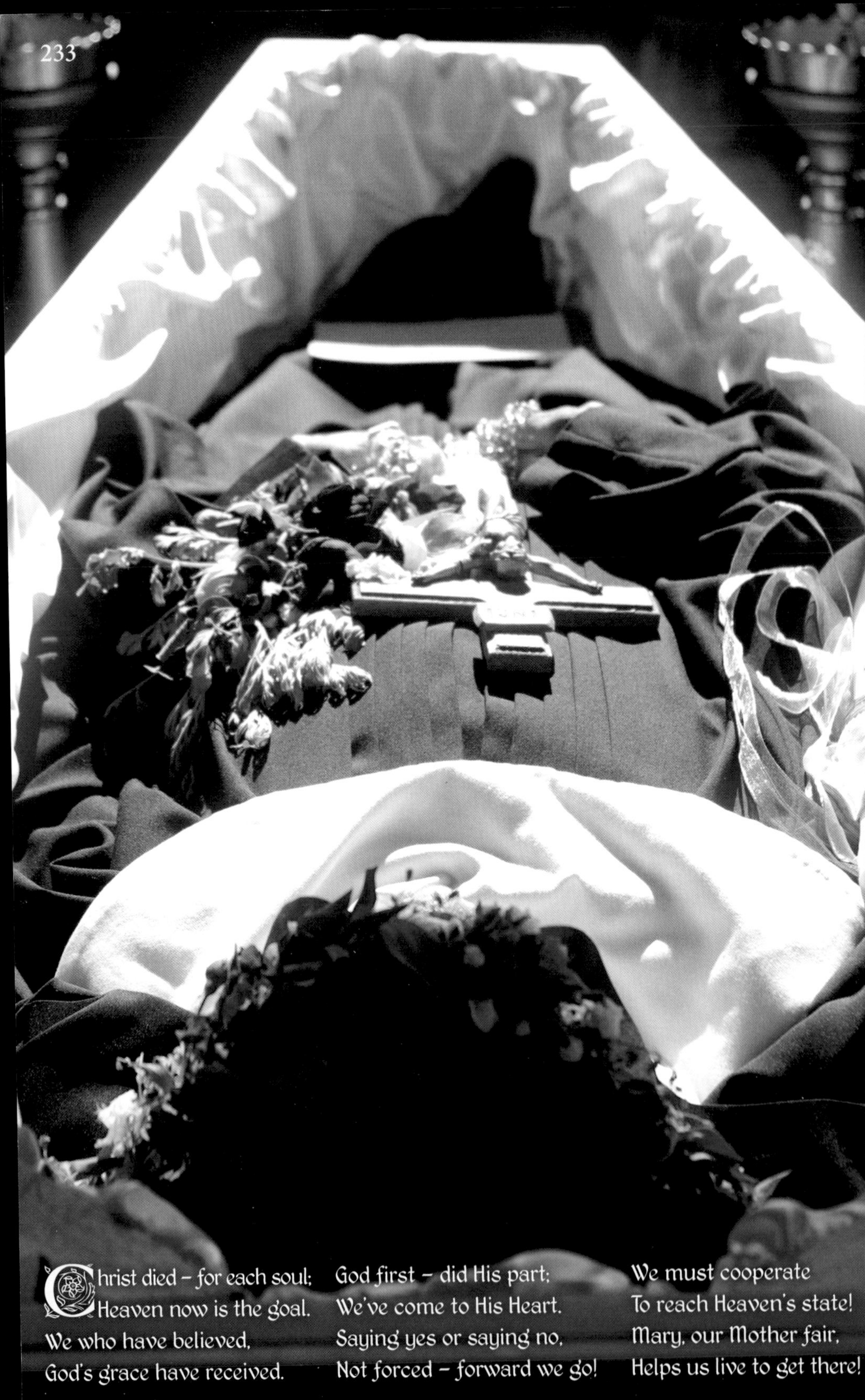

Christ died – for each soul;
Heaven now is the goal.
We who have believed,
God's grace have received.

God first – did His part;
We've come to His Heart.
Saying yes or saying no,
Not forced – forward we go!

We must cooperate
To reach Heaven's state!
Mary, our Mother fair,
Helps us live to get there!

Mother Abbess addressed the community, exhorting all the Sisters to show their gratitude through generosity:

GOD IS SO GOOD TO US! He wants to give us more than we could possibly imagine. We simply have to have greater faith, and the whole canopy of heaven is opened to us. Our dear Sr. Wilhelmina is a saint in heaven! How blessed we are. We can never, never forget how much He has blessed us in so many ways. So let's be generous with Him, and hold nothing back - especially the amount of faith in our hearts, and absolute confident trust in His mercy and tenderness towards us. And just as important, our loving obedience to His will, manifested by our superiors and the circumstances around us, following the beautiful example of dear Sister.

LORD, my Love, my Life, My Light, my only Leader.
Before Thee, let me bow down and adore;
For the whole world let me be an interceder –
At Mass each day I treasure more and more
THY wounds, Thy blood, all Thy pains and crucifixion –
WILL soon there take place my own resurrection?
I want what Thou wantst
Granted to perfection.
BE it in haste, to heaven home,
Lord, let me fly!
DONE be Thy Will,
Thy Will be done,
Lord, let me cry!

SISTER'S NAMESAKE
Sr. Mary Elizabeth, prays by the grave of her foundress.

Sister Maria Battista *tells Sister Wilhelmina it is time to receive Communion at the Dedication of the Abbey Church.*

Special Thanks

to the many who have contributed images and information, firstly to Winnie Sullivan, personal friend of the Lancasters and research assistant; and to Sharon Knecht, Sr. Wilhelmina's successor as archivist of the Oblate Sisters of Providence. May God reward both. Deep thanks also to Brigadier General Keith T. Holcomb for military research; Rebecca Jackson and the extended Lancaster and Madden families; Christine Mucker, long-time friend of Sr. Wilhelmina; Roger and Priscilla McCaffrey of Roman Catholic Books; Catherine Lucy of the Carondelet Consolidated Archive; Lauren Sallwasser of the Missouri Historical Archives; Eric Fair of the Archdiocese of St. Louis Archives; Ann Knake of the Jesuit Archive Research Center, St. Louis; Dr. Patrick Hayes of the Redemptorist Archives; Kristen Keane of the Sisters of the Blessed Sacrament Archives; Dr. Shannen Dee Williams of Villanova University; Dr. Dennis McInerny, formerly of Our Lady of Guadalupe Seminary; Robert Mueller of the Ste. Genevieve History Committee; Betsy Johnson of Mercy Heritage Center; Gerard Kuijpers of Regionaal Historisch Centrum; Matthew Shibler of America Needs Fatima; Barbara Ernster of the Blue Army; Marcia Maranski of Keep the Faith and The Latin Mass Magazine; Jeff Ostrowski of CC Watershed; Alejandra Chavez of Holy Trinity, Orangeburg, SC; Sean Fitzpatrick of St. Gregory's Academy; Nancy LaRoza of Fraternity of St. Peter Headquarters; Bradley Arteaga of Arteaga Studios; Tracy Dunne, Photographer; Judge Michael Lehr, Photographer; William Yap, photographer; Katie Marquette, Photographer; Shara Bruch, Photographer; and Tommy Canning, Divine Mercy Artist.

Prayerful thanks also to the priests and religious who contributed sources and images: Bishop Robert W. Finn, Bishop Emeritus of Kansas City-St. Joseph; Bishop Edward Rice of the Diocese of Springfield-Cape Girardeau; Abbot Placid Solari of Belmont Abbey; Rt. Rev. Michael Stinson, FSSP, District Superior; Msgr. Charles Pope of St. Cyprian/Holy Comforter Parish; Fr. Robert A. Skeris, ThD of CUA Centre for Ward Method Studies; Fr. Vincent DeRosa of Old St. Mary's; Fr. William Define FSSP; Fr. Zachary Akers, FSSP; Rev. Col. Frank Ziemkiewicz, OSB of Benedictine Priory, Savannah; Deacon Patrick Simons of the Ordinariate of the Chair of St. Peter; Frater Bernhard Huber, OSB of St. Benedikt's Monastery, Reichenstein; Mother Abbess Isabelle Thouin, OSB of Sainte-Marie des Deux-Montagnes, Quebec; The Sisters of Jesus Crucified, Elmhurst; Mother Julie, Superior of the Sisters of Charity of Our Lady, Mother of the Church; to Sr. Anna Marie McCormack and Sr. Annuntiata Houghton.

Photo Credits

Wikimedia Commons: pp. 4 (bottom right) 5 (top left) 10 (top right) 19 (right) 20 (inset) 35 (bottom) 36 (all but center) 37 (inset) 39 (right) 47 (left inset) 60, 65, 79-80 (bottom) 81 (left) 87 (top) 96 (except bottom) 97-98, 100-104 (except top photos & bottom of 102) 127 (center & bottom) 131 (top) 139, 141, 145(center) 165 (lower inset) 191-192
Regionaal Historisch Centrum: p. 4 (center left)
Missouri Historical Society: p. 3 (all) p. 4 (two at top) pp. 15-16, 17 (bottom) 18-19, 20 (central) 28 (top) 32, 35, 43-44, 45 (bottom) 48, 49 (bottom) 53, 70 (top)
St. Louis Archdiocesan Archives: pp. 4 (St. Elizabeth's) 38, 54 (inset)
Georgia Historical Society: pp. 5 (top) 13 (2nd left & bottom) 17 (upper)
South Carolina Historical Society: (center p. 5)
Institute of the Sisters of Mercy of the Americas, Mercy Heritage Center: p. 8 (top left)
Belmont Abbey: p. 8 (3rd left) p. 14 (top)
The Lancaster Family: pp. 7, 9-10 (bottom) 14, 27 (right) 28 (center)
Benedictine Military School: p. 14 (bottom)
Sisters of the Blessed Sacrament: pp. 10 (top) 56 (bottom)
Sumner High School: pp. 18 (small insets)
Sisters of St. Joseph of Carondelet, St. Louis Province Collection, Casrondelet Consolidated Archives: pp. 21 (bottom) 27 (left) 39 (top) 59-60, 61 (left and top right.)
Jesuit Archive Research Center: p. 24 (center left) & pp. 34-35
New York Public Library Archives: pp. 26 (center left) & 47 (right inset)
Lucille Brantley: p. 26 (top)
Oblate Sisters of Providence Archives: pp. 28 (bottom) 56, 67, 69 (inset) 77-78 (except top) 79-80 (top) 85-86 (top) 87 (except top) 91 (bottom) 92 (bottom left) 100, 102 (top left) 107 (except center) 116, 122, 124, 131 (center)
West Point Military Archives: p. 33
Our Parish at Work (courtesy of Winnie Sullivan) pp. 36 (center) 39 (left) 40 (bottom) 41-42, 46
Dwight Eisenhower Library: p. 37 (center left)
Markoe Family: pp. 38-39 (bottom)
Institute on Religious Life: p. 40 (second on left)
Loyola University Museum: p. 42
Blue Army: pp. 47 (top) 107 (center)
Arteaga Studios, St. Louis: pp. 53-54
Redemptorist Archives, Philadelphia: pp. 66 (bottom & center inset) 113 (inset)
Tumblr: 78 (top) 167
Diocese of Springfield-Cape Girardeau: pp. 62 (inset) 129 (center inset)
Maryland Historical Society: pp. 71-72, 74 (bottom) 96 (bottom)
St. Cyprian Parish: p. 85 (except top & center)
Fraternity of St. Peter: p. 90, 216 (insets)
Archdiocese of Baltimore: pp. 91 (top)
EpicPew: p. 92 (top)
Catholic University of America, Centre for Ward Method Studies: p. 92 (two lower left)
Dr. Patricia Grey: pp. 101-102 (top)
Holy Trinity / St. Theresa Parish, SC: p. 103 (top)
Flickr: pp. 133 (top-created by Dennis Jarvis-and bottom) 136
Keesler AFB: p. 127 (top)
St. Mary's Church: p. 140 (top)
Born of Wonder / Katie Marquette: p. 140 (bottom)
Sisters of Jesus Crucified: p. 147 (bottom)
St. Gregory the Great Academy p.149

Artwork Credits

Titian (Tiziano Vecelli:): pp. i, 82, 181
Carl Bloch: pp. iii, 123, 145, 164, 206, 227
Winslow Homer: pp. 1-2 and 50 (top)
George Peter Alexander Healy: p. 5 (lower right)
Francisco Lasso: p. 5 (top corner)
Xanthus Smith: p. 5 (lower left)
Eastman Johnson: p. 7
Rafael Flores p. 10
Edmund Blair Leighton pp. 13 (top) and 120
Jules Bastien LePage: p. 13 (bottom)
John Singer Sargent pp. 19-20
Hugues Merle: p. 23
Charles Bosserson Chambers pp. 25, 49, 63
Giuseppe Molteni: p. 34
Carl Müeller: p. 50 (bottom)
Heinrich Hoffmann pp. 51, 75
Bartolomé Esteban Murillo pp. 59, 189, 232
Giovanni Battitsta Gaulli Baciccio: p. 66
St. Peter's Basilica, the Vatican: pp. 65, 76
Joseph Legare: p. 67
Jan Adam Kruseman: p. 73
August Kraus: p. 91
Gertrude Käsebier: p. 93
Etienne-Hippolyte Maindron: p. 94
Michelangelo Merisi da Caravaggio: p. 106
William Adolphe Bouguereau pp. 115, 170, 211
Olga Boznánska: p. 118
Leopold Kupelwieser: p. 126
François Joseph Navez: p. 131
Rembrandt van Rijn: p. 133
Guercino (Giovanni Francesco Barbieri): p. 134
Anonymous / Unknown: pp. 139, 256
Master of St. Wendelin, Kruth: p. 142
Adrien Guignet: p. 146
Sir Francis Bernard Dicksee: p. 150
Ary Schaffer: p. 162
Jules Joseph Duban: p. 172
Eugène Alexis Girardet: p. 176
Francesco Hayez: p. 180
Raphael (Raffaello Sanzio da Urbino:) p. 181
František Ženíšek: p. 185
Jules Joseph Meynier: p. 190
Anton Raphael Mengs: p. 201
Pietro Perugino: p. 204
Carlo Dolci: p. 205
Phillippe de Champaigne: p. 209
Eugene von Blaas: p. 210
Eugene Burnand: p. 216
Almeida Júnior: p. 217
James Doyle Penrose: p. 218
"The Hour of Mercy" p. 222
© Tommy Canning, used with permission.
Giovanni Battista Sassoferatto: end

If there is anything I would want to pass on to the community, it would be this: Devotion to Our Blessed Mother. True Devotion to Our Blessed Mother.

– Sister Wilhelmina in her final years

UT IN OMNIBUS GLOFICETUR DEUS PER MARIAM